WHAT TO EAT?

Hattie Ellis

What To Eat?

10 Chewy Questions About Food

Portobello
BOOKS

Published by Portobello Books 2012

Portobello Books
12 Addison Avenue
London
W11 4QR
United Kingdom

A CIP catalogue record for this book is available from
the British Library

1 3 5 7 9 10 8 6 4 2

ISBN 978 1 84627 215 8

www.portobellobooks.com

Typeset by Avon DataSet Ltd, Bidford on Avon, Warwickshire

Printed and bound by CPI Group (UK) Ltd, Croydon, CR0 4YY

To Tim

Contents

Introduction

Food has become very complicated. It used to be just the stuff on our plates. Helping after helping was put on a fork and swallowed. But now we sit down to plates piled high with issues. Food is bad for you; for other creatures; for the planet. Or conversely, particular ingredients are praised to the skies as miracles that will cure every ill. Buy some pricey goji berries and live forever!

We live in the midst of a stream of fast-moving media delivering headline after headline of competing claims. The juicy steak for supper comes from a cow fed on soya grown in destroyed rainforest; the juicy steak is delivering much-needed iron and energy to make you zoomy and bright. The anchovies on your pizza are threatening the ecology of the oceans. But then oily fish also provide essential, healthful fats. The beans in your daily cups of coffee grind down the poor and damage your nerves; but coffee-growing helps the economies of the most deprived countries in the world and coffee protects you from cancer and depression. The wheat in your loaf is drenched in fungicide and sends your glycaemic index soaring. Then again, bread is a good-value carbohydrate that is the founding block of a healthy food pyramid. Fruit is good and cheering; but can it be local when less than 10 per cent of British fruit is home-grown? White meat good; red meat bad – but is grass-fed lamb better for you than grain-fed poultry? Now we need to follow what the animals eat as well. Aaaagggggghhhhhhhh!

Belief after belief comes and goes, without the time or chance to digest chapter and verse of each new gospel. Just when you start to get to grips with one dilemma, another grabs your attention, and yet another expert gives an entirely different answer. They speak the last word. Until you hear the next.

All this hubbub is quite apart from the other needs in life. We may want to eat ethically and healthily – assuming we know exactly what that is – but do we have the time, the interest, the opportunity and the cash? Besides – pray forgive me for bringing this up as a priority – whatever happened to pleasure?

In the early 1990s, one of my first jobs was researching food 'issues' for the BBC television programme *Food and Drink*. Most of the programme was about the pleasures of food, but I was on the dark side. My section was about the rip-offs, the health problems, the food quacks, the faulty fan ovens, the hopes – then failing hopes – for antioxidant supplements. A trained cook and food writer, I occasionally looked with longing at the other pieces being filmed in the studio, which were all chocolate cake and chardonnay. I was allowed to cross over once, to help out on an item on jelly. But most of my time was spent scouring the *New England Journal of Medicine* or calling up supermarkets to ask why additives derived from pork were unlabelled, or delving (just a little too literally) into the unsavoury subject of fish worms in ceviche.

Both sides of food matter; both the yum and the yuk. Ever since then, I've been trying to cross the line in both directions: to bring the pleasure of food to bear on the underlying issues, and vice versa: to understand more and do my best whilst retaining my love of food and not being put off by the negative.

But it can be hard to do and certainly to discuss. When I started thinking about food issues twenty years ago, you certainly wouldn't have talked about such matters at the table, like a spectre at the feast. Nobody wants to be a food prig. Then in the late 1990s, something changed. People would turn to me over supper and ask questions. They really wanted to know. Perhaps it was the slow knock-on effect of Mad Cow Disease, a food disaster that truly shook consumer confidence; perhaps it was an increasing interest in food in general. Talking about food was once regarded as something of an eating disorder in Britain, but that has changed a great deal.

Yet all this information, all these questions and all this choice can make life complicated. I often found myself in a supermarket aisle in a state of momentary not-quite-sureness, hand dithering between the Fairtrade imported and the 'traditional' home-grown; between the premium and organic; the value-added and the two-for-one. What to eat?

The question has become more difficult as financial belts have tightened. Many people feel the need to shuffle their overall budget and evaluate their choices. This is certainly true for me. Freelancing fees dropped in the credit crunch and my household expanded when I met a man who has three teenagers with hefty appetites. Our budgets merged but our tastes and priorities were not necessarily the same. I could no longer just grab everything I liked in a general feel-green flow of goodness. Each item had to provide value. Was it more important to buy organic or to get plenty of fresh fruit and vegetables of whatever type? Could savings be made without cutting corners? I needed to know more detail about each food in order to back up my choices and decide on the priorities for our budget. I needed to sort the wheat from the guff.

The world is full of specialists, campaigners and monomaniacs. All the people behind the reports and the headlines are spinning their line from their particular angle. It struck me that one voice was often missing, even though it is the most common and practical. My angle is that of the eater and home cook. I decided to eat my way through food dilemmas from the point of view of someone who loves food and wants to find the answer 'Yes!' I was not necessarily going to radically change the food I cooked – sudden shifts never work in something as habitual as what you eat – but I could make alterations, provided I knew them to be worthwhile and enjoyed the food that made a good change. In the end, I wanted to establish good habits on the grounds of health, the environment and food ethics.

So I jotted down questions when they cropped up as I did my shopping, stood over my pans and browsed through menus in cafés and restaurants. Friends, family and fellow food writers gave me the questions that niggled or puzzled or simply intrigued them. Their questions ranged from specific details ('Is red wine good for me?') to basic principals ('How should I cook my food to get the most from its nutrition?'), from the inquisitive ('Why does cheap bread not go dry when good bread does?') to the wry ('What can I get away with?') and the frustrated ('How can I get my ten-year-old to eat vegetables?'). Eventually I distilled these into the ten questions, or quests, that are the basis of this book.

To find out some answers, I went to experts in every field – farmers, scientists, nutritionists, cooks – to discover what they thought and what they themselves eat and drink. I read books and articles ranging from scientific papers to the freebie rag picked up on the train; all gave me matter to chew on.

I knew from past experience that the route through any particular food question can sometimes be straightforward – easy to see and simple to act upon. In other cases, it was bound to be more complex. 'What to eat?' is often *not* a simple question to answer. Beyond this, eating is a personal matter, and you have to find the best answer for your own tastes and circumstances rather than following a theory to the letter.

But the twists and turns along the paths of enquiry would, I hoped, reveal much about what was on the plate, even I did not reach an 'answer of answers'. Sometimes I was going to reach an 'answer for now (and watch this space)'.

Most of all, I wanted to enjoy what I ate and get closer to it. Culture, history and stories were a part of my quest. The more food is about pleasure, engagement and knowledge, as well as nourishment, the more it becomes a good part of your daily life.

This book explores 'what to eat' with a question mark, not a commanding exclamation mark or even a full stop. Nonetheless, at the end of each food quest, I wanted to discover some rules of thumb about what to eat. They are on three levels.

First of all are the simple, straightforward ideas that can be put into practice on any high street. Without this practical aspect, ideas about food ethics and nutrition – the green and the good – remain as useless as paper pies. These I call 'easy'.

Then come the more complicated solutions that are worth a degree of effort. We all have different levels of interest and commitment, and some foods and issues we want to bother about more than others. These I call 'worth the effort'.

Finally each quest ends with a wish list for the future; a vision to look beyond the pragmatic decisions of today to the possibilities of the future. 'Pie in the sky,' some might call this; I prefer 'hopes and dreams'.

As a starting point, it has seemed to me necessary to clear away some of the fuss, to get back to basics and look at food as food again. First of all, what is it, physically? How is it grown? What does it do to me? And what have we done to it, as consumers, farmers and food producers? So I went back to the beginning, to the letter A; and in this case A is for Apple.

1

What is a Good Apple?

The apple is the starting point of any primer of good food. A is for Apple; an apple a day keeps the doctor away. Each crispy bite does you good and tastes good.

But some apples disappoint. You open wide for a big bite and get a certain juiciness but scarcely a shade of flavour apart from a generic sweetness; or, worse, a dull muzziness, with little taste and a cotton-wool texture. The shinier and more colourful the apple, the sadder it feels to be let down. And it is the most apparently beautiful apples that are often the least good to eat.

My first question to chew upon was focused on a single food: what is the goodness in an apple? First of all, I wanted answers in terms of taste, and the difference made by growing, storage and variety. There are around 20,000 kinds of apples in the world, and around 2,300 in Britain alone, yet my local shops only seemed to have a few and many of these were imported. Why were there so many types yet so few that were widely available? And I wanted to know about the other benefits of an apple: does an apple a day really keep the doctor away? I was after the best apples to eat for both health and happiness.

★

To find answers, I started by going right back to the origin of the apple to understand it better. In the first place, why are there so many different kinds of apple?

In the Garden of Eden, Adam and Eve were invited to pluck freely from every tree that was 'pleasant to the sight and good for food'. This is a perfect summation of the apple tree, with its boughs frothy with fragrant blossom and then laden with fruits swelling to a ripe juiciness. The apple, it turns out, is not actually named in the Old Testament as the fatal fruit; botany scholars believe it would have been perhaps an apricot or a pomegranate, given that apples thrive better in cooler climates. It was Renaissance artists who put the apple into Eden, following from Greek and Roman mythology that depicted golden apples as objects of temptation and desire.

The literal start of the apple has a storybook setting. In the Heavenly Mountains of Tien Shan, on the eastern borders of Kazakhstan, a forest grows that is, in parts, 90 per cent wild apple trees. Yellow, red, green, even near-purple fruits of every shape and size grow in profusion. The trees even emerge from cracks in the pavement in the local city, Almaty (formerly Alma-ata, or 'grandfather of apples'). It was the great Russian geneticist Nikolai Vavilov (1887–1943) who first pinpointed Tien Shan as the original Eden. His theories were backed up by decades of travelling around the world to discover the origins of cultivated plants. He believed that the place with the greatest variety of a species was the likely location of its start. (Vavilov tirelessly collected varieties to build up a seed bank that could help feed people in the best possible way. With appalling irony, he fell foul of the Communist Party and died in a Soviet prison of malnutrition.)

The reason that Tien Shan has quite so many types of apples, and that there are so many types around the world, is that the genetic make-up of the apple is especially diverse. The trees need to be cross-pollinated, either by another kind of domestic apple tree, or by a wild crab-apple, and the resulting fruit does not grow true to its parents. Every pip reshuffles the genes and can lead to a new variety. An apple can be squat and gold, oval and streaked, red and round – and any number of other combinations; and it can taste of nuts, honey, spices, nail polish and other flavours, and yet still be an apple.

The apples in Tien Shan and today's orchards produce crops in three different phases. First come the earlys. These can be noticeably fragrant and red, the colour blushing down through their skin. This bright beauty and alluring scent is there to attract the beasts who will carry the pips and spread the trees. When you are drawn to a pink-flushed early eating apple such as Discovery, you are responding to the same temptations as a bear climbing a tree in a wild forest in central Asia.

The next crop of apples have a harder, often quieter-coloured skin and firmer flesh. They have evolved to lie for longer on the forest floor, to be picked up or to set seed where they lie. This trend continues to the late apples, which are very rich in flavour, lower in sugar and more likely to be russeted, with rough patches of brown on the skin. Such mid- and late season apples may be less fragrant initially, but over time develop that wonderful 'Granny's attic' aroma, with skin and flesh that

can have extraordinary flavours of nuts or berries and can sometimes even be distinctly strawberryish – try a Worcester Permain
– or have a peardrop or nail-polish flavour, like a Cox's Orange
Pippin. While the soft early fruits will disintegrate quickly, the
harder later ones will last and mature in cool storage. The rule
is, the later the apple, the longer it will keep.

Once picked, an apple continues to 'breathe'. This exchange
of carbon dioxide for oxygen makes the fruit continue to develop, lose water and juiciness, and eventually rot. Modern mass-
produced apples are picked and put in cold containers with
Controlled Atmosphere Storage (CAS). This gives the air more
carbon dioxide and less oxygen, reducing the rate of respiration
so the fruit is in stasis. Fruit can be kept in this way for six
months or longer, extending the native apple season. The industry claims it makes no difference to the taste. It certainly keeps
apples crisp. Joan Morgan, doyenne of apple experts, gives a nu-
anced view in the authoritative book she co-authored with Alison Richards, *The Book of Apples*. The apples destined for gas
storage are picked early. Once they are removed, they tend to
mature more quickly. 'Traditionalists argue that as a result many
apples now on sale are simultaneously unripe and past their best,'
they write.

An even more unnatural way of extending shelf life is to use
wax on the skin. The wax stops the apple from breathing,
keeping it 'alive' for longer. In the UK, this is not done to the
home-grown crop, but it is perfectly legal to sell imported
apples treated in this way. You are most likely to find wax on
imported American apples. It is interesting that we seem to

have one rule for British growers and another for what can be sold in our shops.

The apple went from the mountains of Tien Shan, then travelled along the Silk Route and emerged into the wider world. Once a good one was discovered, it was seized upon and propagated. In pre-Classical times, perhaps in Babylon or in China, it was discovered that you needed to graft the branch of a tree onto another rootstock to breed the plant 'true', or the same as its parent. Grafting means that each apple tree can then be reproduced indefinitely. Some trees may even have several different kinds of apples on the one tree, a horticultural version of pick 'n' mix.

The Romans fell in love with the apple and they created a goddess of orchards, gardens and fruit, Pomona. The Latin word 'fruor', meaning 'I enjoy', became the origin of our word 'fruit'. They took the apple to the far northern reaches of the Roman Empire, to the British Isles. In each place the apple arrived, new varieties thrived according to how they were suited to the climate and growing conditions. The early settlers to North America, for example, took apples but found they only thrived when grafted onto native rootstock. The adaptability of the apple's genes has led to great regional variation and means that each country and each area has its own lexicon of fruit that suits its place.

Some have become best-sellers, despite coming from one pip in one apple in one place. Every Bramley apple is descended from a single tree, still alive in a private garden in Southwell,

Nottinghamshire. It's said that another famous apple variety was originally found on a tree growing in a creek on a farm in Australia by Maria Smith, who had emigrated there from Sussex with her husband and children. The variety was grown locally and began to win prizes twenty years after her death in 1870. It was named after her as 'Granny Smith'.

The proliferation of apple varieties reached its height in Britain with the Victorian market gardeners, as nurserymen and keen amateurs vied to find their 'top of the crop'. Britain, with less sunshine and cooler temperatures than other apple-producing countries, is less suitable for some varieties. A condition of the trademark of one of the latest commercial hits, Pink Lady, is that it is not permitted to be grown north of the Loire. But our climate has the advantage of being able to produce a wide variety of flavours and an emphasis on interesting sweet and sharp tastes rather than a uniform sugary blandness. More than two thousand varieties are still found in the British National Fruit Collection at Brogdale in Kent, an inspirational place to visit. Here you can see the variety that inspired Sir Isaac Newton to discover gravity and the types taken across to America by the Pilgrim Fathers, as well as all the apples that make the most interesting eaters and cookers today.

But much of this astonishing variety is not seen as commercially viable and has dwindled away. The French and others subsidized their orchards; we gave grants to cut ours down. Since 1950, nearly 60 per cent of our native orchards have gone – around 170,000 acres. The British climate – both physical and political – makes apple growing less profitable than in other countries. The mainstream UK apple growers decided they should specialize to compete with imports. In the economies of scale, the axe fell on the less mainstream varieties. In the last twenty years, Cox's Orange Pippin, a Kentish variety with a distinctive and complex sweet-sour taste, has become the prime apple amongst the eaters and is now just known as a Cox. Another popular apple is Egremont Russet, generally just called a Russet, which has 4.5 per cent of the English market share. The other kinds – and there are eighty varieties considered commercially viable by the trade organization English Apples and Pears – account for less than half of one per cent. Bramley is the only cooker you see in supermarkets, though there are many other kinds: Grenadier, Burr Knot, Norfolk Beefing, Small's Encore, Onion Moonstreak, to name but a few – and what names!

It is not just the variety per se that creates quality. The infamous Golden Delicious is a case in point. An American variety, originally from West Virginia, it was brought over to Britain by the great nurseryman and fruit lover Edward Bunyard in 1926. At its best, it can be honeyed, juicy and sweet. The variety was greatly taken up by former Algerian colonialists who came back to live in France in the 1960s. United States Marshall Plan money for the revival of post-war Europe was put into orchards, and growers were encouraged to plant great acreages of apples, particularly Golden Delicious, in the Loire and Rhone valleys. The fruit, too bland for French tastes, was largely exported to Britain. These mass-produced apples became a symbol of poor 1970s eating: cheap, yes, but neither golden nor delicious. The apples are picked too early to gain their characteristic golden blush and to develop flavour. The good ones look much more appetizing than the usual pallid yellow; they have a suntan, having been left on the tree for the right amount of time and exposed to enough sun to pick up some taste. The details of production make a real difference to the food that we eat.

The British apple eater's year divides into two halves. There is the northern hemisphere season that starts when the first English apples arrive in July and August and lasts until the stored ones run out in the New Year. After that, we have imports from the southern hemisphere, from countries such as New Zealand and Chile. For reasons of freshness and food miles, I was most interested, in this instance, in home-grown apples and their flavours and availability.

New Covent Garden wholesale market is the place that determines what apples are available in many greengrocers and restaurants – indeed, most places other than supermarkets – and illustrates the commercial reality of apples everywhere. Long rows of sellers line great corridors of shed-like buildings in Vauxhall in South London, their boxes piled high and opened up with luscious fruit to tempt the eye. The prices go up or down depending on who's talking with whom; whether the grapevine says a new cargo is due to land shortly, or has been delayed; whether your credit is good; and what else is going on in the market at that very minute, according to the mysterious way that news flies around like pollen in such places. At every step, the name of the game is about making instant calculations on every margin.

Rob, a dapper-suited wholesaler with a quick eye and tongue, gave me the low-down as we stood chilling in his cold store in the market. He dismissed the flavour of a box of perfect, Kermit-green Granny Smiths – 'You might as well bite into a beer mat' – but at 18p per apple, compared to 23p–25p for a handpicked Russet from Kent, this was going to be the choice for the commodities dealer who was supplying schools or fruit bowls for conference halls. Their interest in variety boiled down to a depressing choice: 'Red apples or green apples.'

I had a bite of one of Rob's Russets, which in commodities parlance might be called a 'rough brown apple', with its matt skin. It was superb: honeyed, nutty, firm, fresh. Anyone would gnaw it to the core. What led to the disappointing cotton-wool apples, I asked? Rob reckoned much of it was down to storage and transportation. A bog-standard apple might be a year old or more by the time it came out of storage and had been transported. It might have been driven across Europe by a lorry driver who turned off the refrigeration unit in order to get some quiet kip in his lorry cab at night. Such are the unseen differences that affect the quality of what arrives on the shop shelf.

Rob had good apples – if very few kinds – but not many customers were apparently interested in taste. It was almost as if the apples were not there to be eaten. And many of them, it was true, would not be. We throw nearly a third of our food away, not least apples. There is supposedly a syndrome by which people buy good, healthy food like fruit and vegetables, feel they have done their duty and don't bother to eat it. But listening to Rob had me wondering. Which came first, the poor apples or the wastefulness? Perhaps we buy and throw away for a good reason: the apples don't taste good. Put like that, is a good apple really so expensive? If you buy a delicious apple for 40p and eat it, isn't this cheaper than buying two apples at 30p and not getting round to eating more than a few bites?

If people were to get more interested in different kinds of apples perhaps the large-scale market would supply them more. Rob said it took eight years or so before an orchard was established. No wonder that the choice of apples in mainstream retail stays on its beaten, boring track. The change is a near decade-long turning circle for the vast ocean liner.

But there are signs that commercial supertankers are finally turning around. Media stories of the great variety of apples have helped stimulate consumer interest. And bigger factors than mere taste are at work. Exporters such as Chile, who traditionally sold to Britain, are turning instead to Eastern European countries, with less exacting regulations than the British supermarkets. China, by far the biggest apple producer, with more than six times the tonnage of the next country, America, is producing low-price apple concentrate that affects apple prices worldwide. Most of all, the rising price of oil is making business look at food miles and imports. The net result is an increase in home-grown apples. There has been a reversal in the chopping down of orchards. Now four out of ten UK apples eaten are home-grown – up from a third – and new orchards are being planted following a commitment to home-grown apples by the supermarkets, including Tesco, the biggest seller with 30 per cent of the fresh apple market. Furthermore, the smart, greener supermarkets are attempting to sell more unusual varieties of apples, sometimes calling them 'tree-ripened' to distinguish them from those that are picked early and put in gas storage.

I began to munch my way around the various apples on sale. The tree-ripened interesting English varieties in the upmarket supermarkets were fine, if expensive and highly packaged. But a telling and unexpected discovery was that some of the very best apples I ate, in terms of flavour, were two-for-one bargain bags of Coxes from a budget supermarket. They were crisp and bright, with the balance of acidity and sweetness that makes this such a good apple. They knocked the socks off the far more expensive imports. This sort of cheap fruit was available at that time, in October, in every supermarket. As it was early in the season, the fruit would have been more or less straight off the tree rather than stored. It shows that seasonal eating is not some vague foodie ideology. It makes a sizeable difference in terms of both quality and price.

As I grazed through the supermarket ranges, it was clear that their selection looked good, piled high and wide, and was certainly better than it had been a couple of years before. But with a few exceptions in the more upmarket supermarkets it still boiled down mostly to this: cheap, bland, imported apples; one kind of cooker (Bramley); a few more interesting imports such as New Zealand Braeburn; and a couple of fresh English varieties – but only a couple. This was at the height of the season of our most celebrated orchard fruit.

★

Easily the best selection of English apples on sale in my neighbourhood turned out to be in the farmers' market. There were
two apple stalls that operated throughout the season, from midsummer to the spring. The fruit had been picked for the market
or stored naturally, without gas. There were no apples on sale in
the summer at all; but when they were available, you knew the
fruit was going to be good. A big advantage of a farmers' market
is that it forces seasonality and more traditional farming methods upon you; the small to medium-scale farmers who sell directly do not have the money for fancy tricks such as Controlled
Atmosphere Storage.

The stall for Home Cottage Farm was nothing more than a
pile of crates with seven kinds of apples, sold by a gentleman
sporting Pop Larkin side-whiskers. His personal favourites were
Lord Lambourne and Laxton's Superb. He showed me how to
tell them apart – the Lambournes have a naturally waxy skin
whilst the Laxton's are more pointy. His farm did not use sprays
on the apples at all, he said, but did spray the trees early on in the
season, before the apples formed, to get rid of codling moth.
This meant that they lost a lot of some varieties. He pointed to
his current cookers – Lane's Prince Albert, a splendidly Victorian apple – and said that only one in five of them was good
enough to sell. The rest could be sold for juice or cider,
although they would fetch less money. 'People don't cook with
apples these days,' Pop Larkin said. 'My daughter will eat an
apple pie when they come round to our place but at home they
eat rice and things.' In other words, a particular kind of English
cooking, with puddings for 'afters', was now so old-fashioned as

to be almost obsolete. 'Good Apple Pies are a considerable part of our domestic happiness,' wrote Jane Austen to her sister Cassandra on 17 October 1815. Was such a dish, such a source of contentment, now in danger of becoming food history?

I began to experiment with apple puddings, initially using cookers. These varieties have a higher percentage of malic acid and taste sour when raw, but mellow on cooking to release plenty of flavour, whereas some eating apples can become relatively bland when cooked. A number of such apples are termed 'dual purpose' since they become eaters as the acid softens over time in storage. The sourness of all apples lessens in cooking and even very sharp apples did not need as much sugar as I had initially thought. You discover this when you make a baked apple – surely one of the simplest of puddings: cut a hole in the middle to remove the core, put in a spoonful of mincemeat, or chopped nuts and dried fruits mixed with just a little honey and some orange juice, and bake until soft. The acidity of cooking apples and their relatively high percentage of air means they collapse to a fluffy purée that is good in both a sauce for pork and in some puddings. I also found out that eating apples also make good but denser purées that work well in an apple charlotte, the intense apple mixture surrounded by a shell of crisp, buttery bread.

I wanted to get even closer to the apple, to stand amidst the boughs of an orchard. That seemed far away from my London flat; but it was much closer than I thought.

In 1990 the charity Common Ground, champions of the local

and distinctive, put on an Apple Day in Covent Garden featuring a hundred varieties for people to admire and taste. What is now a plaza of fancy shops and street entertainers for tourists was once London's wholesale market for fruit, vegetables and flowers. Before that, it was the orchard of a convent where apples grew, hence the name. This Apple Day was the start of a gradual revolution. It takes a long time to create an orchard, but the inspiration, infectious generosity and creativity of Common Ground's approach has planted pips in many likely and unlikely places, and these are now bearing fruit including a number of community orchards around the country.

The very best apples I tasted on my explorations were not bought from shops or markets at all but were absolutely free for the picking. They came from a number of modern Edens: the community orchards that I found, to my surprise, on my doorstep in London.

From inner city to outer suburb, I followed the footsteps of a photographer, Katy Peters, who has been chronicling these hidden orchards. Katy had been through the *London A–Z* and had discovered no fewer than 130 orchard-related names. The names were often all that remained of places that really had once been Nut Walk or Cherry Lane. Many of London's orchards were at one time a horse-and-cart's ride from the centre, and were fertilized by the dung of city horses. Where I live, in Ealing, there were once 250 market gardens. My nearest community orchard, Blondin Community Orchard, is on an allotment site on what used to be Brentford Nursery, which once specialized in fruit trees and offered more than three hundred apple varieties.

One of the most inspiring of the community orchards was Butterfield Green in Stoke Newington. When I wandered in, just a street or two from layered urban grime and aggro, a young mother was showing her daughter how to pick and eat raspberries from a bush and an elderly couple were sitting peacefully in the summer sun on a bench made from recycled wood. It was a surprising spot to discover, and instantly both joyful and calming.

It used to be quite different. The orchard has been planted in an area that had been a sterile and unfriendly, roughly grassed-over BMX track. Gated at both ends, people left their dogs there while they went to the pub. One day a local woman, Annie Wilson, got into an argument with the owner of what is termed a 'dangerous dog'. The man proved to be no more friendly than his hound and threw dog faeces at her. This episode of dog-rage was the end of the line. Annie leafleted the whole area and a group was formed to make improvements. They hit on the idea of an orchard, and just a few years later the place has been transformed. 'The orchard has made us a community,' says Annie. 'We've got to know each other through this.' 'There are lots of bits of ground in London that people grumble about and they don't think they can do anything,' says Pat O'Leary, another of the organizers. 'But a group of us turned what was basically a dog toilet into an orchard.'

The London community orchards were enchanting in many different and often unexpected ways. There was the orchard behind a high wire fence in the middle of the White City estate. Pears, plums, damsons, greengages and apples were tumbling off the boughs, there to be looked after, sat amongst and enjoyed by those who went to the Nubian Life Resources Centre for Caribbean and African-Caribbean elders. I found other orchards on the corner of housing estates and near tower blocks. All these trees somehow obliterated the sharp angles of their surroundings and people were instinctively drawn to these beautiful places. I trekked out to the eastern fringes of the city, past the Festival of Britain bus shelter at Newbury Park underground station on the Central Line, and then onwards to find the remnants of an orchard from a country estate that now lay under the current housing estate. When I arrived, two teenagers were cooing to each other like Adam and Eve, sitting upon a bench under a tall apple tree, she with a bottle of pink alcopop, he with cans of Fosters lager.

Then there was the Chinbrook orchard on an allotment site in Bromley. Dozens of trees had been planted here, but the new orchard had become overgrown. Four amateur gardeners, who met on a Royal Horticultural Society evening class, decided to pull it round. One of their first tasks was to learn how to prune fruit trees. 'You want to get rid of dead and diseased branches and ones that are crossing, shaping the tree so air circulates around the fruit,' explained one of the rescuers, Jan Fish. 'What you want is vigour and shape. It's more of an art than a science.' She spoke of how good it was to work as a team; to have another pair of eyes to back up your decisions about which branches to lop off and which to save. You could feel her sense of achievement in bringing this sleeping beauty back to life.

Standing in these orchards, I saw how you could cup an apple in your hand and tell if it was ripe by whether it would come away easily. In them, I finally tasted England's wealth of apples. It started with a windfall Pitmaston Pine Apple at Chinbrook. A small apple, raised at the end of the eighteenth century in Herefordshire, it really did taste of pineapples. At Fenton House, a hidden National Trust gem in Hampstead with a beautiful traditional orchard, I saw some apple varieties that went back to when the house was built in the seventeenth century. You cannot pick these for yourself but the house holds an annual Apple Day in September when twenty-odd apples are sold fresh, and more are available as pressed juice. Soft, hard, blushed, juicy, dry, waxy, sweet, sharp, flesh as white as snow, skin as red as rubies, neon-green, pale yellow, golden: here was the bounty of the apple. It was a long way from the mountains of Tien Shan and the entrepreneurial Victorian market gardeners, yet here it was in all its glory, to be shared and celebrated.

So much for quality and variety. What about health? 'An apple a day keeps the doctor away' was originally a marketing slogan dreamt up by American apple growers at the start of the twentieth century. Many apples were then made into alcohol, what is called 'hard cider' in America. When Prohibition got its iron grip on booze, the apple growers were keen to promote their fruit as something good to eat instead. At this time, evidence was emerging about the health aspects of food, especially the newly named vitamins. In the subsequent century, this evidence has accumulated and the marketeers' point has endured.

But does an apple a day keep the doctor away? There are all

sorts of goodies in apples, including vitamins and many other micronutrients, as well as two types of fibre. When I looked into the figures, it emerged that apples are a good enough source of vitamin C but way down the pecking order compared to other fruit and vegetables. An average apple – and note that this is an average – has 6mg/100g. Compare this to blackcurrants (200mg/100g), red peppers (190mg), broccoli and kiwi fruit (90mg), Brussels sprouts (80mg) or oranges (50g). They come below peaches (7mg) but above pears (4mg). On further questioning, however, it turns out that different apple varieties have different quantities of vitamin C, varying from 3mg to 28mg or more. A single old-fashioned Ribston Pippin has more vitamin C than a whole pound of Golden Delicious, according to Common Ground's *The Apple Source Book*. The very best way to eat an apple is raw, as vitamin C is destroyed by heat, and to eat it peel and all. This is where the micronutrients are concentrated, and also, crucially, the flavour. Try eating two segments of an apple, one peeled and one unpeeled. The difference in taste is striking.

Vitamin C is just one small part of the apple's goodness, and apples are great to eat for all sorts of other reasons. Apples are mostly sugar and water, and we are led to feel that sugar is a bad thing. Yet there is a vast difference between biting into an apple and eating a spoonful of sugar. The apple's sugars come in a mouthful that contains other parts of the apple, most crucially fibre. Fibre is the stuff that forms the structure of plants and is hugely beneficial in terms of how you digest what you eat. The insoluble kind in apples moves food through your body at just the right pace, enabling you to absorb the goodness in the apple through your gut wall and without your blood sugar suddenly going into peaks and troughs. Apples contain the soluble fibre pectin, which is the stuff that sets jams and jellies. (Rowntrees used to use pectin from apples grown in the Vale of York to set their Fruit Gums; a quaint notion in these days of industrialized food.) Pectin, along with vitamin C, is thought to help lower cholesterol. A French study concluded that two apples a day were required rather than one, double the dose in the American slogan. A team at Cornell University in New York State is doing some interesting work analysing how the micronutrients in apples seem to prevent cell and tissue damage in the body. This is particularly true of the peel, and yet another reason to eat it. The Cornell research findings so far are from test-tubes not humans, but all the same they make me even happier to enjoy a good apple – or two.

I became interested in all the other apple products available. Dried apples are both delicious and contain vitamin C and fibre but they are usually made from peeled apples, so not as good as fresh. I sometimes have some for breakfast and for snacks, putting a small packet in my bag to nibble on. It is easy to cut thin slices of apple, dip them in a flavoured sugar syrup and dry them in a very low oven to make your own apple chips. I have also tried different types of farm-pressed juice in the interest of tasting my way through varieties, getting the English apple taste out of season in the summer, and supporting the smaller growers who cannot sell all their fruit fresh.

Then I got into cider. Cider in the past has suffered from

being too cheap. In an effort to boost sales of a native drink, its tax has been low in comparison to other alcoholic drinks. It became gut-stripping, head-swirling scrumpy – made from real apples but sometimes on the rough side – or produced from apple concentrate as a cheap way for teenagers to get drunk. Happily, advertising campaigns by the big producers, aimed at bringing cider to the mass market, has also stimulated interest in the far more interesting artisan ciders. One of the best places to sample them is the English Cider Centre in East Sussex, where you dodge the drunken wasps to get to a room filled with 120 kinds of draught cider and perry (the pear cousin of cider) and 160 bottled types. A number of English ciders were appley and with a gently sweet quality that, like French ciders, can make it such a great accompaniment to food, particularly curries and other hot dishes.

A fine book, *Ciderland*, by the poet James Crowden, gave me some clues as to the difference between traditional French and standard English cider. French producers make their medium cider using a process called 'keeving'. This means you do not ferment your apple juice to the point where all the sugar is turned to alcohol. Instead, you add chalk and enzymes to draw off the proteins in a 'brown hat', stopping the fermentation and keeping more of the natural sweetness of the apple in the cider. This method was practised in some parts of England up until the Second World War. Then it was yet another skill that got lost in the rush towards cheap food production. A number of craft producers are reviving it. I am sure that if more did so we would see an even bigger surge in the English and Welsh cider revival.

As an added bonus, English cider apples, native to the West Country (cider is made with eating apples in the east of England), have especially high quantities of antioxidants. Your winking cup of cider is full of them to the brim, and this is why cider was once taken on board ship to prevent scurvy.

When cider gets too sour, it can be made into cider vinegar. Health foodists rave about this. I was intrigued to be told by a cider maker that she was regularly getting called by vets – a reasonably hard-headed lot – looking for supplies of cider vinegar to give to domestic horses and racehorses because it was so good for their joints. The folklore dosage for cider vinegar is to have a couple of teaspoons with a teaspoon of honey. This sounds to me like the basis of a rather tasty salad dressing and – proven or not as a health food – it is certainly very good on a big bowl of rocket leaves, a sliced avocado, a little cheese, some toasted walnuts – and some unpeeled apple slices, naturally.

There is one final apple issue to touch upon. It's well known that these fruits have been amongst the most sprayed crops, a disturbing thought when you consider that you want to eat the peel because this contains many of the micronutrients and a lot of the flavour. My initial findings on apples and pesticides raised some interesting issues.

The latest government figures, from the Pesticides Residues Committee, are available on the Internet. When I looked in 2008, they showed that out of ninety tested samples of apples on sale in the UK, just twenty-six, including the six organic apples tested, had no pesticide residues at all. The rest all had some of at least one kind. Of these, nineteen had detectable traces of two kinds of pesticide; nine had traces of three; five had traces of four sorts and one had traces of five pesticide residues in total. Two Chilean apples tested had traces of pesticides beyond what is called 'maximum residue levels', i.e. what the government is officially worried about. One had unacceptable residues of diphenylamine, which is sprayed onto apples to prevent something called 'scald'. Some of the apple industry's instructional pictures on the Internet show terrible pictures of fruit scarred by pesticide misuse. Clearly this was damaged fruit and would not be eaten, but these are potent chemicals – strong enough to cause industrial accidents to the people using them, as well as affecting the food they are applied to. I am not sure I want to eat such pesticides, even if greatly diluted. Beyond this, two English apples in the study had traces of a fungicide, carbendazim, that has been put on the Friends of the Earth list of the 'filthy four' and was banned from orchards in 2006, though in this case not entirely effectively.

Apples are notoriously difficult to grow without sprays. But Peter Kindersley, the owner of an organic operation, Sheepdrove Farm, has planted eighty acres of orchards in Herefordshire using apples developed in Eastern Europe at a time when they couldn't afford to buy pesticides behind the Iron Curtain. I spoke to one producer in Kent, who grew both conventional and organic fruit, and he praised the best level of conventional horticulture, using such methods as integrated crop management that uses bugs to kill other bugs, rather than using chemicals, and he was critical of the fact that copper sulphate can be used as a fungicide on fruit classified as 'organic'. This is done under 'derogations' from the main guidelines, according to the regulating body for organic foods, the Soil Association, and very little is in fact used.

During the course of this project I would look further into the issues of pesticides, and of organic food in general, but as far as apples go there seem to be two way of looking at the matter. The government's pesticide report states that none of the residues found in their apple samples would be 'expected to pose a health risk'. The upside of chemical use is twofold: productivity, which affects price; and cosmetic perfection, which we are all meant to care so much about. I'm not so sure that, given the choice, people wouldn't pick a bit of roughness on the skin to fewer pesticides. The unsprayed farmers' market apples might have been a bit blemished, but they were the best commercial apples I bought, and were the same price as standard supermarket apples. Pesticide use matters on trees because it will accumulate in the soil; you cannot just suddenly move the orchard to fresh new ground, and completely unsprayed orchards are special places to visit, full of insects and birds.

I once spoke to the food writer and anti-pesticides campaigner Moyra Bremner, who put the matter of orchard chemicals in this light. Even if the quantities of chemical toxins are small, they are still present. She asks: 'Imagine you have two dishes and you are giving them to a child. Which one would you choose: the one containing poison or the one without?' Extreme, perhaps; but thought-provoking.

WHAT TO EAT?

Easy. Buy British in season, from midsummer to late winter; spot tasty bargain apples in the 'misshapen' bagfuls in supermarkets; taste your way through fresh-pressed apple juices; try good cider instead of wine and give it a go with curries and other spicy food; cook with apples as well as eating them; add cider vinegar to your store cupboard.

Worth the effort. Go to farmers' markets and farm shops to try different apples throughout the season; revive apple puddings; get to know your nearest community orchard and celebrate Apple Day, on 21 October or the nearest weekend.

Hopes and dreams. More British varieties will be grown and reach a wider market; cheaper second-grade fruit will find its way into schools to be pressed for juice bars; good apples will be sold as snacks in schools, local shops and works canteens; apples and cider will once more be seen as a national treasure and the health of the nation will be toasted with delicious artisan cider.

2

What is the Best Breakfast?

Breakfast used to be a big deal in Britain. 'To eat well in England you should have a breakfast three times a day,' advised the writer Somerset Maugham. He'd made his home in the South of France, surrounded by ripe tomatoes and bouillabaisse, and you can feel the edge of an insult in these words. But there's also truth. Breakfast is the occasion for bringing out a surprising number of our classic British foods, from porridge to marmalade, with the 'Full English' and kedgeree at the summit.

Such foods developed when breakfast was still a proper meal. I'd read about Victorian and Edwardian breakfasts, the sideboard groaning with lamb chops, smoked fish and three kinds of jam to spread on your hot buttered toast, and wondered about the reason for such a feast.

According to *The Great British Breakfast* by Jan Read and Maite Manjon, breakfast was originally one of two large meals in the day, the other being taken at around 4 p.m. When the Industrial Revolution brought people into cities, we no longer worked close to home and we came back later at the end of the day. Electric light meant the shape of the day was no longer dictated by when the sun rose and set. Dinner got later and lunch slipped into the gap, making breakfast a less important meal.

The Edwardian rich still ate a big breakfast, and a few crumbs from the feast have fallen down through the decades. As a child in the 1970s, my school day usually started with a three-course meal. Cereal and fruit juice were followed by 'cooked' – eggy bread, beans on toast, the dreaded runny yolk of the poached egg (a substance that still gives me a slight phobic shudder – how primal eggs are!). Then came toast with butter or, later, Flora, this new stuff in a brightly packaged tub that adults suddenly took to eating. It spread more easily than butter but the taste was entirely forgettable; there must be some other mysterious reason to eat it, I surmised. There was jam, Marmite and then marmalade, which had a special aura. People stated firm preferences for different kinds – thin or thick shred; the type of citrus fruit; dark or light. Every year our kitchen was full of a sticky orange fug from a cauldron brewing an arcane domestic spell. My step-grandfather called marmalade 'jeely pieces', a Scottish way of referring to 'jelly marmalade'. The special phrase was another indication that marmalade was the pick of the pots. Cereal was less mysterious: Cornflakes or Weetabix. But it had its excitements. Sugary Frosties were a Very Big Treat. The odd plastic toy could be found in the bottom of a box – a present from Tony the Tiger – he's grrrrrrrrrrreat!

On high days and holidays I also remember Mum and Dad carefully picking out chunks of flesh from the hairy-boned skeletons of kippers. It seems slightly quaint now, this leisurely application to an eating task, with the clink of cups on saucers, the rustle of newspapers and conversation about the plans for the day.

Breakfast in my present-day home is now taken at different times in different ways by different people. It is far too fragmentary to come together as a shared meal. From looking at my own past, I realise how much is lost once a meal is scattered. The rich culture of breakfast can even be reduced right down to the 'breakfast bar', a cereal snack you can eat on the way to work. So we've gone from buttery, savoury kedgeree, fragrant and golden with spices, or the pert yolk of a fried egg, or a comforting bowlful of apple purée and creamy yoghurt to … a piece of flavoured chew. I wondered how to get back to having a proper breakfast and what the best one is to eat?

Breakfast can be reduced to such a basic unit of nutrition as the breakfast snack bar because the functional nature of the meal is clear. First and foremost, the food you eat now is about energy. You haven't eaten for perhaps twelve hours and your body needs a quick shot of calories to get you up, up and away. It is to 'break your fast' and power you through the morning. And yet often we fail to do this well – or at all. A survey by the Breakfast Cereal Information Service concluded that four out of ten teenagers didn't have any breakfast (half of them said they got out of bed too late – an all too believable reason).

This falling away of breakfast came to me drastically at a conference organized by the British Nutrition Foundation. In the coffee queue, I got talking to a home economics teacher who taught seventeen- and eighteen-year-olds the basics of catering. You'd think such students would have an interest in food. But it turned out to be a 'sink subject'. They were pushed towards catering (or childcare) if they were good for nothing else – a depressing indictment of priorities on both counts. The teacher told me how on her first day she looked at her new class and saw a lack of concentration in their faces and bodies. She hoped it wasn't simply that they weren't interested. A few questions revealed many hadn't eaten any breakfast. Some had scarcely supped the night before because of lack of money, effort and organization. Her first task was to get the class to cook breakfast. It wasn't a revolution, but it was a start.

When I looked again at my own breakfast habits, I realized that it was not a meal that involved much effort or pleasure any more. In the weekdays, it had become stripped down to the merely functional – and it wasn't even that useful. Usually, I had two slices of toast, one sweet (marmalade, jam, honey) and one savoury (Marmite, sometimes tomato ketchup – a strange quirk of taste left over from childhood), both with quite a slather of butter. The bread came from a variety of loaves, sometimes white, sometimes brown. As often as not, I was hungry by about 11 a.m. and got into snacking, the hand wandering towards the biscuit tin. I'd end up at lunchtime with a mind adrift from concentrating on anything much apart from food.

I happened to go on a press trip to Jamaica at around this time. The buffet bar in the Holiday Inn had its amusements, principally looking out of the window at preparations for a series of beach wedding parties and a company of cheerleaders in matching outfits on a team-building holiday. But even these got upstaged by the breakfast. What fascinated me was the way it laid out the main fault line of breakfast today. The hotel's all-inclusive meal deal offered an American breakfast, eaten by most of the guests. This was more or less what we ate in the UK – let's call it 'the Western diet' breakfast: processed breakfast cereals, toast, muffins, croissants, Danish pastries, rolls, brioches and cake. I suddenly saw it as a beige carpet of processed wheat and sugar that could be rolled up and out anywhere. Everything had been made in a factory, put in warehouses and taken to as many places as possible, to be scaled up or down as identical units.

In contrast, the Jamaican breakfast alongside contained proper dishes that had been freshly prepared. It included the country's national dish, saltfish and ackee. Ackee is a curious food plant in that it is poisonous unless the fruit is picked properly ripe. Whole families have died after eating unripe fruit at a meal. Correctly picked, however, it has delectably creamy curds of flesh and a distinctive taste of its own. Tinned ackee is available in the UK, picked and processed so there is no risk of poison, but it isn't the same as fresh. In my Jamaican breakfast buffet, the delicious and delicate fresh ackee was mixed with saltfish – dried, salted white fish that is soaked in water and cooked. It was a deeply savoury and unusual dish to eat at breakfast, though surely no stranger than a British kipper. Effort, knowledge and culture were repaid in taste.

I asked my Jamaican friend who would eat this sort of food at breakfast? People like his nephew who mended telegraph poles all day, he said. A cooked breakfast was regarded as crucial if you are going to do any kind of physical work. I knew from way back when that proteins were 'body-building' substances. Did this have any relevance to me? Sitting at a computer and diddling around at a keyboard may not seem like hard work. But the brain is also a physical entity – it uses a quarter of our energy – and I notice that when I'm thinking hard then a good breakfast makes a big difference. Could it be that protein was now a component missing from the start of my day?

Because of its functional nature, breakfast has become a forum for nutritional claims, full of 'modern' foods that boast their health credentials like foot-in-the-door salesmen. Spreads such as Flora and highly packaged and marketed cereals flash the fact they are low-fat or the right fat, with 'added vitamins' sprinkled in like sugar. The probiotic yoghurt on your cereal helps your digestion and makes you leap through the day – according to the adverts. Then the meal is washed down with juices that are again 'fortified' by these mysterious 'added vitamins'.

As a food writer, I am partly fascinated by nutrition and partly frustrated by it. On the one hand, it can tell me more about what's on the plate. On the other, it can reduce food to a pile of technical terms. I felt there must be a way to learn about breakfast from nutrition without being reductionist.

To start off, I wanted to know more about proteins and carbohydrates and consulted my bookshelves. For my basic knowledge, I went to the most solid-looking book on the shelf, Fox and Cameron's *Food Science, Nutrition and Health*, a student primer now in its seventh edition. It was 320 pages of closely written text with tables, chemical equations and the odd line illustration to illuminate matters along the way.

Since nutrition-speak is part of our culture, it is common now for people to talk of 'carbs', as if they are some separate kind of food on its own that can be bought in packets like sugar or cereal. People talk of 'comforting carbs' as if of a cosy blanket to be tucked over your tired body – or your hangover – and they are shorthand for foods such as bread, buns, biscuits and crisps. But what are they, literally?

Carbohydrates are made up of three essential elements: carbon, oxygen and hydrogen. Plants make carbohydrates by mixing carbon dioxide (CO_2) with water (H_2O) in the presence of light (photosynthesis). The end products of photosynthesis are carbohydrates. I could now hear the 'carbon' and the 'hydro' in the word. These circulate around the plant like sweet petrol to give energy and substance to cells of every kind – be they petal, stem or leaf. We humans are far less elegantly self-sustaining and cannot make our own carbohydrates. So we have to get them from eating plants, or the animals that eat the plants.

Whilst carbohydrates provide us with C, O and H, we also need N, or Nitrogen. This is one of the crucial elements of protein. Fox and Cameron have chemical equations showing constellations of Cs, Os, Hs and Ns. The book explains that proteins are made up of crystalline substances called amino acids. These build our cells and are also essential for our immune system, metabolic processes and movement. There are eight amino acids that are termed essential; we cannot make them in our bodies and so have to eat them. Animal proteins, such as meat, cheese and eggs, contain these essential or 'complete' amino acids. Plant foods are not complete but become so when eaten in the right combination. Beans and grains, eaten together, work in this way, and quite a number of dishes, from beans on toast to Jamaican rice and peas, are eaten together through folk wisdom without any knowledge of the science. Native Americans even evolved a way of growing corn, beans and squash together; the 'three sister plants' that are, when combined, nutritionally complete.

I read about how the carbohydrates we eat quickly circulate around the body, as sugar sap does around a plant. This is why they are useful at breakfast, when you want to get going. If you eat more carbohydrates than you need, they are stored as fat that can be remobilized as energy when necessary and, if unused, will build up and sit on your tummy. Protein, however, cannot be stored and we need to eat some every day.

How much protein do we actually need? I remember hearing that we need 1 gramme per kilogramme of body weight. Fox and Cameron state that you need a bit less than this. As a 'woman, 19–50 years' (my category), I needed 46.5g – but that was for someone who was 60kg and I was 65kg. Getting out my calculator, I reckoned I needed, proportionally, about 50.3g. I measured this out in random common foods that were all in my kitchen: chicken, cheddar, chickpeas, and then cashew nuts, since it also began with C and I had them on the go for a pre-supper snack. To work out their protein content, I used the other solidly chunky nutrition book on my shelf, McCance and Widdowson's *The Composition of Foods*. This has tables of every food with all parts measured out, be it vitamin A, zinc or protein. The tables calculate how much of each nutrient is in 100g of the food.

I worked diligently through the tables, using a ruler to keep my eyes on track. A portion of 100g of chicken is three-quarters of a breast and I'd usually eat a whole one, meat and skin. This would be around 34g of protein, so around two-thirds of what I needed for the entire day. A 50g lump of cheddar is a decent but not very greedy hunk and this has around 13g of protein. Half a drained can of chickpeas has around 11g. A couple of handfuls of cashew nuts (weighing 20g) has around 5g.

Delving further into McCance and Widdowson, I came up with some interesting discoveries. Yoghurt, an animal product and therefore something I generally thought of as protein, has more carbohydrates than protein. A baked potato is, as I thought, mostly carbohydrate, but it also has nearly 4g of protein, getting on for around a tenth of what I need to eat in a day. Perhaps most surprisingly, two slices of brown bread has 8.5g of protein. One of the most striking statistics you hear is that three crops – wheat, rice and maize – provide 50 per cent of the calories and – rather more surprisingly – a whole two-thirds of the world's protein. Of these, wheat has the highest level of protein.

So plants are useful providers of protein as well as meat, and it wouldn't be difficult to get an adequate amount of protein from these vegetable sources if you got them in the right combination. If you eat a reasonably varied diet, you should get enough, since protein is present in the cell walls of all matter, and therefore all foods – grains and other plants as well as meat. Yet I hadn't realized, also, that meat is quite such a nutritionally powerful and concentrated food. Even a small amount will soon give you the protein you need – indeed, soon far more than is necessary.

I felt a touch impatient at working my way through the nutrition tables, just as I do label-worriting in the supermarket. But I had also learnt from looking at the detail and this knowledge started to feed through to my breakfast. I saw how protein is an important part of a meal, and made more effort to include some. And I also saw how it could be got in a small package. A piece of advice picked up in a magazine, *Waitrose Food Illustrated*, is that you only need a piece 'the size of a pack of cards' of concentrated animal protein, such as meat or cheese, at a meal. After this, I could appreciate more the value at breakfast-time of an egg, or a piece of ham on toast, or a slice of cheese. Quite a bit of protein can also be got from foods that I had previously thought of as 'just carbohydrate' such as bread; meat is simply the most convenient and densely packed way of doing this, but not the only way. I realized more fully that foods could contain all kinds of macronutrients – protein, carbohydrates and fats – just in different quantities. If you ate a reasonable number of different fresh foods, you would cover the bases. The old saying about having a 'balanced, varied diet' is evidently true.

In my quest for the best breakfast, I wanted to look further at plant proteins. There is a good alternative to the dreary processed carbohydrates of the Western diet breakfast: wholegrains. These are grains that are kept more intact than their processed cousins. As a general rule, I'd picked up that food that is kept closer to its original form tends to contain more goodness and be easier on the body and better for you.

One of the reasons that oats and wholegrains are praised is that their glycaemic index (g.i.) is low. This is one of those phrases that often crops up now when food conversations takes a nutritional turn. It refers to the way that different foods affect your blood sugar. The higher the g.i., the more quickly the food raises the glucose in your blood. If this happens a great deal it affects your insulin levels, and this hormone affects how much food you store as fat. It was originally codified by scientists at Oxford University who measured how much blood sugar went up two hours after eating sixty-two foods. The benchmark of 100 was given to the response after consuming glucose syrup. Compared to this, white bread has a g.i. of 72 and apples of 39; white bread is a high g.i. food and apples a low one. A more accurate way of measuring food is to look at the 'glycaemic load' (g.l.), which takes into account how much of a particular food you are likely to eat. Carrots may have a high g.i. but a lower g.l., for example.

At the Holiday Inn buffet in Jamaica, I'd spotted a dish containing wholegrains with low g.i.: the porridge – or rather, the porridges, for there were several. One type was a golden cornmeal, the others were made of oats. It wasn't like the porridge I'd grown up with, but full of spices and sweetened with coconut milk. I took a spoonful. Delicious. I ate my bowlful to the last scrapings, Goldilocks-style. Porridge is traditionally eaten by Jamaican kids as a good energizing breakfast and you see it on the high street in Jamaican take-aways alongside the fried chicken and curried goat.

I've had my porridge eras. We're always being told it releases carbohydrate-energy slowly and keeps you going for longer. But faced with a bowl of what is essentially a dull grey-brown sludge, I sometimes don't feel inspired to swallow much and then get hungry late mid-morning, and not in a way that just an apple can fix. Perhaps I wasn't eating it correctly? I came back from Jamaica determined to make what I called 'unpenitential' porridge.

My Jamaican friend was taking me around Brixton market when a helping hand appeared. 'Eh, Miiiister Porridge!' my friend shouted out in that shy Jamaican way. Mr Porridge is famous in Brixton, London, and Kingston, Jamaica, for his concoctions which are sold from the back of a van. He smiled with the glint of a gold tooth. I watched it flash as he described over the next five minutes how he'd make his brews, stirring coconut milk, nutmeg, allspice and Demerara sugar into either an oatmeal or a cornmeal base, sometimes along with, let's see ... (he looked around in the vast storecupboard of the imagination)... mmmm, today with just a little bit of ... rosewater. It all sounded much more appealing than grey goo.

The next day, I went to look at the oats in the supermarket. As with any food, once you start looking, there are so many types. There were acres of porridge oats that were simply processed, flattened out grains, and even instant porridge with the tag 'Just add water'. I've learnt that there's an unfortunate trade-off between convenience and flavour (and certainly price). So I went to the other end of the scale. People had told me that pinhead oatmeal was 'the Tops', and I found some in a fancy tin.

The first time I made some, it was very, *very* hard work. I just didn't have the time and application, or the arm and jaw muscles, for this task. You might call it an 'inconvenience food', if overtly wholesome. However, soaking the oats the night before made a big difference. Plenty of people advise two parts oats to water but life is much easier if you go three to one, or even a bit more. But I rarely have the backbone for these hardcore oats at breakfast-time and more often, if eating porridge, I go for rolled oats. I still try to remember to soak the grains the night before, sometimes with some dried fruits, which flavour the water and grains.

I make my porridge with water rather than milk and also add some salt to the cooking pot because plain grains need it. Many breakfast cereals contain a great deal of salt, but when making my own porridge I can use just a pinch. Most important of all is what you put on top. Plain porridge is like bare toast: neither appetizing nor, in the end, effective. I'd always tended to have milk and some sugar or honey on it, which makes it nicer to eat and keeps me fuller for longer. Now I thought it good to also add bits and pieces from the fruit bowl and the storecupboard, particularly dried fruits and, inspired by Jamaican porridge, nuts – there's some good protein – and also spices; perhaps a cinnamon stick, a grating of nutmeg or some crushed cardamom pods. If I have some cream in the fridge I add a splosh, and it definitely keeps me fuller for more time. I discovered in my nutrition books that fat takes longer to digest than carbohydrates. It makes a big difference not just to the pleasure of the dish but how much it sustains you.

When I am in more of a rush, I have decided that oatcakes are another good way to eat my oats. You'd never dream of having a bare oatcake. It acts, rather, as an easy vehicle for some protein and fat to keep you going. An oatcake with peanut butter, or some butter and honey, or a piece of ham or cheese, is easy and delicious.

However much I got into oats for my breakfast, it is wheat that makes up the largest part of the breakfast diet. In the US, some 20 per cent of all the calories eaten in a day come from wheat. I wondered how we in the West came to have this concentration of calories in one single plant – and in largely one form, white flour?

Wheat was originally a wild grass that spread its seed as it ripened. It is thought that over a time-scale of perhaps a couple of centuries, early man picked up on the mutated plants that did not just shed their seed by letting them fly off in the wind or fall to the ground, but instead grew a 'shatterproof' stem that clung onto the grains for longer. This meant the seeds could be gathered, threshed and stored. A similar process happened in the domestication of wild maize in America and rice in the East.

Wheat is a powerful symbol, as well as a daily staple, seen as nothing less than a cornerstone of civilization. Being able to store grain allowed humans to settle and organize society. With food assured, different tasks could be distributed to different people, not least food production. This freed us up to build the pyramids, form parliaments, write poetry, create the Internet and so on.

The reason that wheat, in particular, became pre-eminent in the modern world is as much about culture as agriculture. Wheat became a symbol of Christian purity; its very name is thought to be related to the word for 'white'. In Medieval Europe, rye and other grains were seen as second rate compared to the pure wheat of Christian countries. The attraction and symbolism of wheat was so strong that, even though it was harder to grow wheat and other grains in the wet climate of northern Europe, farmers persisted. When grains were taken over to New England, it took some time before the wheat grain took to the soil, but again the European settlers kept on trying.

Wheat became so important because it is so good to eat and has miraculous properties when leavened by yeast and baked. The grain is especially high in a substance called gluten. This is formed from proteins in the flour when they are kneaded with water. Gluten has the elasticity to stretch and hold and it is this that gives a loaf its spring. Other grains, such as rye, have less of it and oats have none. So it is wheat that makes the lightest and most glamorous of loaves.

But the main point of bread is the energy it gives you. If an average slice of bread weighs around 30g then, according to McCance and Widdowson, three slices offer around 220 calories of energy – a tenth of what I, as a women, need in a day, and what's more it comes in the form of quickly mobilized carbohydrate, as well as giving me a good heft of protein.

Was this staff of life as strong as it used to be? My lesson from apples was that the detail of production matters. Was the same true of both bread and the flour it is made from?

I looked first at flour, such an ordinary bag in the kitchen and yet again with so many variations. Traditionally, wheat was milled between grinding stones. The industrious Victorians invented a more efficient way to mill flour between rollers that unfortunately removed some of the vitamins and minerals. Craft baker Andrew Whitley, in his campaigning book *Bread Matters*, gives a dispiriting list of the loss: vitamin E (86 per cent lost), zinc (78 per cent), calcium (60 per cent), iron (76 per cent) and so on. Some of these are added back into the flour, but it still does not have the same nutritional composition as stoneground flour. The calcium, for example, is added as chalk.

Then there's the type of flour. Wholemeal flour is just the whole grain, ground up. White flour is what you get when you sift off the bran and internal wheatgerm. The latter is full of vitamin E and in time goes rancid as it contains oil. But the food writer Elizabeth David says in *English Bread and Yeast Cookery* that many think taking the germ out of the wheat berry is like taking the yolk out of the egg. Roller mills reduce wholewheat down to perhaps 70 per cent of the original grain in order to make white flour. When stoneground, even white flour is more nutritious, with more like 80 per cent of the original grain.

I've visited a few mills and found them charming, timeless places, the restored ones often run by enthusiasts who take a great deal of care with their craft. There is something mesmerizing about the rhythm of the revolving stones, be they powered by wind, water or electricity. The flour had more flavour and character than the standard type.

This process isn't just a small-scale, artisanal craft. Doves Farm, the foremost specialist stoneground flour millers in the UK, sells 100,000 tonnes of flour per year. Founder Michael Marriage comes from a family that's been milling for some four centuries. He worked in West Africa for a couple of years in his twenties in a project that sought to bring better agriculture to subsistence farmers. It was partly seeing the inroads chemical farming was making that lay behind his decision to make an organic food business on returning to the UK: 'You could see nice pristine areas being polluted,' said Michael. As for health, he was concerned that the cocktail effect of eating different kinds of pesticide could be bad, even if individually they seem to be within 'safe' limits.

Michael explained how roller-milling wholemeal flour involves breaking up the grain, sifting out the branny bits and adding them back in. But he said some millers add bran from different wheat. Somehow this goes against the wholesome honesty of the product. More seriously, he said they don't necessarily put the valuable wheatgerm back in, as they should. 'With stoneground wholemeal flour, you know what you're getting,' he said. The wheatgerm oil also gets spread nice and evenly in stoneground flour, giving it a different character.

As for the wheat itself, Michael Marriage is interested in the older varieties, and when we spoke he was about to launch a 'heritage' flour using sixteenth- and seventeenth-century varieties of wheat that he had grown from a seed collection. He described the flavour of the bread made from it as 'hedgerowy' and interesting, even if it didn't have as good a rise as bread made from modern wheat flour, which has more gluten and holds its height. He was also about to produce a flour from einkorn, the original kind of wheat grown, domesticated in the era when, as he put it, 'wheat domesticated us' and we stopped being hunter-gatherers. Einkorn is still grown in the Fertile Crescent in the Middle East, but he had found a variety more suitable for growing in a northern climate. The flour makes purple-red, cakey bread that is highly nutritious and very nice to eat.

By the end of the twentieth century, the home-baking flour market seemed to have gone into terminal decline, with sales dropping 5 per cent year on year. Then in the new millennium, automatic breadmakers became popular. Michael says sales of his flours always shoot up in the first week of January, when people start using their Christmas-present breadmakers. They don't stay that high – the millers' trade group is thinking of having a 'get the bread machine out of the attic' campaign. But the overall trend against stoneground flour has increasingly reversed, not least because the economic downturn has led to a renewed interest in home baking. And when people get their hands on the raw material of bread, they realize that a bag of flour is not just a bag of flour.

It isn't only the flour that has been degraded in the modern loaf. It is also the way of making the bread itself. In 1961, the infamous Chorleywood Bread Process (CBP) was invented by the British Baking Industries Association. This speeds up the process of breadmaking and allows bread to be made from the lower-protein wheat grown in the UK rather than from imported flour. It was also a clever way for the industrialists to add water and air to make the flour go further and produce the bread more quickly – time is money. Clever for the makers, yes; but not so good for the eaters. The taste of CBP bread is strange when you come back to it after eating real bread for a while. It is pappy in texture and has less flavour, character and nutrition than a 'proper' loaf.

Some think CBP bread is more sinister. One of Andrew Whitley's most disturbing arguments is that such bread is loaded with additives to make the process work. These include enzymes, some derived from genetically modified organisms, which do not need to be listed on the label as they come under the category of 'processing aids' rather than ingredients. Enzymes can be allergens but, more broadly, Whitley feels it is wrong not to tell people what they are eating, for ethical as well as health reasons. They can be derived from substances you might not otherwise eat, such as pig pancreas, which he points out would be unacceptable to vegetarians and some religious groups.

Around 80 per cent of the bread in the UK is now made by this 'fast-baking' method. But the rest is not, and it is perfectly possible to find a real loaf if you make just a small amount of effort. Traditional bakers use a slower fermentation that produces more flavour. Less water and air is added, so there's more bang for your bite. There are other benefits. Whitley quotes a study that shows that fermenting dough for six hours, rather than the thirty minutes of the CBP, removed 80 per cent of the acrylamide found in bread crusts, a substance which has been fingered as possibly carcinogenic. It also means that more of the B vitamins are conserved. There is certainly more taste and better nutrition in traditionally made breads, especially those using stoneground flour, as is often the case with traditional bakers.

I wanted as much taste and goodness in my breakfast toast as possible. I met a man who gave me some more clues. Andrew Wilkinson of Gilchesters Organics was sitting behind a stall at the Real Food Festival in London. This is an event full of the genuine artisanal producers who safeguard traditional methods, because the organizers have taken the enlightened step of subsidizing participants so the small guys can take part. After having spent a fair amount of time travelling the byways and lanes and alleys of the UK to track such people down *in situ*, it was a novelty to find so many gathered in one place, like a fantasy farmers' market.

Andrew turned out to have a wealth of knowledge on the fundamental subject of flour and bread. After the Army and a spell as an estate agent, he realized he wanted to farm. He sold his house and bought a smallholding in the North-East of England. Then he discovered there was little research into what kinds of grains he should be growing in this wet and windy part of the world. It used to be that grains were developed that were particular to their place; this has gone.

Andrew went to his old university, Newcastle, and embarked on a Ph.D. on organic wheat production. Eight years on, he was something of an expert, not least through growing trials on his own land. 'After a lot of painstaking research, I've discovered that the further back in time you go, the better the food,' said Andrew. 'Whether it is rare-breed cattle or corn, it is better. For millions of years, plants and animals have just gone about structuring their cells in a very slow, orderly, time-honoured fashion. As long as you get the soil nutrients right, it'll go on and do its own thing.'

Following his beliefs, Andrew planted spelt, one of the precursors of modern wheat. Spelt is the opposite of modern wheat. It grows well on poor land, and without artificial fertilizers, which is why its present revival has been brought about by organic farmers. Andrew's daughter calls his forty acres of spelt 'the jungle' because the plant grows to nearly six feet high. The output is only a quarter of that of modern wheat and the individual grains are bound up in their casing and so need to be de-hulled. It is hard work and the flour consequently costs more. It is, however, more nutritious than modern wheat. A study published in the *Journal of Agriculture and Food Chemistry* showed that most nutrients were higher in spelt, sometimes by 20–30 per cent.

Andrew explained another piece of bread chemistry. One of the building blocks of wheat is phosphorus. This is a powerfully charged chemical, so much so that in its pure form it is used in explosives. When you add water to flour in bread making, the phosphorus binds many of the other nutrients that are good for you – calcium, iron and zinc – and locks them up so that they are less digestible. However, there is a way to get around this: you raise the acidity of the bread. We somehow figured this out long ago, said Andrew, by making sourdough bread. This is a traditional way of making a bread rise by using a yeasty mix, which you keep alive in the fridge like a wee beast by feeding it with flour. This method means lactic acid gives a delicious, slightly sour flavour to the bread. A sourdough starter not only makes the bread rise but lowers the pH and so makes the goodies in the bread more digestible. Another advantage of sourdough bread is that it causes fewer of the 'spikes' in blood sugar that may be linked to obesity and diabetes.

Like Andrew Whitley, Andrew Wilkinson is convinced that the rise in wheat intolerance and the more serious coeliac diseases is connected to the way that modern bread is made. For breakfast, he has two slices of bread: a wheat-and-rye sourdough, buttered, with a slice of ham, and a slice of toasted wholemeal spelt or wheat bread spread with honey. It was not unlike the default breakfast I'd got into – my two slices of toast, one savoury, one sweet, but with better bread and better toppings. Sometimes just a small adjustment makes a great deal of difference, and this is certainly the easiest route to making a change.

It was important to me to get my daily bread right for my breakfast, as a nutritional cornerstone. In the spirit of diversity, I realized it shouldn't always be wheat. Sometimes I eat rye bread, occasionally spelt, sometimes a home-made loaf full of nuts and seeds from a friend's recipe. Sometimes I have oatcakes, and these do seem to power the morning well, as long as they are alongside some sort of cooked breakfast. Sometimes it's good old soft, fluffy CBR rolls, warmed in the oven and eaten with butter and honey. They are noticeably less good at powering me through a work morning but they remind me of childhood Sundays, and this is when I tend to have them, when less energy is needed and there are bigger feasts in the day.

Bread is the bedrock of what we eat. Getting it right was satisfying in many ways. It got me back into visiting good bakers. I also got back into making bread from time to time. This is an effort if you don't do it all the time but always worth doing, not least as an antidote to the computer keyboard. Andrew Whitley has a vision of how schools could bake their own bread and corporate workers could take a break from their desks and go and bake at lunchtime, engaging with something more real. I liked the yeastiness of his thinking. Anyone who wants to engage children in cooking knows that you do so most quickly by two means – sugar, naturally enough, but also dough, not least by making pizza. Anyone who bakes knows that it quite simply makes you feel better, whatever your mood. Dough feels alive in your hands, and indeed it is, as the yeasts multiply. The loaves themselves may be different from the kind of bread you buy from a baker, who has a far hotter oven and different sorts of skills; but they are still, essentially, cut from the same cloth.

My journey so far had shown me that the goodness in food is never just about nutrition. What really engaged me, beyond my own experiences, were people and their own stories, whether read in a book or gathered from talking to them in a shop, or a market, or a trade fair, or over a meal.

In the case of bread, the good food people come in two strands: the craft people who follow tradition and know that it works; and the inspired individuals who are new to their trade and learn about it from every source they can. Both kinds are there in abundance in the bread world and are most easily accessed through a directory of bakeries put together by the Campaign for Real Bread, set up by Andrew Whitley and the real food charity Sustain. You can now also cast about locally, because another type of baker is on the rise. This is the keen amateur who sells to his or her neighbourhood without going through a shop. Rather like a 'veggie box' scheme, they can sell to people who pay a set amount each week and get the 'loaf of the week'.

Nigel Wild is one such community baker. He has made a part-living for many years from baking this way. Wherever he goes, he builds an oven. There's currently a straw-bale one in his back garden in Newcastle. He also uses it to forge knives, having grown up in the steel city, Sheffield. 'I do believe in transformative processes,' he muses. 'There is something very rewarding about putting a couple of ingredients together and the heat of the oven turning them into something so different.' Baking, he believes, is basic yet magical.

Nigel is as grounded as all the other bakers I've talked to. His education included a spell in an agricultural college where he saw that farming had moved a long way from what had inspired him on a holiday on a farm in Cornwall as a teenager. His judgement on the farming industry in the 1970s is succinct. 'It was thoughtless and dangerous and some of the people in it were moronic,' he says. 'You could get a degree without growing a vegetable. It was about the uses of hormones and growth enhancers for animals. It was seriously and profoundly wrong. Any one with half a brain could see it was just for profit and not for the quality of the food. They didn't respect the land, or people, or animals.'

The experience radicalized Nigel. He left farming and after a while helped set up the Red Herring, a co-operative bakery and café in Newcastle. At this time, he became part of a Peace Tax movement, refusing to pay the government money that would be used for armaments. His 'bread not bombs' stance – he offered to pay the £155.25 owed in tax in the equivalent value of bread rolls – led to a spell in prison, where he worked in the kitchen and discovered just how poorly the prisoners were fed.

On his release, Nigel returned to the Red Herring café, a place frequented by everyone, from professionals to policemen to the local criminals. Everyone appreciates good bread, if it isn't too pricey, Nigel believes, and the prices were kept reasonable.

It's true: bread really is the staff of life and it doesn't cost much more to eat the really good stuff. But it does take an effort as, still, the best is found in independent bakeries or from these small individual bakers, rather than in supermarkets.

Breakfast cereal is a type of food that doesn't make sense to me any more, though I ate it as a child. Kids and teenagers wolf down bowlfuls all through the day. The appeal is largely to do with the sugar and also the crunchiness and noise of it. Texture is very important to kids, and sound: snap, crackle and pop. Cereal is such a useful and convenient food – shake, splosh and spoon – that I sometimes wish I could find a way to get it back into my life. Yet for me it has as much attraction as horse nuts.

No wonder, since breakfast cereals are a product of late-nineteenth-century America puritanical health freakery. The inventor of the first breakfast cereal was John Harvey Kellogg, a doctor who set up a health 'sanitarium' in Battle Creek, Michigan. Breakfast cereals were the product of his efforts to flake cereals to make them easier to eat for people with no or few teeth, and were initially intended for chewing – JHK was a fan of mastication, as many such health gurus were. It is a supreme irony that Kellogg, evangelist of the good chew, had invented a form of food that requires hardly any at all, as the flattened, puffed and generally processed grains dissolve in their milk to a dull pap.

Worse was to come. Kellogg's brother and business manager, Will Keith Kellogg, realized they were on to a winner and bought up the company's shares. He added sugar to the corn flakes, thus becoming estranged from the health-orientated John Harvey, and set breakfast cereals on the road to being, for the most part, so processed, sugary and filled with additives that they 'might as well be cookies', as the American nutritionist Marion Nestle puts it.

The cereal manufacturers realized that kids were a great market and that television was the best way to reach them. By 1976, 43 per cent of all Saturday morning commercials in the US were for highly sugared cereals. In the UK, it is telling that breakfast cereals really got into their stride with the launch of ITV in 1955. Kelloggs now has a global advertising budget of £1 billion. With the UK children's breakfast cereal market worth £0.5 billion, a hundred new cereals launched in a year and seven hundred competing for a child's plate, it's a jungle out there and Tony the Tiger is just one of the big cats on the prowl.

I accept the fact that it is sometimes the easiest food you can get into a child at breakfast time but can't help but notice that when offered the alternative of a cooked breakfast children tend to take it.

Adults are more likely to be suckered by health claims than cartoons. I remember in my childhood being mystified how adults would earnestly chew their way through pure bran. We now know that eating rather more delicious wholemeal bread and lots of fruits and vegetables are gentler and more effective ways of getting your fibre than scouring your insides with these harsh brown chippings. The bran craze has gone the way of other health fads.

On a less penitential note, I tried to get into muesli. It's full of goodies and would be so convenient to have around. I've tried grating apple into it, as the original Swiss recipe prescribes. I've tried adding yoghurt. I've tried fancy expensive kinds and home-made kinds. And for me it's still horse food. Others I know feel differently, and that's lucky for them, because muesli is convenient and good for you.

After much experimentation, the only kind of cereal I actively like is granola, which is at least slightly cooked, since the grains, nuts and fruits are coated with oil and toasted. It is easy to make yourself. Heat some maple syrup with a little oil and vanilla extract. Toss some rolled oats, nuts and dried fruits in this and put them on a baking sheet at a low temperature (140°C) for twenty minutes or so. Stored in a jar, granola is a far more inspiring cold breakfast cereal than most others I've tried – and better value if you make it yourself.

★

My other jolt of energy in the morning comes in the form of a glass of orange juice and quite often a spoonful of marmalade. Not only do they brighten my dozy palate but the mere sight of either cheers me up. The very colour 'orange' is named after the fruit, fittingly enough: what could be more orange than an orange?

In fact, ripe oranges can be green, the pigment protecting the fruit from the sun, and they are picked and eaten that way in some of the hot countries where they grow, such as Thailand. In places like Florida, such fruits are gassed with ethylene to turn them orange again and sometimes a dye, Citrus Red 2, is added to the outside of pale fruit. The natural wax is often washed off to tidy up the fruit and replaced artificially to reduce moisture loss, thus extending shelf life. Perhaps an orange is not always as natural as it seems.

Looking at this more closely made me wonder how we came to drink orange juice in the first place and how oranges have become such a talismanic part of my breakfast table in the distinctive and curious Brit-food, marmalade?

Oranges came originally from China, and the kind that came to Europe was bitter, like the type used in marmalade. 'Marmalade' was originally a fruit paste in a solid block made from such oranges, as well as from other fruits. This sweetmeat has been eaten in England since the fifteenth century and is still familiar today in the form of the Iberian quince paste, *membrillo* (and, at a less elevated level, the corner shop fruit pastille). From the eighteenth century onwards, the Scots took to making a thinner orange jelly containing pieces of the cut-up peel. Sugar was starting to become cheaper and this was a way of stretching out the fruit to a spreadable jam. Marmalade became embedded in our culinary culture and Spanish producers now grow this kind of Seville orange for the British breakfast market.

It was only in the seventeenth century that the modern sweet orange arrived in Europe. The diarist Samuel Pepys records his first glass of orange juice on 9 March 1669. After downing a pint, he wrote: 'It is a very fine drink; but, it being new, I was doubtful whether it might not do me hurt.' Well, was it good for him? And how has it changed?

I remember cans of frozen orange juice in my 1970s childhood, when the deep freeze was a large magic cavern of great wonder and modern technology. This canned juice had been super-concentrated and frozen to make it easier and cheaper to transport than the fresh kind. Food scientists working in the US after the Second World War claimed a 'technical breakthrough' when they discovered that adding a little fresh juice at the end of the production line put back some of the flavour, since so much had been lost in the processing. But why not just keep the flavour in the first place?

During the 1980s, freshly squeezed orange juice became popular. Nowadays you have different kinds, including 'with bits'. The early kinds could be incredibly acidic and not entirely appealing but have since improved in flavour.

Yet whatever the vitamins, the main component of orange juice is sugar. What's more, it's in the form of fructose. I consulted my nutrition books. Fructose turns out to be a sugar that can be problematic in the modern diet. Fructose is not absorbed straight into the blood stream, like other sugars, but is metabolized in the liver. It seems to act differently on the hormones that control appetite. The net result is that drinking fructose means you are likely to eat more, and it also converts what you eat and drink into fat an amazing fifteen times more readily than other sugars.

The main problem with fructose, as far as society is concerned, is not the kind in fruit or orange juice or any other fruit juice but the type of fructose you get in fizzy drinks, which comes from High Fructose Corn Syrup, an invention of the food industry that comes from cheap subsidized maize and is now endemic in the food system. It is the reason sugary drinks are so cheap and therefore widely consumed in such quantities, and the reason they are so bad for you. All the same, fruit juices are also high in fructose, even if they are more natural. A smoothie can have more sugar than Coca Cola. Before I knew this, I used to buy big cartons of smoothies as a sort of liquid fruit salad. But since discovering the way fructose works, I've become more cautious.

This played out on my breakfast table in two ways. Fruit is best of all eaten whole, as the fibre helps you digest it more slowly. The sugar in fruit comes packaged in its own antidote, if you like, and my breakfast fruit is more often apples or pears or berries on cereal or porridge, or eaten with yoghurt. I also began to squeeze my own fresh juice from reasonably cheap juicing oranges. It has become one of those morning half-asleep routines that I do, just with a manual squeezer. After learning about fructose, I felt this was the right way to produce orange juice because the effort of doing so means I enjoy a super-bright glassful but don't drink too much. It adds a little time to the morning routine, but has become part of giving breakfast a bit more space and importance, and getting much more from it as a result, not least in terms of taste. Drinking carton orange juice at breakfast time isn't a big deal, but as an adult watching my middle-aged spread, I concluded that I'd personally stick to a smaller, fresher glassful. Most of all, of course, I do this for taste.

All this picking apart of my breakfast helped me understand its foods better. But there are dangers to doing this. American author Michael Pollan, in his ground-breaking book *In Defence of Food: An Eater's Manifesto*, argues against what is called 'nutritionism'. This is the way that the food business has developed a meta-language of nutrients, understood by a priesthood of experts and spread by the food industry to sell products. Then journalists see a story in a 'miracle' or 'evil' element in food. And so the headlines roll out and we blindly follow one element of food without looking at our platefuls and our diets in the round. Nutritionism means that health is seen as the main point of food, not culture, pleasure, sociability and all the other elements of eating. It pulls food apart and so often becomes reductionist and misses the point.

Part of the problem, Pollan argues, is that the study of nutrients is a comparatively young science and its findings can be based on flimsy evidence. It is notoriously difficult to draw firm conclusions when there are so many individual elements in a single food, let alone in an overall diet. Overblown claims or fears about a particular part of food lead to broad-brush advice that is later retracted or refined. The classic example he cites is how, in the 1980s, fat was claimed to be the Baddy and low-fat diets became *de rigueur*. But now many scientists say fat is an important part of the diet and food-related diseases such diabetes have increased even as people have been eating less of it.

Pollan's conclusion is that, whilst the elements of diet are not entirely understood, it is best to eat a time-proven common-sense diet of real, fresh foods – those that our ancestors – even grandparents – would recognize. 'Eat food. Not too much. Mostly plants.' This is the conclusion of *In Defence of Food* and one I wanted to explore further and bring back to my home table.

One major point I got from Pollan was that it was important to think more about the culture of food. The person who most vividly took me into the way we eat breakfast was not one of Pollan's grandmothers, with folk knowledge in her bones, but a hip thirty-something.

Seb Emina had run a cult blog, the London Review of Breakfasts, for five years. The idea came into being for a negative reason, he explained when we met up. He'd gone out for breakfast with some friends and paid £8.50 for a 'Full English'. 'We were expecting something quite nice,' he said, 'but there was no bacon and the eggs were underdone. It reeked of the chef's distain for the customer. He obviously wasn't even looking at the plate. He thought it was easy to cook a breakfast and didn't think about it.

There was this big epiphany that nobody ever reviews the English breakfast, even though it's the meal we go out to most of all.'

The blog emerged from a spare morning at the computer. Such is the power of the Internet Age that a good idea can go public within an hour. Seb wrote a mission statement, coined the name – a riff on the literary weekly, the *London Review of Books* – and continued the puns with pseudonyms for the writers. He writes as 'Malcolm Eggs' and was soon joined by Damon Allbran, Koffee Annan, H.P. Seuss, Mabel Syrup and others. One calls herself Grease Witherspoon, 'which works on every level a pun can,' said Seb. A bank of some seventy contributors has been built up, including the arts editor of a major newspaper, a literary publicist, a poet and a Radio Three producer. Occasionally there is a post from a foreign correspondent – a recent one had come from the Forces canteen in Basra in Iraq, written by a certain Private Yolk (a documentary filmmaker embedded in the British Army), who depicted the Trenchard Lines Mess with its choice of cereals and space for body armour. Sometimes they have opinion pieces, or 'Opp Eggs', like the Op Eds (Opposite Editorial) page that you get in newspapers.

The LRB reviewing style might be called literary tongue-in-cheek. H.P. Seuss, in particular, has become known for his full-blown literary experiments. Some people would log on just to insult him in the comments strands following his reviews. 'He went through this heyday,' reflects Seb. 'Then he went a bit "prog", a bit experimental, as these people do. The last I heard of him, he was on a train to Morocco.' (This turned out to be another literary spoof; H.P. Seuss was sitting in Stoke Newington contributing an essay to the LRB's book on breakfast.)

I had met up with Seb in one of my local haunts, the Walpole, in Ealing. Seb divides his breakfasting venues loosely into 'greasy spoon' caffs and 'silver spoon' restaurants. He reckons you can have excellent breakfasts in both type of establishment. One of his current favourite caffs was a Post Office workers' canteen in King's Cross that boasted a superior sausage. At the posh end, he was a fan of the Bistrotheque in Bethnal Green, a place so hip it didn't even have a sign outside, minimalist décor inside and a pianist who played heartfelt piano covers of pop songs.

The Walpole was one of the rarities that had a foot in each camp; a caff that pleases many types. It is frequented by local workmen, who come in waves and stoke up with full-blown fry-ups. It also has the likes of home-baked ham and a decent bubble and squeak and brings in brunchers and people who want loose-leaf tea.

Our breakfast conversation, once tea arrived, turned to what exactly counted as a breakfast dish. Seb was exploring the meals of different countries and had just eaten a Malaysian breakfast at the canteen below the Malaysian Cultural Institute in London. He talked of the 'head and hoof' soup of Iran, the rice porridge of China, and the way every country has its particulars. 'It's the only meal that has this strict set of rules,' he said. 'They are unspoken but really there.'

Then the food we ordered arrived. So, of course, did the food dilemmas. For me it had been a problem that the café didn't have free-range eggs. The waitress told me the eggs were 'British'. In terms of welfare that meant the birds had been caged in Britain. They would at least be safe as our birds are vaccinated against salmonella. Recent egg food-poisoning cases had been tracked back to imported Spanish eggs from non-vaccinated hens. Even without this risk, I didn't want to eat an egg from a bird that spent its sorry life in a small, shut-in space.

The bacon, sausage and ham were also problematic. I'd become aware of how pigs were often industrially kept in barren conditions. So, what to do? In the end, I had a slightly strange medley of bubble and squeak, baked beans and lamb's liver, with the thought that sheep are one of the least messed-around of livestock, feeding on grass without the intensification of chickens and pigs. I felt that familiar annoyance that everything had got so complicated.

As our plates arrived, I took out my Smartphone and took a photograph of my plate. I looked up to see that Seb was doing the same to his ham, egg and chips. Then I took a photo of him 'tweeting' his image. Luckily the workmen seemed to be stuck into their grub and didn't notice this media circus.

We tucked in, and I asked Seb about the energy element of breakfast. As a teenager, going through the growing pains stage, he said he would fill a mixing bowl full of cereal and chomp through it, even before eating supper. Now, unless eating out and reviewing, he might have porridge or a particular kind of seed-rich bread. He confessed that sometimes a Full English left him feeling a bit tired, with an energy crash about an hour after the initial buzz, followed by a craving for chocolate. Food that gives us energy can also take it away if you eat too much; the very act of digesting so much can tire you out.

Perhaps it was a question of not eating too much rather than what you ate. Then again, you could have a large meal that kept you going. My cooked breakfast at the Walpole, dished up at 11-ish, sustained me right the way through to a light supper. The lamb's liver had been a slightly weird food to have for breakfast but tasted good and might have been on an Edwardian sideboard, covered by a silver dome. Knowing just a little bit more about the nutrition in food had turned out to be helpful. I'd picked up how to eat-to-last: good carbs plus a bit of protein and a proper saucing of attention.

Reflecting on my conversation with Seb, I realized that breakfast food is slightly weird – just think, for example, of having a lunch that was half a grapefruit followed by fried pig and egg. Odd, isn't it? But not at the breakfast table, even though this is the most conservative time of day, when you don't want many shocks so soon after leaving the amniotic comfort of the duvet. As in every culture, we have breakfast foods that are so entrenched you just don't think about them and that is that. Everyone else's breakfasts are, of course, just plain weird. We have porridge, an oat 'soup' – fine; the Chinese have congee, a savoury rice 'soup' – yuk.

But why not eat other kinds of food at breakfast? Other cultures eat savoury foods for breakfast that they might eat at any other time of day, for example the Continental habit of having a plate of cheese and ham. I was already often eating a piece of cheese on top of an oatcake. Emboldened by reading about other cultures' savoury breakfasts, which included dishes eaten at other times of day, I started to have spoonfuls of leftovers from last night's supper. A piece of ham with a poached egg turns out to be very sustaining, or the odd cold lamb chop – very 'Edwardian breakfast'. Remembering my childhood holiday breakfasts, I sometimes top my oatcakes or toast with smoked salmon or leftover fish. Fishcakes are a breakfast dish that has slipped into supper. I would now make a couple of extra ones and move them to the morning.

To do this, I did need a two-course breakfast – cereal and toast, or a cooked breakfast and toast or cereal. I often have a poached egg on toast, or perhaps with a piece of ham. Sometimes I gently fry tomato slices in olive oil with some herbs and sometimes I have a bacon buttie. Quite often I have a couple of pieces of fruit chopped up and brightened with a squeeze of lime. All this takes a bit more time, and that's a commitment in the working week. But it is worthwhile and it certainly helps me work better.

Finding the best breakfast has meant not just a shift in content but a change in how I think about the meal in the first place. Part of this journey was trying to figure out how to understand and use nutrition a bit better. Whilst I'm wary of 'nutritionism', having a bit more knowledge of what is in food is helpful because breakfast is, in the end, the most functional part of the eating day, and it helps to think about that explicitly. As a consequence, the meal has begun to work better. The energy I get from it is of a better quality and lasts longer. No longer do I start to snack at noon and to feel my attention disperse for the hour or so before lunch.

Yet, crucially, my changes and understanding did not come about just through following 'dietary guidelines' and their ilk, but from an understanding of the foods all round, including their culture, history and, most of all, taste. I gleaned all this through reading, media-swimming, conversations and listening to people tell their stories. Once I understood what I was eating better I could stop picking food apart and just get on with eating it. That, I realized again, was the best way of all for my quest to discover what to eat.

WHAT TO EAT?

Easy. Squeeze fresh orange juice; sit down to eat rather than getting ready with a piece of toast in your hand; expand what you consider suitable for breakfast; eat more savoury foods and use up leftovers; eat sourdough bread and toast; try a variety of real breads; find the best oatcakes.

Worth the effort. Use your storecupboard to make non-penitential porridge; make your own granola or muesli; find the best local bakeries and bakers; explore different kinds of stoneground flour.

Hopes and dreams. That we will get back to real bread made from real flour; that people will bake at least occasionally for pleasure and get back in touch with dough; that we will start to take time, every day, for breakfast and not see it as a rushed, gulped-down meal; that we will return to enjoying food and not label-worrit or be suckered by the packet claims of nutritionism.

3

Should I Eat Like a Caveman?

The sight of the Western diet breakfast buffet kept returning to me. It had made me realize more fully just how much today's food supply, for all its apparent choice, had become concentrated on just a few staples, specifically industrialized carbohydrates such as highly processed wheat and sugar. Of some two hundred thousand wild edible plants, only a couple of hundred have been domesticated for production and twelve now provide 80 per cent of the world's annual tonnage of food: wheat, corn, rice, barley, sorghum, soybean, potato, cassava, sweet potato, sugar cane, sugar beet and bananas. Does this concentration matter?

Furthermore, our diet is now composed of foods that are largely different from what our ancestors ate. Agriculture, which brought us dairy food and grains such as wheat, started around 10,000 years ago: a mere blink in the eye of evolutionary time. But for 2.5 million years before that we ate what was essentially a wild food diet, hunting animals and gathering a wide variety of wild plants.

A number of nutrition theorists are now drawn to the idea that we need to pay more attention to this distant past. The trend began in the 1970s, when gastroenterologist Walter Voegtlin self-published a book called *The Stone Age Diet* in which he proposed that we should look at what our bodies evolved to eat. Similar ideas were taken up by others, in particular by Loren Cordain, a professor in the Department of Health and Exercise Science at Colorado State University who has published many papers in scientific journals on the subject and popularized it as the 'Paleo Diet'.

The Paleo Diet promises good health and weight loss in one prehistoric package. 'I didn't design this diet – nature did,' Cordain writes. 'This diet has been built into our genes.' He believes we are Stone Agers living in the Space Age. For all our food factories and convenient 24-hour supermarkets, our bodies are still fundamentally the same now as when we were hunter-gathering in the savannah. Yet look at what we eat. He says some 18 per cent of calories in the typical US diet come from refined sugar; 24 per cent from cereal grains, most of which are refined; 10 per cent from dairy products; and another 17 per cent from refined vegetable oils made from farmed crops. So around 70 per cent of calories in the average western diet come from foods that our ancestors wouldn't have eaten in their current form.

By eating as we do, Cordain argues that we are running our bodies on fuel it's not designed to use. His analogy is that the modern diet is like putting diesel into a petrol engine. And what are the consequences? The diseases of modern society – heart disease, cancer, diabetes and so on.

So, what to do? Translating the Stone Age diet to the modern plate means, broadly speaking, 'Eat more lean protein, eat fewer carbohydrates and eat the right kind of fat'. Cordain thinks the best plateful means you get half your calories from lean protein such as chicken and fish and much of the rest of the balance from fruits and vegetables.

Protein is at the heart of this diet and the proportion Cordain recommends is far more than we normally eat. Perhaps the point of the diet is that it makes you eat less. Protein makes you feel fuller for longer – two to three times longer according to Cordain – than other foods. I'd certainly found that eating more protein – a poached egg for breakfast, some cheese on an oatcake, or peanut butter on apple quarters for snacks – worked in this way. There's only so much protein you can eat in a meal, whereas you seem to be able to go on eating slices of toast or biscuits forever. Perhaps eating more protein means you eat less food in total and have fewer weight problems.

Looking at Cordain's figures, I was interested to see that the protein content of common foods is not quite what you'd think. Eggs, cheese, bacon and nuts, which I'd thought of as high protein foods, are far less protein-rich than seafood, offal and lean meats. Eggs are 35 per cent protein but halibut is 80 per cent; cheese is 28 per cent whereas sirloin steak is 65 per cent. Nuts are just 10 per cent protein but they do tend to contain more healthful oils, particularly walnuts. The figures made me see, once again, how animal protein is especially powerful in nutritional terms.

It's also about what the protein replaces. Cordain's next point is that our diet is high in carbohydrates such as potatoes, sugars and white flour that give you a quick burst of energy. The ancestral diet, however, would have led to far fewer such surges and drops in energy, even though it was gathered from the wild rather than picked up at the shop. This is an argument, again, for wholefoods and goes back to the glycaemic index issue.

The Paleo professor then looks at the type of fat in our modern diet. I'd been struck by the fact that towards a fifth of the calories in the American diet came from vegetable oil, presumably from fried and processed foods. This is a great deal, and the quality of the fat must matter. Cordain focuses on the area of omega-3 and omega-6 fats. All fats are made up of fatty acids of different kinds, of which omega-3s and 6s are two kinds. These are what are called 'essential' fats since they are needed in the composition of our cells (as opposed to the storage fat that hangs around your waist). But the balance between omega-3 and omega-6 fatty acids is very different from those of our ancestors. It's thought that we evolved with an omega-6 to omega-3 ratio of no more than 4:1. A shift towards processed vegetable oils and animals fed on cereals rather than grass (which changes the composition of their fats) means the balance between these two is now more like 10:1, 20:1 or even 100:1.

The problem is that the composition of omega fats makes a difference to your cell membranes, hormones and something called the 'eicosanoid function'. The latter was a term I'd never come across. A quick Google search told me it was about immunity and how your body copes with inflammation, which affects blood pressure, cardiovascular disease and arthritis.

I still wasn't entirely sure exactly what omega fats themselves were and wanted to try to pin this down. In the meantime, I looked at the oil I use every day in the light of the Paleo Diet.

Flaxseed, rapeseed and mustardseed oil have the best balance of omega oils (i.e. the ratio of omega-6 to omega-3), according to Cordain. Beyond these, walnut oil is all right (5:1) and so is olive oil (13:1). Flaxseed and mustardseed oil are strong-tasting and not widely available. I'd tried cold-pressed rapeseed oil, a relatively new British product, but sometimes found its taste cabbagey – it is also from the brassica family, after all. I like the idea of using a home-grown oil and so I decided to give it another go. A friend suggested I think of it as 'nutty' and that helped – a bit. You could also think of it as pleasantly grassy. I also discovered that the different kinds you can buy do vary in taste so it is worth trying different ones, if you can. But after a few bottles I was still more enthusiastic about rapeseed oil in theory than in practice.

Then at a press event held by the posh cold-pressed rapeseed oil producers, the doctor promoting the health benefits of the oil said that ordinary rapeseed oil, which is the majority of cheap vegetable oil in the UK, has the same sort of health benefits. The cold-pressed version – at least five times the price – was better in terms of taste, she said. Since I'm not all that keen on the taste in any case, I changed my basic cooking oil to plain vegetable oil, checking on the label that it was rapeseed.

For a superior dressing oil, I am happier to use walnut oil – though you need to ensure it doesn't hang around and become rancid. It's expensive and certainly not for frying. Such oils are mostly made in France and Italy but I also found a delicious cobnut oil made by Richard Dain, a producer in Kent, and got a great deal of pleasure from the bottle I bought. Every drop is a treat. Paying attention to the nutritional quality of oil, and buying nice types is good news because it makes you more aware of what you are eating and you tend to savour, not to slosh.

For everyday use olive oil is still my all-round favourite. Even if its omega-6 to omega-3 ratio was higher than some, it was significantly better than others. It compares well to some others, on Cordain's terms: corn oil is 83:1 and sunflower oil has no omega-3s at all. Most importantly, it tastes so good. But was this nutritionism? I certainly wasn't going to suddenly switch to mustard oil.

For me the Paleo Diet provides some more interesting clues in another area of what to eat. I noted that Cordain's statistics reveal how the micronutrients (e.g. the vitamins and minerals) in our diet are way below those of our ancestors. He reckons that the Paleo Diet has, as an average, up to ten times more of these than we are typically advised to eat, and far more than most people actually consume. Cordain's figures show that a plant and high-quality protein diet is extremely nutritious and strengthens the argument that we should eat a wide variety of fruits and vegetables.

The basic premise of the Paleo Diet argument seemed interesting. But there are criticisms.

Firstly, hasn't the human body largely adapted to the modern diet? After all, it has been some time since man first tilled and maid first milked. We do seem to adapt to foods that become common, even if there is a debate about how well we do this.

Take milk. It's estimated that three-quarters of adults around the world cannot entirely digest the lactose protein in dairy foods and drinks, but in areas where milk has been consumed for a long time this percentage is much lower. Only 5 per cent of northern Europeans are lactose-intolerant, and East Africans, who are pastoralists, have also adapted.

Another criticism of the Paleo Diet is that it's all very well to look back to the Stone Age in theory, but what about in practice? Cordain's Paleo Diet book was like every other diet book I've ever read: plausible enough, until you look at the menu plans. The recipes were somewhat unappealing – typical examples were marinated cauliflower salad dressed with flaxseed oil and onion flakes and the likes of 'Paleo Correct Meat Loaf'. Cordain allows two 'open' meals a week when you can eat anything – and, praise be, fall on a glass of wine – but for the rest of the time, so many foods are discouraged. As much as possible, no dairy and no wheat – nor any grains, not even wild rice; no beans (he says that, like cereals, they contain 'anti-nutrients' that stop you digesting other foods); no starchy vegetables such as potatoes and sweet potatoes; no foods with salt – so no ketchup, no olives; no fatty meat – leg of lamb, bacon, sausages; and no sweets or sugars, including honey. What does that leave?

On the other hand, Cordain's theory did give me pause for thought. Just to take one food, modern refined sugar, it is very different from sugars that originate in plants and would be totally alien to a Stone Ager. I discussed the modern diet with a friend. She'd been working in Ghana and had taken some fudge along as a present. A tribal woman put a piece in her mouth and immediately spat it out. Sugar in this concentrated, processed form was so alien that it felt poisonous. A great deal of sugar has crept into our diet. Once you eat less, you certainly notice the over-sweetness of many processed foods such as breakfast cereals and even savoury foods such as baked beans. Honey would have been an occasional treat for our ancestors, found in the wild and gathered in the face of the bees' stings. Such sweetness was certainly not a daily food to be eaten in quantity.

Pondering the wider issues of the Paleo Diet, I went to my local noodle bar for lunch. More food quandaries. For a start, the noodles were a Paleo no-no (they were made from wheat or rice). Most of the stir fries were made with fatty meat or meat from animals that would certainly have been factory farmed and so were off my menu for different reasons. The fish, in theory, should have been fine but I was starting to think more about how we harvest sustainably from the sea and had a few questions on that score. In the end, I went for aubergines in a 'sea-fragrant' spicy sauce, which probably had too much salt for a caveman, and – on Paleo principles – refused the rice. It felt all wrong eating this rich dish without the blander, less dense accompaniment of rice. I wasn't sleepy that afternoon – as can be the case after lunch – but I was certainly hungry a couple of hours later and went off to hunter-gather some chocolate biscuits.

All in all I felt the Paleo Diet was most useful in the way it made me look again at the basic assumptions of the modern Western diet. In particular, it made me wonder more about the benefits of the diverse, largely plant-based diet that man has

eaten for nearly all of our existence. The specific practicalities of
the Paleo Diet, however, made it hard to swallow whole.

I thought it would be interesting to look at each step of our
evolution and see what further clues it could give me about
what to eat. Some theorists have gone much further back than
the Stone Age diet. There is one area of enquiry about the evolution of food that goes way, way back into the past. In one
sense, it is too big to put in your mouth; on the other, it is in
every morsel you eat. The idea is this: what we put on a plate
goes back to the start of life itself.

'The chemicals that make up the body were born in a star.'
This striking sentence comes from *The Driving Force: Food,
Evolution and the Future* by Michael Crawford and David Marsh.
For 99.8 per cent of human existence we ate a wild food diet.
But the book goes further back, to the biochemical origins of
life and how we evolved from inanimate matter to cellular slime,
to creatures, to mammals, to humans. I knew I was related to
apes, but what about to rocks? It was all slightly trippy.

Crawford and Marsh take an evolutionary approach to the
question of what is good nutrition, arguing that for all stages of
our development, the essential building blocks of life remain the
same: the billions of cells in our bodies still need particular
chemicals to function. These are replenished by food. In the
book, they write of the 'interior sea', the products of digestion
washing into our cells to build and nourish them individually
and the body as a whole.

Professor Michael Crawford is known for championing

one particular source of nutrients: omega-3 fatty acids. I read up to discover that fats are made up of chains of atoms. Fats with long chains have a greater fluidity than those with short chains, such as saturated fats. This is why butter – largely saturated fat – is solid at room temperature and vegetable oils – largely long-chain fats – are fluid. Fats are one of the building blocks of cells, and the human brain, in particular, is rich in these fluid fats. When people talk of fish as 'brain food', this is true in a literal sense, because these long-chain omega-3 fatty acids are an important part of this organ. The constant motion and thinking of humans needs liquidity; Crawford says the human brain has 1,000 billion cells, each of them making 6,000 or more connections with other cells. Long-chain fatty acids help this to happen. The omega-3 lobby argues that eating plenty of omega-3 rich foods in pregnancy is important for foetal brain development, and we need to eat them all through our lives.

Various research institutions have become very excited about omega-3s. There have been trials with supplements for children to show whether they can improve their concentration and even IQ. Some claim a difference; some not. There is better evidence that they may be helpful for your heart, and some evidence that they may help in the prevention of cancer. Even if the exact benefits of omega-3s are still being assessed, they certainly seem to be beneficial.

How to get them? Omega-3 fatty acids are found in their most useful form in oily fish such as salmon, tuna, mackerel and herring and also, to a lesser degree, in many other forms of seafood such as cod, scallops and prawns.

There are sources other than fish. Omega-3 fatty acids also exist in flowering plants and their seeds, as I'd discovered from Loren Cordain's Paleo Diet. *The Driving Force* explained that these evolved at the same time as mammals and are another form of the fat. You also get these fats in animals that have eaten the plants, such as grass-fed cattle and the milk from grazing cows. Organic milk has been shown to be higher in omega-3s. (But if you want to get the benefit, you should use full-fat milk and not skimmed.)

But plant oils are just a small part of the story; it is the omega-3s found in fish that are the most nutritious. A group of UK lipid scientists is currently lobbying to stop food manufacturers advertising their wares as being beneficial because of their omega-3 content when they are using the cheaper plant type rather than the more expensive type from animals.

The American Heart Association recommends we eat at least two portions of fish a week. Fish differ in the amount of omega-3 fatty acids they contain. The United States Department of Agriculture food figures, quoted by Dr David Servan-Schriber in his book *Anti Cancer: A New Way of Life*, say you may want to eat, for example, 120g tinned tuna or 70–350g of fresh. The huge disparity in the amount you need to eat – from a small portion to a vast one, in the case of fresh tuna – is because species, diet, packaging and cooking methods all make a difference and these are difficult for the consumer to assess or control. You could also get a decent amount (1g) of omega-3s from eating 45–100g of farmed salmon, 60–250g of mackerel, 60g of herring, around 100g of farmed trout, 400g of cod, 450g of haddock, 80–200g of oysters and 550g of scallops.

It sounds like a good idea to eat more fish. I resolved to have fishcakes for breakfast from time to time and more smoked fish for lunchtime salads and sandwiches, as well as eating fish for supper at least once a week. Yet it didn't sound possible to consume the right 'dosage' without supplements. But when I tried to take the supplements I found the taste too disgusting – like the notoriously stinky cod liver oil of my parents' childhood. On the whole, I believe getting the right balance of nutrition in your diet isn't about popping pills but eating the best food. Having more good fish is the best way to go. But what is a 'good' fish in terms of sustainability? That was another food quandary to chew upon.

I wanted to move on from the swampy origins of human life to a later step, from ape to human. Martin Jones, Professor of Archaeological Science at Cambridge University, collected many fragments from the past to write his absorbing book on early food, *Feast: Why Humans Share Food*. He uses archaeology as a stepping stone to walk across time and relate how we eat now to how we ate then. Since the material evidence is so fragmentary, he believes we should also look for parallels in the way we are now. The fundamentals of human behaviour haven't changed all that much since we evolved from apes. Cavemen and women feasting on a fresh meat kill can be compared to modern humans eating a TV dinner together, the flickering screen replacing the hearthside gathering with its darting flames. Sociability, hunger and a need for a focal point are present in both situations, however far apart they might seem at first glance.

The opening page of Jones's chapter on apes and humans shows two photographs. One is of Jones, debonair with bow tie and wine glass at a Cambridge college feast. Below is an adult male chimpanzee. His hand, like Jones's, is clasped. But whilst Jones's hand is bent in a conversational gesture as he chats with his fellow guests, and his other hand holds a glass, the chimp grasps the head of a red colobus monkey that he is about to eat. In other words, we've moved on.

Whereas we have mealtimes, the chimps in Gombe must eat for around half their waking life to get enough calories. If they are lucky, they might snaffle a monkey head. One of the reasons they don't hunt as much as humans, and therefore don't eat as much meat, is that their groups are less organized into sharing. It is therefore too big a risk to go off on an uncertain hunt and risk possible starvation rather than gather lots of static plants to eat immediately.

The foundation of our evolution from apes to humans was the use of tools. This gave humans more access to better food, which powered our brains to grow. Jones lays out the evidence that chimps, in fact, also use tools, for example when bashing open nut shells with rocks. And they have a great knowledge of natural history that is passed down from one generation to the other. In the bush, mothers show their offspring what to eat, how to take food from a pod, pick out a stem or cope with hard fruit. In other words, it is learned rather than innate behaviour. The range of food they eat is also flexible. A comparison of two groups of chimps, one in Gombe forest in Tanzania and the other in the Mahale mountains 140 kilometres away, showed that less than 60 per cent of the foods suitable and available were eaten by both groups of animals.

But the human diet diverged from that of chimps and we moved onwards and upwards. We had more sophisticated tools and a greater knowledge of what to eat and how to get it. An upward spiral, powered by better nutrition, meant bigger brains and better use of tools developed together. Being better with our hands allowed us to crack open bones and eat the nutrient-rich bone marrow. This led to a bigger brain and so better use of tools, and so on.

Evolutionary change is about the economics of energy, and this has much to do with diet. It takes a great deal of energy to digest plant foods. A famous example is that it takes more calories to eat and digest a cucumber than the cucumber delivers back. Meat, in contrast, is rich in energy and you don't need to eat so much. As we ate more meat, our guts could become smaller and more efficient. At the same time as our guts got smaller, our brains got correspondingly bigger. More meat meant more excess calories to build and fuel a bigger brain. More brain meant more organized hunting and food sharing – and more meat. It is not so much 'we are what we eat' as 'we are what we ate'.

Having a bigger brain meant that we could organize and feel comfortable in larger groups. Chimps are also notably social but our bigger brain means we can recognize more individuals. This has led to a degree of sociability that recurs in different societies.

Jones says the size of the average Christmas card list – 100–200 names – is the same size as contemporary hunter-gatherer groups. Sociability and society caused changes to our diet. When you have bigger organized groups, you have the foundation of food production and modern society. The next step, farming, was around the corner.

I wanted to discover more about how human food moved on from our ape and early human past. The man to help turned out to be a Harvard professor with a background in primates. He thinks he has unlocked the rest of the mystery of what made us humans: cooking.

Richard Wrangham is a Professor of Biological Anthropology at Harvard University and also director of the Kibale Chimpanzee Project in Uganda. He started out by conducting field studies with the eminent primatologist Jane Goodall at the exciting time when apes were being studied properly for the first time. For his work, Wrangham would go into the jungle from dawn until dusk. Sometimes he would take his own food but at others he would eat what the chimps ate. 'It was impossible to fill your belly with what they ate,' he says. 'Most of it was too tough, too dry, too fibrous, too bitter, too hot or strong-tasting.' In short, what chimps eat is very different from human food today.

Some twenty-five years later, Wrangham was lying in front of a fire at home, organizing notes for a lecture on human evolution, when something clicked in his head. He suddenly wondered how long humans had been around a fire like this. It got him thinking about his time in central Africa. There were, he believes, two significant steps in human evolution. The first was going from apes to *Homo habilis*, or 'Handy Man', which was half ape, half man. The second was going from Handy Man to a much more modern type of human, *Homo erectus*, from which our species *Homo sapiens* came. These two changes happened between 2.5 and 1.5 million years ago. Meat-eating lay behind the first shift. Wrangham believes that fire was central to the second. The reason is simple: it enabled us to cook.

Cooking, crucially, allows us to digest more calories from food while using less energy. It is, in effect, a form of pre-digestion, softening the food, breaking down its physical structure and converting it into more digestible matter. Charles Darwin called the harnessing of fire perhaps man's greatest invention other than language. But only now are we starting to see quite how important it may have been. Cooking our food continued and accelerated the process begun by meat-eating. Most primates eat a largely plant-based diet and have a gut adapted to digesting this. Our gut, however, is around 60 per cent of the size that would be expected in a primate, just as our brain is more than twice the size it might otherwise be. Wrangham's idea is that meat wasn't the only important step in evolution; cooking saved us energy that was diverted, instead, to building a bigger brain.

To investigate the digestibility of raw and cooked foods, Wrangham hooked up with a physiological ecologist called Stephen Secor who uses pythons in his work. A python is a highly economical creature. After eating a meal it does precisely nothing except breathe and digest, like a snoozing human stretched out on a sofa after a big lunch. By measuring how much oxygen the python produces before a meal and during digestion, Secor could work out the energy requirements for digestion.

Nobody before had looked at the difference in the energy cost of digesting raw and cooked food. The result was significant. Grinding up food, thereby increasing its surface area, reduced this cost by 12.3 per cent. Feeding the python with cooked meat reduced it by 12.7 per cent. When the food was both ground up and cooked, it reduced the energy needed for digestion by 23.4 per cent, or nearly a quarter less than raw food.

Meat is not the only kind of protein that is better, in calorific terms, when it is cooked. Body-builders used to eat raw eggs as 'protein-building' material. In fact, cooking increases the protein availability of eggs by some 40 per cent. So it turns out that it isn't just the bare calories in food that matter, but the way they are prepared and digested.

Wrangham said at a talk he gave in London that the research into calories was only just starting. The calorific content in food is measured by a gadget called a bomb calorimeter. This burns the food and measures the energy released. But not all that energy goes to our bodies. It all depends upon its 'bioavailability' and how it is digested. Some of it is eaten by the microbes in our gut and not by us all. Weightwatchers in the US is apparently looking closely at this new research. It is potentially a very big story. A calorie may not be just a calorie, a subject that I wanted to return to.

The python experiment and the whole of Wrangham's book, *Catching Fire: How Cooking Made us Human*, made one fact increasingly clear. We like cooked foods – even apes do, choosing cooked over raw if they are given a choice. We like soft, easily chewed foods, and these are the ones that we digest the best and get the most calories from. We like energy-dense foods that give us get-up-and-go. Where is it leading? Not, perhaps, to the place that the Paleo Dieter might think it would. Rather, it is the route towards burger, chips and a super-sweet milkshake. What did we evolve to eat? Modern fast food. It presses all our Paleo buttons. And yet our modern way of eating is leading us towards the diet-related illnesses of the contemporary developed world: heart disease, stroke, cancer and diabetes. What we evolved to eat, in one sense, is not necessarily what we *should* be eating.

The most present and tangible aspect of the Paleo Diet is wild food. I went to meet a man who had spent a good deal of time gathering and eating it. Professor Gordon Hillman is an ethnobotanist who works with the British bushcraft expert Ray Mears. He grew up on the Sussex Weald, where his family had a garden nursery, and spent much time out and about learning about the plants of his area. Whilst studying the genetics of wheat at university, he realized that the real questions about what to eat came from much earlier, from before agriculture, and that some of the answers could be found growing in the fields and woods where he walked.

As we settled down by Hillman's wood-burning stove, he said in passing that Ray Mears was brilliant at getting different kinds of heat from fires for different kinds of cooking, and I thought back to early man discovering fire and cooking. Then we got down to another aspect of the past and its role in the present. For Hillman, the likely key to eating well is biodiversity. You need to eat as wide a range of plant foods as possible. Our ancestors would have eaten a much larger number of such foods and benefited from their good nutrition. And you don't even need to eat to get all the benefits. 'These plants are transpiring a huge range of compounds into the air – thousands of different kinds,' said Hillman. 'You get them in greater dosages than you get in homeopathy. It's bound to have an effect.' Walking in proper countryside always makes me feel good and it felt like a magical (if unprovable) idea that the very air you breathed was a complex, beneficial tonic.

As for types of food, Hillman is very much in favour of eating greens and is drawn to bitter flavours, such as those in sea kale, which often indicate foods are potent. 'I love greens generally,' he said. 'There's a real need for them. You get a huge variation and they are the most physiologically active part of the plants with a huge range of micronutrients.' Wild greens, in particular, are good news. He uses plenty of wild garlic leaves and sorrel, as a stuffing for baked fish, for example. Nettles are his ultimate green leaf: the best of the lot for micronutrients and a nutritious source of protein. As for other plant foods, he eats lots of apples and said they always seemed to sort out any digestive problems.

But wild foods have a problem: diminishing habitats. It is hard to find good locations for wild plants. 'Even woodlands are often coppiced these days and the ground shaded out,' said Hillman. 'The richness that would have been in British woodlands, with many glades and open areas, has been reduced. You'd think the countryside is everywhere, but in the average wheat field there's nothing but wheat. The herbicides have got rid of all the weeds so there's a monoculture without an insect around, because they've all been killed by insecticides, and no fungi on the floor to break down the leaves because a fungicide's been used, and yet leaves are a rich source of nitrites.'

Hillman extended his concerns to animals. Having worked in places such as Turkey, he'd seen cows eating an utterly free-range diet. They browse through the leaves on the trees and eat a wide range of plants, self-medicating from herbs when necessary. This is in contrast to animals fed a monoculture of grass. 'Cows as we see them in the fields around here are all suffering from diarrhoea,' he said. 'They're sick animals. We're eating the flesh of sick animals. It can't be good for you.'

The professor's main piece of advice about animal proteins is to eat oily fish in order to get the best source of omega-3 fatty acids. He eats a piece of smoked mackerel every day. It was clear to Hillman that meat was an important part of caveman eating. On the five-day bushcraft courses he'd worked on with Ray Mears, the vegetarians were soon driven to become carnivores. 'They get very hungry and start eating meat – and fatty meat, too,' he said. 'Your body knows what it wants.'

Then I asked what the professor ate for breakfast. Sometimes he has rye bread with olives. He tries to avoid breakfast cereals as even the best can be extremely high in sugar and salt. Then he showed me a big basket of acorns in his hallway. This was his breakfast staple. He first shells them and puts them in bags improvised from mosquito nets to dangle in the Cuckmere River south of the medieval Michelham Priory for a fortnight. This process gets rid of the tannins and transforms them into a substance that's good to eat. Then he mashes them up and makes patties to bake. 'It's my favourite food,' he says. 'I'll eat it for lunch, too, given half a shot.'

Clearly, not everything about Gordon Hillman's kitchen was directly applicable to my own. But he did give me some useful ideas, not least about the power of wild plants, and a respect and concern for the countryside that are their source.

I wondered how wild food could fit into my diet. The wild is not so very far from us. All our everyday foods have wild ancestors. If you look around, such plants are still present. My own path to understanding this came when I started looking into the wild carrot, *Daucus carota*. Its white froth of flowers was easily spotted as I walked along the dry, chalky soil of the South Downs Way in high summer. When I pulled one up, the root had an unmistakable smell of carrot. Yet the form was weedy and the taste acrid. Such wild carrots have been in Europe for a long time; prehistoric carrot seeds have been found in excavations in Switzerland. It made me wonder how it turned into the fat, sweet root of today.

If you grow generations of the wild carrot in the right soil, the tap-root swells and sweetens up, and this is probably how enterprising farmers bred the modern carrot. Like aubergines and spinach, the new root arrived in the West with the Moors, who came through North Africa to Spain. In seventeenth-

century Britain the plant was seen as such an exotic import that
the young carrot's feathery leaves were even used to decorate
the attire of courtly Stuart ladies.

There's a mystery as to why the wild plant wasn't tamed into
a domesticated food in Europe as it had been in the Middle East.
In his *Oxford Companion to Food*, Alan Davidson takes the answer
back to the wild. The fragrant seeds have long been gathered
and used in herbal remedies. They were traditionally mixed with
honey for cough cures and powdered and drunk in wine. For
medicine, the wild plant was favoured over the cultivated. An
eighteenth-century physician complained: 'The shops are often
supplied with old seeds of garden carrot instead of the fresh
seeds of the wild plant. This is one of the ways efficacious
medicines are brought into disrepute. But the remedy consists of
everyone gathering the wild seed fresh for himself.' Davidson
thinks that since the wild carrot was regarded as a useful medicinal plant, there was no reason to turn it into a root vegetable.
Once again, I saw the potency of wild plants on a pharmacological level.

The story of the carrot connects past and present – and also
shows why we don't eat much wild food: I couldn't see myself
gathering wild carrot seeds like a twenty-first-century druid.
There are few wild foods that are still widely gathered.

Blackberries are a notable exception. Why do we still pick
them? First of all, they are common as well as delicious – 'as
plentiful as blackberries' writes Shakespeare in *Henry IV Part 1*
– and continue fruiting for many months, from midsummer
right through to mid-autumn when the Devil is said to spit on

the bush at Michaelmas (29 September). Seamus Heaney's poem *Blackberry-picking* captures this fall from grace. The first berry was 'Like thickened wine: summer's blood was in it,' but the poem ends with the autumnal rot of the fusty fruit and this turning point of the year.

Cultivated varieties of blackberry have been developed with fewer thorns, juicier fruits and a less pippy texture. But while they may be more consistent, tame berries lack the thrill of the wild, and you wonder if they contain the same quality of nutrition since they are molly-coddled by cultivation rather than producing different sorts of micronutrients to survive in the wild.

Other aspects of wild food matter. In his seminal book on wild food, *Food for Free*, Richard Mabey says that the most complex and intimate relationship most of us can have with the natural environment is when we eat it. Blackberries, he suggests, provide 'just enough discomfort to quicken the sense' as you reach past its prickles to the juicy prize. We are outside, hunter-gathering, and perhaps this touches something of my inner cavewoman.

We eat some wild foods that we don't realize are foraged. One commercial food that is almost entirely wild is the Brazil nut. Its tree is part of the rich diversity of the forested Amazon basin. This area is an arborial Eden where there are thought to be more than a thousand types of tree in a square kilometre. The Brazil nut's existence relies on a specific connection within the complex web of the natural world. It is dependent on pollination by large-bodied bees that can lift the coiled centre of the

Brazil nut tree flower. In a further twist, this bee needs a specific orchid with a smell that attracts the females so they can hook up with the males. Biodiversity depends on such precise webs which all survive together – or not, if one part goes.

There is something altogether untameable about the Brazil nut, quite apart from its complex pollination story. At up to 150 feet high, the tree is one of the tallest in the forest. It soars up virtually branchless until it spreads to a 100-foot-wide canopy at the top. Here grow dark brown pods that look a bit like coconuts, and inside are the brazil nuts in their shells, clustered like the segments of an orange. The shape of the tree makes it impractical to cultivate and harvest the pods by machine. Instead, teams of *castanheiros*, or nut collectors, wait until the ripe pods fall, often in windy or wet weather, between late November and early June. The workers steer clear on turbulent days, and keep a sharp eye out at all times. The heavy pods fall from a great height at considerable speed and can injure or even kill.

Sales of Brazil nuts have gone down in recent years and some of the trees have been lost to deforestation as land has been turned over to grazing cattle or growing soya for animal feed. A wild source of protein and fat gives way to the farmed. Yet even as this happens, people are getting more interested in the pharmacological power of this difficult nut. It contains exceptionally high amounts of selenium, a powerful antioxidant. Just 25g of Brazil nuts can provide you with ten times the recommended daily allowance. People in some countries such as the UK can be deficient in selenium as it doesn't occur in high levels in their soils. When the UK imported wheat from selenium-rich

Canada, this was not a problem. Now we grow most of our own, and we eat less of this mineral. The quantity of selenium in a Brazil nut can, in fact, vary greatly, so it is a hard to know how to get your dose in a precise way. Nonetheless, rather than just finding Brazil nuts a hard-to-crack curiosity at Christmas, I began to keep a packet of the shelled kind in my fruit bowl and peck at one every now and again, occasionally thinking of the *castanheiros* dodging death-by-nutting.

There is an edginess to wild food. It does its own thing and we must follow. This refusal to bend to man's bossy nature delights those partial to a spot of foraging and adds an extra element to how you respect your food. The number of neo-wild gatherers is growing. After Richard Mabey in the UK (and before him Euell Gibbons in the US) wrote about wild food, it has become something of a cult as people latch on to its unusual potency.

I felt this strongly for myself when I spent a spring and summer working on a television series about wild food, *A Cook on the Wild Side*, with the food writer and broadcaster Hugh Fearnley-Whittingstall. I was given a hire car, pointed in the direction of three areas – Norfolk, the west coast of Scotland and the New Forest – and told to come back with people and places to film. There are certain times in your life that lay down a growth ring. The richness and vitality of those days spent largely outdoors finding and filming were such for me. Over the summer, my hair went a shade lighter from the sun as I stood in fields and walked through woods talking to travellers who poached fish (in both senses), mushroomers, hunters, wild-plant beer brewers and eel catchers. It wasn't just the food that was wild but also the people, who all had such finely tuned instincts. They were real country people, as interesting to watch as birds and full of well-honed knowledge.

Most of all, it was the taste of wild foods, eaten *in situ*, that was extraordinary. They revealed to me again the fleeting beauty of freshness, such as I'd experienced from the fish caught and eaten in childhood. It could be as simple as an oyster gathered, or 'guddled', from the clean waters of the Isle of Mull and put on a barbecue to poach lightly in its own juices. Then there was an eel pulled from a small river on the Suffolk–Norfolk border. It was killed, skinned, filleted, put on a smoker and, still twitching with muscular spasms, finally contained in a sandwich with grated, freshly dug horseradish root. A gamekeeper browsed the hedgerows and gave me a raw nettle leaf to eat, folded in such a way as to keep it from stinging. There were mushrooms and samphire – rock and marsh – a feast of feral raspberries in a ruined house, pea-plumped pigeon, musky elderflowers and squirrels that really did taste slightly nutty. And 'dived scallops', literally *just*-dived scallops, with an astonishing sweet minerality.

The main lesson for me from foraging in the wild was that foods have a natural history. This is, of course, affected by farming and processing; we are not eating from Eden. But Nature can still be just a small step from what's on the table. One of the most delicious foods I've ever eaten was on a Chippewa reservation in Wisconsin where an elder had taken the sap from maple trees and sat up all night boiling it down to a smoky and rich maple syrup. That is a form of 'processing' that makes a food, and now

I look at any bottle of real maple syrup (as opposed to those made with flavoured corn syrup) and realize it is concentrated tree sap, just as I know honey is concentrated nectar. Understanding that foods originates in Nature brings another layer of knowledge to the table. It also makes you aware that a food can be pushed too far, such as the cardboard-tasting apples I'd come across in New Covent Garden, that had been picked early, stored at odd temperatures and in odd ways, and had suffered as a result: they'd lost touch with what they were meant to be.

Wild food takes you to interesting people as well as foods. I talked to Stephen Watts, a musician and sculptor in his twenties from Sheffield, who epitomizes the unusual combination of liberation and connectedness that comes with 'food for free'.

Stephen used to cycle around the affluent parts of the York-shire city noting all the fruit trees laden with an ungathered harvest. Eventually, he made a map of them and this grew into the Abundance project that has since spread around the country. The idea is to link tree owners with volunteers who gather the fruit and give boxfuls to community groups, or turn it into jams, chutneys and juices. 'A tree might have 200kg of fruit and the owner only wants a bagful,' Stephen explained. 'We are importing apples from the other side of the world when there's all this food here for free.'

An organic grower, Stephen also leads wild food walks around the city. He finds that foraging is one of the best introductions to organic horticulture since it fosters an awareness of wildlife in general and how organic gardening works with nature.

He pointed out that wild food is not so very far from us. 'People have different opinions of what is wild,' he said. 'They tend to say it's uncultivated, that it can live without human interference. I think that's true but it can also be helped by human interference. Blackberries grow far better at the edge of human interaction. I've found as much food to forage in a city as in the countryside.' We talked about nettles and how he blends them into smoothies, juices them and pours boiling water over them to take away the sting. He says you can also put them into bottles of vodka to make a tincture. Nettles are so common they are an easy way to get into the edginess of wild food. The Romans found another use for them. The small Roman nettle found in old towns and castles is said to descend from seeds planted by legionaries so terrified by the tales of cold English winters that they brought over the plant so they could sting some warmth into their frozen limbs. Human interaction and history, again, lie behind a wild food plant.

Stephen extends his sense of wild food to foraging what's been thrown out by shops. He gets rejects from a local ethical store, and then there are the supermarkets where they throw out packets that are past their sell-by date. It has long been a challenge for people to go 'skipping' and get food for free that's not from the hedgerow but from the pavement. This expansion of wild food to include what is called 'freeganism' points up, again, the personal aspect of its appeal. Foraging is also about the freedom; the wildness in yourself. You are not just buying into the modern, shrink-wrapped world of commerce – even if the food you are taking is packaged – but exploring your surroundings as a hunter-gatherer, with an eye sharpened by a quest.

Wild plants may be especially good for our health. They tend to have a more potent taste than their tamed agricultural counterparts precisely because they are especially rich in micronutrients. Before medicines we used such plants for good heath, and they are at the base of many of today's pills, just as strong-tasting herbs have been used for millennia by herbalists in folk medicine.

It's reductive to dismiss this sort of knowledge as merely old-fashioned. Kew Gardens is just one important research institute that takes such plants seriously. They've gathered information on plants that are used to treat ailments, for example the 1,700 species used to treat diabetes, concentrating on substances in the plants that may be useful such as phenolics, terpenoids and alkaloids. Monique Simmonds, head of the Sustainable Uses of Plants Group, says there are estimated to be some 50,000 plants that could be of use medicinally.

Clearly you get a scientifically proven effective dosage from pill medication, but increasingly people regard health as being about general well-being rather than just emergency treatment once something has gone wrong: that prevention is better than cure. For centuries, people have had herb salads to help keep them well or have eaten watercress and wild greens soups as a spring tonic. Anyone can grow herbs in a pot and add them to food or infuse them in hot water for a mug of herbal tea. It may not be a pill; indeed, it may even be better, perhaps, if taken regularly over a lifetime rather than in a large dose in an attempt to cure ill health.

Professor Dean Ornish of the Preventative Medicine Research Institute in California has for three decades pioneered the idea that changes in lifestyle can reverse the risk factors for conditions such as heart disease and cancer in a matter of months. He says there is now a greater convergence of opinion on what is a good diet, and that this means generally eating a wide range of fruit, vegetables and unrefined grains. He believes we should try to eat nutrient-dense, low-calorie foods and use the 100,000 protective substances found in plants.

This is knowledge that hunter-gatherers had at their fingertips. Archaeology shows that when humans became farmers their health initially suffered badly. Archaeologists have found that skeletons shrank because of impoverished nutrition when we relied on a few crops rather than nature's diversity. You'd think farming would make food more secure, but this is not necessarily so.

I spoke to Alex Laird, a medical herbalist and founder of Living Medicine, a charity that seeks to promote an understanding of the power of plants. She suggested that the potency of plants is clear through how you eat them. 'You might eat four ounces of carrots but that amount of thyme is way too much,' she said. 'There's a symbiosis between animals and plants and our taste buds are carefully calibrated to know what to do.'

Alex's approach, like that of Dean Ornish, is that pleasure makes a diet sustainable and what is right for you is a matter of personal preference. 'It's not about being perfect,' she said. 'You can have delicious refined things, but not as the standard.' For breakfast, she makes smoothies with a hand blender, adding some oatmeal rather than flaked oats because this is a less refined product. If this is the sort of food you eat all the time then you can have a fry-up from time to time, she says; just not all the time.

Like the researchers at Kew, Laird believes that we can rediscover our past plant knowledge and reinvigorate our food with it. Part of this is complexity; we should aim at the biodiversity-on-a-plate of our hunter-gatherer forbears.

Biodiversity, however, is under threat. Kew Gardens is behind the Millennium Seed Bank that aims to collect seeds from a quarter of all the world's plants by 2020; a number that chimes with the fact that roughly a quarter of all plant species are threatened with extinction. You can visit the seed bank in Sussex in a modern building where seeds are stored in pots like a fantasy kitchen full to the rafters of pots of spices. They are saved and kept safe, to sprout again and be reproduced should the need arise.

This approach also applies to saving the biodiversity of particular species. The Global Crop Diversity Trust, which Kew is part of, points out that in 1949 there were 10,000 kinds of wheat in China but by the 1970s there were just 1,000. Likewise, Mexico has lost 80 per cent of its maize varieties and India 90 per cent of its types of rice. We do not know when climate change or other events may mean we need to develop and cultivate other varieties of a particular species. The wider our choice, the better. Biodiversity matters on a global scale as well as to the individual.

For my own part, I have found it easy enough to get into the habit of having two or three kinds of leaf or vegetable and a herb or two in a salad instead of one plain leaf, and perhaps adding some seeds as well. When I make a sandwich for my own or my partner's packed lunch, I now find myself looking through the kitchen to see what I can add. Cheese and tomato, yes, but then why not add a chopped-up spring onion, a few leaves from our basil plant, some pickle and slices of radish? This so much more delicious as well as more nutritious. I'll chop up three kinds of fruit for a breakfast fruit salad instead of just having a banana. Having less of more is the key.

As for the type of plant, buying heritage varieties of vegetables from a farm shop, farmers' market or even some enlightened supermarkets, or growing some yourself, is a vote for diversity and certainly an accessible and engaging way to eat like a caveman.

One organization especially champions traditional diets. The Weston A. Price Foundation's website has two slogans that caught my eye. First comes its mission statement that the organization was 'for wise traditions in food, farming and the healing arts'. Then, next to a picture of a beaming family were the magic words, 'They're happy because they eat butter.'

Dr Weston A. Price (1870–1948) left his Cleveland dentistry practice to travel around the world on a quest to discover the cause of tooth decay, a disease that had become prevalent in the developed world. He sought those with beautiful teeth and 'stalwart bodies' and he found them in what he called isolated primitive peoples. Price's 1939 book, *Nutrition and Physical Degeneration*, analyses the diets of fourteen such groups, among them people from Switzerland, the Outer Hebrides and

Polynesia, Aboriginal people in Australia and the Maori in New Zealand. All of them had different diets, but there were some crucial common denominators. In particular, they were free of the refined foods of the modern Western diet, such as sugar and white flour. The foods they ate, like that of a Paleo Diet, were instead remarkably rich in nutrients, having at least four times as much calcium and other minerals as the Western diet and ten times the fat-soluble vitamins A and D from the animal foods they ate, including butters, fish and offal.

The foundation continues Price's work of promoting unprocessed food and traditional diets. *Nourishing Traditions* by Sally Fallon is the foundation's cookbook, full of recipes that stay away from the four main evils: refined grains, sugar, canned foods and pasteurized milk (the foundation is a big promoter of raw milk). The book's introduction attacks the opposite of traditional foods, the 'fast foods, fractionated foods, convenience foods, packaged foods, fake foods, embalmed foods, ersatz foods' of modern eating. Fallon argues that processing removes nutrients from food, for example by ultra-heating or filtering foods, techniques that make for a longer shelf life but take away their original qualities.

Another striking aspect of the foundation's work is its championing of animal fats and its anger at the 'diet dictocrats' who are especially down on them. Instead of being bad for you, the foundation says that these provide plenty of fat-soluble vitamins that we need. The diets of the Swiss and Cretans, for example, are all high in animal fats and yet these countries are known for their longevity. And farmed and wild meat are not the only things that are important. It is possible to get vitamin A and D from plant foods, but it is also true that meat and animal products such as eggs are especially rich in them – so much so that you don't need to eat nearly as much of them as we do today. Offal (so called because they are the internal organs that are cut or fall off the carcass) is especially rich in the vitamins and was regarded as nourishing by the healthy groups Price encountered. I am not a big offal fan, but that's partly because it has such a different taste and texture to other foods. Nevertheless I wanted to find ways to eat more of it, especially livers, which I find the most appealing.

Another of Price's observations was the attention paid by these groups to parental nutrition. Many groups even believed in premarital nutrition to help produce healthy offspring. Price found that some wouldn't allow girls to be married unless they'd had a period of special feeding, perhaps for as long as six months. It is now common to stress the importance of good nutrition for foetal development, and some also stress the importance of this before conception.

Whilst some of Price's theories seem like biological predeterminism – 'a decadent individual cannot regenerate himself' – his observations about the nutritional richness of traditional diets and foods were thought-provoking. His pro-fat arguments are in direct opposition to the current received wisdom that fat, especially animal fat, is 'bad'. There are many, such as Dean Ornish, who advocate a low-fat diet. It's hard to imagine that our Paleo ancestors ate a great deal of fat, simply because it wasn't available in the way it is today. You first had to catch (or

scavenge) your animal, and it would have been leaner than today's farmed creatures. All the same, for the most part, Weston
Price's arguments and observations were helpful in broadening
out my approach to the past. You don't have to go back as far
as the caveman, but to a more recent and attainable past. The
change in our food is from traditional foods to industrialized
ones, not just from wild food to agricultural.

Price found two cooking techniques in particular were common to all the groups he studied. For one, they made mineral-
and gelatine-rich broths from bones. Stocks and soups are a
satisfying part of cooking from scratch, and there is sometimes a
bowl of nutritious chicken stock in my fridge. They also ate
fermented foods. What are they?

In 2010, I attended the Oxford Symposium of Food and
Cooking on the subject of fermented foods. Fermented foods
include bread, beer, yoghurt, pickles and cheese. Even chocolate
is made using wild fermentation, the bugs on the pods beginning
the process of turning an indigestible plant into the chocolate
bar on the shop shelf. It seems a touch odd, in our ultra-
controlled world, that such an everyday product relies on a wild
process engineered by microbes. Yet of course the world teems
with microbiological life. For all the paranoia about bacteria and
food poisoning, with shelves full of antibacterial wipes and sprays,
the processes of tiny life are the basis of food everywhere.

Bacteria are fundamentally important in making the nutrients
in the foods we eat more available, rather as Richard Wrangham says cooking does. They digest fibres our human body

can't, making food quicker to cook as well as digest. Bacteria ferment foods in various ways, one of the chief ones being the lactobacillus bacteria that produce the delicious lactic tastes of many foods including sourdoughs and beers. The acidic medium they produce makes it more difficult for harmful bacteria to thrive, and hence makes food safer. Fermented foods often enliven a dull diet, their strong tastes becoming almost addictive, be it soy sauce or pickles.

Harold McGee, the American who has done so much to popularize the science of food, gave one of the talks at the symposium and took us into an extreme close-up of what we eat. 'Most foodstuffs start as living cells,' he said, showing an artist's picture of plant and animal cells so magnified that they looked like something from outer space rather than inner. It took me back to *The Driving Force* and the idea that we began as cellular life ourselves.

McGee explained how some fermented foods are partly about proteins that are broken down by enzymes to make them more savoury. One example is Jabugo ham, the cured Spanish ham that is matured in temperatures that now artificially imitate the fluctuations of the farmhouse buildings where they would originally have been hung. The temperature changes over the seasons, between 14 and 30 degrees Celsius; the latter is body temperature, a good temperature that biological processes clearly favour.

At the Oxford Symposium, you break off into one of three rooms where people give papers, some with extremely erudite titles on esoteric subjects. Yet somehow these talks are always grounded because they are about food and full of people and shared experiences. I heard one symposiast, June di Schino, talk about kimchi, the lactic-acid pickle that is a staple of Korean meals. It was part of a way of life, with women still making it together in groups; you'd never dream of making kimchi on your own, she said, and likewise you rarely find a single kimchi vase. She was referring to the pot it is made in, one of the oldest vessels used for preserving, and showed many beautiful examples of these in different materials. You could see how bacterial and human cultures worked side by side.

A striking conclusion from all the talks that weekend was how the processes of fermentation that used to belong to ordinary home kitchens are now mostly industrialized. Partly this is said to be for reasons of health and safety – bad bacteria can certainly be dangerous, and we have largely lost the folk knowledge of what's good and what's not. The message was that we should try to keep such kitchen crafts going, and rather than being frightened by the small chance of a problem, instead rebuild our knowledge. A number of books are currently appearing, to try to revive such domestic arts. Traditional foods need this basis of craft to keep them going, whether by inspiring you to do it yourself or by instilling a greater sense of respect for the makers of cheese or cured sausage.

Late in the weekend we returned to the main hall to find the air full of a delicious sour smell from hundreds of little pots of fermented vegetables. These had been made by Sandor Katz, a self-styled 'fermentation fetishist'. There was something attractively wild about Katz himself, his benign energy giving off a ferment of ideas. He'd got into wild and more natural foods when he went to live in a 'Radical Faerie Community' in Tennessee after becoming HIV positive and deciding to pay the utmost attention to his body.

Fermentation is universal, said Katz, as we crunched into our pots. It is at the core of what it is to be human. People speculate about its origins, but it predates recorded history. 'We always knew it; we didn't discover it,' he said. How absurd, then, that we have this war on bacteria when we ourselves contain so many bacteria. Bacteria are at the heart of the cycle of life and death. They mostly work in our gut, but also elsewhere; for example, a woman's vagina has lactobacilli that, amongst other functions, help reproduction and these are picked up by the baby on its way out of the womb like initial armour for the big, bad world outside.

I enjoyed Katz's talk so much that I read his book on wild fermentation and another on alternative food cultures called *The Revolution Will Not be Microwaved*. In some people, a strong focus can be monomaniacal. But Katz was genuine and humane. He'd thought and lived through his ideas and there was an underlying wisdom in the way he shared them. This was a twenty-first-century approach to traditional foods. I liked the way it also looped back to the far distant past and connected us to it. After all, bacteria and other micro-organisms occupied the world for the first 2 billion years of the 3.5 billion years of life. They are, it turns out, the stuff of life.

I had been somewhat sceptical about the idea of going back to the Stone Age diet and it is, of course, impossible to do – or at least for me (I've read some entertaining blogs by others who follow this way of eating to a greater degree). But looking at what we evolved to eat turned out to be a useful marker against which to measure the excesses of today's diets. We would do well to eat a wider range of nutrient-rich foods, eat a bit less and exercise more. That's not going back to the cave, but following, broadly speaking, a traditional diet.

WHAT TO EAT?

Easy. Aim for biodiversity on the plate – if you have a salad with two plants, add two more; eat more herbs and oily fish; appreciate nuts; have more raw foods; look for heritage varieties in shops and markets; enjoy traditional foods such as cheese, yoghurt and broths.

Worth the Effort. Forage for wild food, especially wild greens, and grow some types, such as sorrel; experiment with home-fermentation crafts such as making bread from a sourdough culture, and making lactic-acid pickles; find an Abundance group and make jam and chutney; explore nut oils; learn more about the medicinal uses of plants.

Hopes and Dreams. That the insidious taste for sugar is reversed; that fermentation becomes less frightening and the techniques as well as the foods are preserved at a domestic level; that habitats and cultures are kept alive as the basis of biodiversity.

4

What is a Sustainable Fish?

If there is one single question that people raise with the most unease it is this: 'What fish can I eat?' and even 'Can I eat fish at all?'

At the heart their anxiety is the fact that fish confronts us with a conflict of interests. With many food issues, the environmental and health benefits run parallel. There may be questions of cost and accessibility, but the basic principles are reasonably clear. But the subject of fish seems to put the green and the good in direct collision. On the one hand, fish is the most delicious and fashionable of healthy foods. We are increasingly aware of the health benefits of eating fish, particularly the likes of salmon, tuna, herring and mackerel. They build our brains, sharpen our vision, help our synapses swim and keep our hearts well-oiled. They may even regulate our appetite by altering a hunger hormone, making fish both filling and slimming. In short, fish is the alpha and omega-3 of good nutrition.

Yet at the very same time as the popularity and status of fish have grown, we have come to look beneath the surface of the big, wild, wet sea and fathom that all is not well below.

The starkest assessment about the state of the marine world came from a four-year study, carried out by fourteen ecologists and economists and published by the journal *Science* in 2006. If we continued to kill and eat fish at the current rate, they concluded, the world would run out of seafood by 2048. Nearly 30 per cent of species had crashed. Some fisheries, particularly of the larger fish such as bluefin tuna and swordfish, had fallen to below 10 per cent of their highest recorded stocks. Some 75 per cent of fisheries were fully or over-exploited, according to the United Nations. The world's oceans and the creatures in them are, at the very least, in an extremely serious state and in some cases dire.

Why are there so few fish in the sea? The problem, in a nutshell, is that there are too many boats chasing falling numbers of fish with whizzy technology such as satellite hunting equipment and nets that are the size of Wembley stadium. An industrial fishing fleet can now decimate a fishery in just 15 years. No wonder the whole industry has gone into a downward spiral.

What is immediately shocking, given the plummeting fish stocks, is quite how wasteful fishing is. A billion people around the world rely on fish for their protein and 540 million (8 per cent of the world's population) depend upon it for their livelihoods, according to the UN. Some 90 per cent of these jobs are in developing countries where people earn more from fish than coffee, tea, rice and bananas put together. Yet in profligate Europe, around half the fish caught in the North Sea are thrown over the side of the boat, dead, because they are illegal to land or not valuable enough to sell.

The reason for so much waste is, in part, the indiscriminate method of catching the fish, by trawling. Beam trawlers rattle along the bottom of the sea, hoovering everything up into a big net and damaging the seabed. The environmentalist Tristram Stuart, in his book *Waste*, draws a powerful analogy by transferring this method of fishing to the land. 'Imagine if the standard method for killing cattle were to use bulldozers to haul a net through the countryside, uprooting trees and hedges, smashing ancient monuments and exterminating along with the cows everything from badger and stoats to lapwings and barn owls, all of which perished slowly by suffocation,' he writes. 'This is what happens every day under the cover of the oceans, despite more sensitive alternative ways of catching fish being available.'

At issue here is not only the fishing method, but a quota system that means the fishermen discard undersized fish and those beyond their quota. They also discard less valuable fish in order to fill their landing quota with the most profitable haul. All this causes genuine chagrin to the fishermen and great disgust to the public when they see it on news and campaign footage.

Expressing this state of affairs just in these terms, however, risks pushing the problem onto the fishermen. They, in turn, are supposed to be under the rule of governments. A large part of the responsibility lies with those at the top, since they have the most power to regulate types of gear and fishing grounds.

But governments, in turn, are voted in by us. Furthermore, we need to ask where the fish have gone. To be blunt, we ate them. The statistics of marine destruction lead back to the fish finger, the tuna sandwich, the lunchtime sushi, the anchovies on the pizza, and the genteel fillet of sole swimming in its buttery sauce on the restaurant platter. This is not a problem we can just push to the side of the plate. We may well, in however small a way, be contributing to the dire situation of the oceans. I now feel slightly sick when I see small fish, caught too young to reproduce, on the fishmonger's slab.

A wake-up call for the general public about the plight of fish came with *The End of the Line*, a passionate and thorough book by the journalist Charles Clover that was made into a campaigning documentary feature film in 2009. Both the writer and the filmmakers of *The End of the Line* are motivated by a love of the sea and an anger at the way it is being abused.

Perhaps *The End of the Line*'s most powerful overarching point is that the sea is a common resource, not one to be exploited to its detriment by one group: the fishing industry does not own the sea. And whilst fishermen may know more about the sea at a working level, they do not necessarily have the overview that matters. Ultimately, our right to the oceans' sustainable future – the state of nearly three-quarters of the planet – is much bigger than the industry's to make a living.

Most important of all is the ability of the oceans to exist on their own terms, richly layered and self-sustaining. Fish are not simply there for us to eat; they are part of a complex ecology that we disrupt at our peril. One answer is to designate large areas of the sea as marine reservations so that the fish stocks can recuperate and the marine environment can be left alone. UK campaigners want 30 per cent of seas around our shores to be kept like this.

Marine reservations are just one suggestion of what we can

do. For all its tales of destruction, *The End of the Line* is an uplifting film. It shows the beauty of the sea and its fish; and it argues that the answers to these problems are known. We *can* do something about this. We *can* catch better and eat sustainably. We *can* look after the oceans, or rather let them look after themselves in their own way. It is a question of political will, following scientific advice, using better technology and implementing more regulation. This does not have to be 'the end of the line'. But how?

Amongst all the bad news, it came as a relief to learn that the answer to over-fishing does not seem to be for consumers to give up eating fish altogether. Professor Callum Roberts, a highly regarded marine conservation biologist at the University of York, says that, properly regulated, fishing can boost numbers. Fisheries science suggests, for example, that taking out the largest, oldest fish allows more feed and growth for the younger, faster-growing fish and, overall, benefits the health of the stock.

As a consumer trying to work out what to do, I started to look into the subject through the websites of environmental groups concerned about the state of the seas. The Marine Conservation Society (MCS) is a UK charity that offers an online and pocket guide to fish, Fishonline. Each species is rated from a green '1', which is in a healthy state, to a red '5', which is to be avoided.

I clicked onto the 'Fish to Avoid' list. It was an uncomfortable read. My eye ran quickly down the sixty-nine 'species to avoid' on the website list. There were a number of classics of the

British table that I liked to eat. In alphabetical order, they were: anchovies, brill, cod, haddock, hake, halibut, herring, plaice, skate, tiger prawn, tuna and turbot.

I thought of Spanish stews with chunks of hake; of my first discovery of brill's pearly texture; the fat Calabrian anchovies I'd eaten that summer on sourdough toast with unsalted butter; the supper-time convenience of tiger prawns, tossed together with some spicy sauce and slippery noodles. I remembered memorable fish feasts, forking the smooth skeins of skate off its cartilage frill, the plump plaice that a fishmonger said had fattened up on mussel spat off the Sussex coast; haddock and chips eaten by the seaside; and the occasional push-the-boat-out treat of turbot, acclaimed by many chefs as the finest fish that swims in the sea.

And then there was tuna, almost meaty in its colour and texture, and available everywhere from common cans to posh restaurants. I had eaten it all my life, from the tuna and sweetcorn bake of childhood camping holidays to ruby slithers of high-end sashimi in my metropolitan restaurant-going twenties. I now ate it every so often for a healthy supper, perhaps baked in a Sicilian dish with capers, currants, onions and Marsala, or fried briefly on the outside so the centre remained that beautiful pinky-scarlet.

Faced with this Fish to Avoid list I wondered: are all these to be struck off my menu? I had that familiar sinking feeling: what's left to eat?

When I looked further, the list was less proscriptive than I'd thought – but more complicated. It was Bay of Biscay anchovies you shouldn't eat, and non-organically farmed or otherwise properly certified tiger prawns. You could eat brill that was not from the Atlantic and caught by 'demersal otter' rather than beam trawling. Demersal otter trawlers have nets towed off the seabed and are therefore less damaging to the marine environment than the beam trawlers that run along the bottom. Haddock was best line-caught or, nowadays, from the newly certified sustainable fishing fleet in Scotland. Halibut was one to avoid but Alaskan halibut was all right. Plaice scored a maximum number 5 on the red 'don't eat' list, but then again it was okay from some fisheries but not from others.

Bluefin tuna, the big turbocharged hunter of the sea, was a no-no because numbers have fallen so much, but the smaller, more plentiful skipjack was fine. Then I had a look on the American equivalent of Fishonline, the Seafood Watch list compiled by the Monterey Bay Aquarium, and saw that the longline fleets that catch skipjack can have a bad rate of 'by-catch' – species caught other than the targeted one – including sea turtles, sharks and seabirds. You need, ideally, to go for skipjack tuna (or other sorts such as albacore and yellowfin) that have been caught by pole-and-line, handline and longline fleets that avoid by-catch. But when you are in a shop or restaurant, you just think of tuna as tuna; you don't tend to dwell on the type or fishing method. However, thanks to vigorous and imaginative campaigning this is changing, and it is now possible to find tins of eco-tuna in most supermarkets.

The Marine Conservation Society also had a 'Fish to Eat' list. This was also complicated. Atlantic salmon had to be organically farmed. Mackerel should come from a certified handline fishery in Cornwall. Particular types of tuna could be eaten, provided they were caught in particular ways. You could eat something called bib or pouting, but only those that were over 20cm. and not in its springtime spawning season. But would you really bother about all this as you shopped for your supper? You get the picture: it's not easy.

In the end, it felt quite complicated to try to pick my way through the ever-changing detail of what should be on or off the menu, even though the MCS has made matters simpler by having three categories, red (to avoid), amber (eat occasionally) and green (fine). But easiest of all would be to be able to trust the shop where you are buying the fish or the restaurant where you are eating out, or for there to be some sort of eco-label on the product to tell you that it is sustainable.

It is clear that such a certification scheme, marking what is or isn't sustainable, is needed in order to make it easy for us to choose the right fish. An international body, the Marine Stewardship Council, or MSC, was founded in 1997 to design a scheme of this nature. It was set up by the international conglomerate Unilever and the World Wildlife Fund in a marriage of commerce and conscience. The MSC certifies around 6 per cent of the world's wild fish caught for human consumption. Internationally, it has 12,784 certified products with 135 fisheries certified and a further 133 being assessed.

To get certification, a fishery has to satisfy three criteria. The fish stock must be in a healthy state in the first place. Then the fish must be caught in a way that does not have an adverse effect on the rest of the environment, be it ploughing up the seabed, taking too many other fish or other creatures as by-catch or adversely affecting a food chain. Thirdly, the fishery must be well managed to ensure that the catching does not get out of control.

It certainly felt like a reassuring solution for consumers. The dark blue fish-tick logo of the MSC can now be seen in some shops and restaurant menus. I had even seen it in a chippie I had just been to in Scotland. Fishermen and fishing fleets that join the scheme and get certification can get a premium for their fish and will be in pole position as the world gets more concerned about the state of the seas. Andrew Mallison, at that time the MSC's Standards and Licensing Director, told me that the organization offers a path through the uncertainties of the world's most tricky resource. 'There is hope and there are better ways of doing things,' he said. 'And the people doing it need to be recognized and rewarded.'

The MSC report *Net Benefits* gives many examples of how this has been achieved. For instance, there is the hake fishery in South Africa that used to have a by-catch of 18,000 birds a year. Simply by putting streamers on the lines and making them sink more quickly reduced this to almost zero.

At the moment, however, there are a couple of problems. Given the 'good news' of the MSC labels, I was surprised to hear that a fair amount of certified fish wasn't given the distinctive blue label in the shops simply because it costs money to use the label. Then I learned that some restaurants had gone down the MSC route but couldn't manage to get sufficient supplies because so much of the stock goes to supermarket chains with their superior buying power, even though the blue tick is not always apparent on the shelves.

More worryingly, there are criticisms that the MSC does not set the sustainability bar high enough. Within its own system of totting up marks, the organization allow fisheries to be 60–80 per cent sustainable, so long as they are actively working towards a higher level. You could argue this gives an incentive for the fisheries to become more sustainable, but does it mean the eco-brand is watered down?

The standards of the MSC clearly need to be maintained and monitored in order to be meaningful. But at least it offers the consumer, fish merchants and fishermen a way forward. The main impact of the MSC blue label scheme is not just in influencing what you can buy yourself (assuming, of course, it is labelled), but in the way it helps fishing fleets to be more sustainable. Crucially, it encourages the big buyers, who tend to have an agenda of corporate responsibility they want to promote to the public, to raise their standards and turn a large volume of seafood towards sustainability.

The large retailers, aware of the worrying state of fish stocks, have been pursuing supplies of more sustainable fish for some time, and indeed have led the way. A number have pledged to sell largely or entirely MSC-certified fish within a few years – and we are talking Walmart here, to give an American example, and not just the more boutiquey retailers that attract more concerned shoppers. This will cover wild fish, not farmed (at present the world's supplies are roughly half-and-half).

It sounds good – but how far is it sorted? A Marine Conservation Society survey of sustainable fish in UK supermarkets in 2009 showed the flaws. Nearly half the retailers refused to take part at all (participation has since improved). The highest was the Co-operative, with 80 per cent. The supermarkets that responded were better at not stocking the 'fish to avoid', such as bluefin tuna, skate, eel and rock, than they were at actively promoting the 'fish to eat', such as pollock, gurnard, tilapia, black bream and dab.

If you look on the labels of packaged fish in good supermarkets, you might think all was rosy. They are reassuring, but as the Marine Conservation Society supermarket survey shows, you still have to be aware of the issues and pick your way through. A supermarket may have a strong sustainable fish policy for its own-brand fish, but other suppliers are responsible for the standards of the fish they supply to the store. And most of the sales may be for farmed salmon, which often has sustainability issues (of which more later) and is rated amber by the MCS except for organic and certain stocks of wild salmon, which are green.

Another challenge to the ethical fish buyer is that you may want to go to a proper fishmonger because the selection and freshness are better than in most supermarkets. But can you find one who takes a stance on sourcing ethically? A number of fishmongers have chosen to do this, but by no means all. In the end, you can feel more secure in the hands of the supermarket in terms of sustainability, but alas not usually for quality, although this has improved markedly in recent years.

When it comes to sustainable fish, eating out is even more complicated. Do you want to be the spectre at the feast by asking about where the fish comes from and how it was caught? Every time I have asked a waiter this question they don't know, and, to be frank, asking makes you feel like a school examiner, not the happy guest on what is supposed to be a night out.

The question of sustainable fish in restaurants has been bravely raised by Charles Clover. In *The End of the Line* he makes the counterintuitive point that a McDonald's 'Filet-o-Fish' is sustainably sourced whilst many of the smartest London restaurants are cheerfully serving up endangered species. If you were to put 'panda burger' on a menu, it wouldn't go down well, and yet they might have bluefin tuna on offer. Clover set up a website called Fish to Fork, which rates a wide selection of restaurants on how they measure up against the Marine Stewardship Council's guidelines.

The result caused something of an outcry. Some restaurateurs felt they hadn't been given proper warning about the survey, which 'names and shames'. On the other hand, Charles Clover's impression was that some thought themselves too grand to respond to the questionnaire and that the issues were not relevant to cuisine as they understood it. But a threatened fish is a threatened fish, whether it ends up in a fish finger or robed in hollandaise. 'People did not know what they were serving and did not know it was endangered,' says Clover. 'Our big contention is that you can't talk about quality food without talking about its source and the sustainability part of the definition. The reality is that listing people – especially if your name is put in the bottom ten – puts a huge amount of pressure on the restaurant. Some of them were not expecting it and they don't like it.'

I wanted to talk to some of the people who supply the restaurant and catering trade, so I interviewed one of the biggest fish wholesalers, Mike Berthet, of M&J Seafoods. His company supplies 14,000 businesses, from works canteens to Michelin-starred restaurants. Sustainability is high on his agenda for very practical reasons. Like many suppliers, he had noticed with increasing disquiet that there were fewer fish in the sea and that they were getting smaller. This was bad news, because fish need to reach a certain size and sexual maturity to spawn and produce the next generations. Tiddly 30–50g fillets, cut from small codling landed from the North Sea, were being turned into battered cod for fish and chips. Mike asked, instead, for bigger cod that could be cut carefully to make the right-sized portion; the smaller fish should be left in the sea to grow and reproduce.

Mike believes the wholesaler should be a 'locksmith' who prevents endangered fish from being sold and in this way helps to influence what's caught. Part of his task is to educate the chefs, who must in turn persuade their customers to eat other seafood. He estimates 60 per cent or more of the people he supplies at least have sustainability on their radar, especially the bigger catering companies who supply schools, hospitals and government canteens, and individual chefs, such as Raymond

Blanc at Le Manoir aux Quat' Saisons, are now high-profile advocates of sustainable fish. People, in the main, now see that there is a problem, and that is a start.

One of the unknowable problems concerning fish stocks is how much fish is caught illegally. At one point it was thought that half of UK landings were illegal. The government is becoming far stricter on this. It is not always easy for anyone to be 100 per cent certain of where the fish comes from. Emily Howgate of The Good Catch, an organization that promotes sustainability within the catering business, says the degree of 'untraceability' of fish is astonishing. 'You wouldn't buy a chicken and be told "We don't know where it was from,"' she says. 'We need to demand that of our fish. It seems to be out of sight, out of mind. But it's a mindset that is shifting.'

Mike Berthet said he was 'hopeful' (though not optimistic) about the future of global fish supplies. He thought that governments were closing the net on illegal fishing – though it could take another five to ten years to do so – and that fishing technology was improving to reduce wasteful by-catch.

After a strongly fought campaign by the television chef and food writer Hugh Fearnley-Whittingstall, the EU has recently shifted forward on the disgraceful requirement to throw away fish that is beyond the fisherman's quota. The EU fisheries commissioner, Maria Damanaki, said that we cannot continue 'this nightmare of discards', and has pledged to reform the present system. So, there's progress – or at least a promise of it.

Mike Berthet was also very concerned about the way

industrial fisheries were moving in on developing countries, who sell their fishing rights for cash and get their stocks trashed in return. I spoke to a friend who had recently visited Sierra Leone. He said the locals no longer had much access to the shrimp, which are all sold abroad. Some of the fish is illegally caught. The UK-based Environmental Justice Foundation has exposed how West African pirate-caught fish find their way into the European market. A shining example of the opposite approach is Namibia, which supports its local, small-scale fishermen, who in turn are prospering by selling well-caught fish at a proper price to a world that wants high-quality seafood. This is one way forward, even if it looks like a small boat bobbing about in a sea of troubles.

'If you catch plentiful species unsustainably then they won't be sustainable,' said Caroline Bennett, an eco-minded fish restaurateur I met at a Slow Food event on sustainable fish. This nugget of wisdom stuck in my mind. I went to see Caroline to find out what she was doing in her restaurants. Her response to the situation clearly went deeper than just switching from an unsustainable species to another that could then, in turn, come under threat.

Caroline at that time ran a Japanese restaurant called Soseki and a small chain of sushi bars called Moshi Moshi. Her first one, in Liverpool Street Station in London, was the first conveyor-belt sushi restaurant in the UK. Sushi originally started out as a means of preserving fish. In pre-refrigeration days, fish was packed in fermenting rice. It was one of the first ever fast foods, served on Japanese streets. Then sushi caught on as a Hollywood, high-end fashion in the 1970s in the US and spread around the world in the 1980s in the restaurants set up for Japanese ex-pats. In the 1990s, sushi went back to its street origins and became mainstream, helped by restaurants such as Moshi Moshi and an awareness of the healthiness of Japanese food.

When I went to the Liverpool Street branch of Moshi Moshi, I noticed there was a Cornish Catch sushi selection. This was subtly different from what a Japanese person would expect to get in a sushi selection, yet entirely appropriate to UK sushi. The fish was very fresh; it had that indefinable, fleeting juiciness that shines and then quickly fades.

I took a five-minute walk from Moshi Moshi through the City to Soseki, Caroline's main restaurant (which she opened, alas, at the start of the economic downturn and has since closed). The venue folded you into Japanese boxes and bars where you sat as if in your own space, as if at home. The restaurant's décor was unusually feminine in its fabrics, colour and intimacy. Caroline and I sat at a booth to be served octopus and beautiful little packages of spider crab. Soseki was based on the *kaiseki-kappo* restaurants of Japan, which serve set menus based on ingredients at their peak. For a number of the set menus, you were given no choice; the chef had a supply of what could be termed 'reasonably sustainable' fish – of which more later – and that was what was on the menu.

Caroline told me that the origins of Moshi Moshi and Soseki were, ironically, linked to the most endangered fish of all. Blue-fin tuna is regarded as the ultimate sushi offering, especially its fatty belly. The California Roll, with its centre of avocado and crabstick, originated because the fattiness of the avocado echoed the *toro*, or fatty belly cut of tuna. 'I set up a Japanese restaurant because I loved the flavours I ate in Japan,' said Caroline, who had studied and worked in Japan for five years. 'Probably the most memorable one was bluefin tuna. On a Sunday morning, you'd wake up and phone friends in Tokyo and say: "Shall we go out for sushi brunch?" because you had that wonderful salty hit of the miso to get over any hangover and the freshness of iodine and the creaminess of this wonderful tuna – it was just what I hankered for. And I wanted to come to London and be able to eat it myself. Because Japanese food was so expensive at that time, opening Moshi Moshi seemed like a good way to satiate my own desires.'

The idea of conveyor-belt sushi took off. Brits liked the idea of grabbing little plates of food as they slowly snaked their way past their place. But every summer there was a problem with bluefin tuna supplies. In 1998, four years after Moshi Moshi's opening, they stopped. 'I remember screaming at my chef, saying, "We call ourselves a Japanese restaurant and we haven't even got *toro* on the menu,"' said Caroline. She thought it was just a hiccup in the supply chain. This went on for a matter of weeks. Then someone said, 'There's probably a real problem – there aren't many left.' Caroline phoned the World Wildlife Fund and Greenpeace. Within twenty-four hours, having made just two phone calls, she realized that there really was a massive problem with bluefin tuna. It was a moment of revelation – not least about how little she knew about one of her most prestigious ingredients. 'That dichotomy of knowledge was so extraordinary,' she said. 'How come these NGOs know there are these massive problems and yet the people using the fish are exacerbating the situation and don't even know what they are doing?'

From this point on, Caroline began to learn about the issues surrounding not just tuna but the marine environment as a whole. She became part of a five-year government initiative, Invest in Fish, travelling to South West England to sit at meetings with supermarkets, fishermen, anglers and conservationists, all brought together in an attempt to hammer out solutions for the common problem of dwindling fish stocks. From this experience, she was determined to find a practical solution to how to get sustainable fish in her restaurants.

One of the main issues for the conservationists is that they want to favour the smaller, inshore boats, known as 'day boats', that use more carefully targeted static nets that do less damage to the seabed, have a far lower incidence of by-catch and catch fewer immature fish that have not had a chance to spawn. Yet both these and beam-trawled fish are sold for the same price at the market, despite being of a completely different quality. The fresher, less bashed-around, more sustainable day-boat fish are lumped in with the industrially trawled catch despite the fact that this is exactly the sort of produce that concerned consumers would pay more for. Caroline said, 'Where is the incentive for any fisherman to change his ways – unless there's a deep-felt conviction that it is what you want to do? For many it is, but it's been beaten out of them by the system.'

In 2004, Caroline started to see a solution. She went along to Slow Food's Terra Madre in Italy, a coming together of small producers from around the world. The large number of visitors were put up in hotels a two-hour drive from the event's centre in Turin. On the way back and forth to the events, she got talking to a fellow bus-traveller, a Cornishman called Chris Bean. He runs a twenty-eight-foot family fishing boat, the Lady Hamilton, out of Helford and uses what is called 'static gear' – nets with specific mesh sizes which he lets down like curtains for the likes of monkfish, ray, sole, red mullet, pollock, cod and ling. He gets handline mackerel and crabs from pots, throwing back the immature shellfish so they can live and spawn. After years of seeing his carefully caught fish being sold for the same price as those caught by industrial trawlers, he decided to market the fish for himself.

Chris promised Caroline he would courier over some fresh seafood. From then on, their partnership has thrived. Caroline and her chefs went to down to Cornwall to try out ways of using the types of fish that Chris lands but can't sell because they don't have the cachet of bass or monkfish, say. A weekend spent experimenting with sashimi was the start of the Cornish Catch box I had eaten in Moshi Moshi.

Chris has now found a way to use every fish he catches. Take pouting, a fish that had puzzled me on the Marine Conservation Society's Fishonline's 'to eat' list. It is what commerce would term a 'rubbish fish'. Chris and his crew take a sharp knife and skin and bone it, and what was worth 30–40p per kilogramme as a whole fish, when filleted and tidied up is worth £1.70–£2.

They've worked through all the fish right down to what Chris calls 'the final frontier' – an unprepossessing fish he calls a morghie (Cornish for 'seadog'). This was formerly sold as bait, but he strips it off the bone and makes it usable by chefs.

There is now no waste at all in what Chris catches; everything is worthy of a posh-plated London restaurant. As well as selling to Caroline, he supplies fifteen other restaurants, gastropubs and fishmongers in the London area. He also has a family-run stall at three farmers' markets in Cornwall, where sales just grow and grow.

In the end, for Chris sustainable fish is a question of quality. 'Trawled fish are generally smaller than those caught in static nets,' he says. 'The fish are damaged, suffocated, dumped on deck and some of them shovelled over the side for the seagulls. I just don't think it's the way forward.' He believes discerning chefs and cooks won't buy trawled fish for much longer because its shelf life is so much less because it is not looked after. 'Once they've tasted our stuff and seen it and smelt it and appreciated the service, they are reluctant to go for anything else. Unquestionably, with a limited resource we should be using the best, catching it sustainably and marketing it at best quality to people who appreciate it.'

When I went to see Chris's stall at Penzance farmers' market, I saw for myself the fantastic range of his catch. As whole fish, he had sea bass, monkfish tail, Dover sole, turbot, cod, pollock, plaice, cuttlefish and John Dory – all locally caught. Pollock, wrasse, huss, pouting and smoothhound were also sold as fillets, and he had some ray wings. By the time I got there at midday there was a line through most of his blackboard list as he had sold out of everything but cuttlefish, wrasse, smoothhound and monkfish. At that time of year, in May, he had masses of cuttlefish and gave out recipes and tastings to introduce people to this less familiar seafood. When he did this, it sold: a bit of effort pays off.

Our friends Jude and Matt cooked us some of the very fresh huss for lunch and we talked about how in Cornwall the land is the edge of the sea, not the other way around. Perhaps the physical closeness to the sea makes a difference to people's engagement, but I imagine that interested shoppers anywhere would like the same sort of connection. But what made this special was that Chris and his family were at the stall and had caught the fish themselves. You saw pictures of the boat beside the fish on sale, and it all made sense.

Caroline Bennett wants to scale up through an operation called Pisces Sustainable Fish in Restaurants. The aim is to pair chefs up with small-scale fishermen, as she has done with Chris Bean. There are challenges. Supply lines, reliability and variety are all problems that need to be addressed. Cornwall has what's called a mixed catch; many different fish swim in the same waters. Other parts of the coast have just a few species. Are people prepared to get what they are given and not what they ask for? It takes a shift of understanding for a diner on a night out.

And like any consumer, Caroline faces the age-old dilemma of quality and cost. She was talking at a conference to some British fishermen who were shocked that she was using farmed bass. 'We've got wonderful bass here, Caroline, why don't you use it?' they asked. 'I said, it's £5.60 per kilogramme for the farmed one and yours is £15–£16 per kilogramme, and they said, "Well that's the price you pay for good bass." To overcome that one and clear my conscience I had to open a much more expensive restaurant, and that's where it gets really nasty: is sustainable food only for the people who can afford it?'

A way for home cooks to source sustainable fish at a decent price has been pioneered in the northeastern United States: Community Supported Fisheries (CSF). The idea is that you guarantee to buy a certain amount of fish every week at an agreed price, then you pick it up from a drop-off point at the same time each week. Fish notoriously goes up and down in price depending on the weather, demand and what everyone has caught. CSF schemes connect consumers with fishermen who fish more sustainably, and give the fishermen a guaranteed price and an incentive to carry on. They are a great idea for the consumer who wants to eat more fish (and good ones). In the same way as getting a veg box means you eat more veg, getting a fish bag means you eat a regular amount of well-caught, delicious seafood.

I came across an example of a CSF in Gloucester, Massachusetts, a charismatic fishing town that has long attracted writers and artists to its shores. It's a salty, sassy, colourful place. *The Perfect Storm*, both book and film, was based here, and Mark Kurlansky, author of the micro-history *Cod*, fished on a Gloucester trawler in order to pay his college fees. Much of its appeal relies on fishing, past and present. But life has not been easy for the modern Gloucester fisherman. The fleet has been largely industrialized and prices for any commodity can drop, even when fish are scarcer. And the fish are becoming scarcer. The area was hit when the cod fishing was banned altogether in the region in the 1990s. The CSF was set up by a group of feisty fishermen's wives and an environmental organization called NAMA (the Northwestern Atlantic Marine Alliance) in order to get a better deal for the fishermen and provide concerned consumers with the kind of fish they wanted.

I went to see Niaz Dorry, who runs NAMA. It was a Sunday morning and I found her hard at work in her office, kept company by Hayley, a rescue dog from Hurricane Katrina. Niaz was a campaigner on toxic waste for Greenpeace before she was asked to get involved in fisheries. At first she was reluctant. At the time, marine environmentalism tended to focus on single species, such as the whale, and she didn't quite see how it could work for a broader campaign. Focusing on just one species, or 'charismatic mega-fauna' as Niaz puts it, can lead to a lack of proportion. Whilst it is easier to connect to a campaign for dolphins or whales, she felt it was much more important to look at the entire ecosystem. She started to read articles on the state of the sea. 'I realized pretty quickly it went beyond the whale to the global movement of capital, just like a company producing toxic waste,' she says. 'In the case of toxins the community, the air, the water were in the way. In the case of the oceans, the whale, the fishing community and the fish were in the way.'

What is needed, said Niaz, is to look at fisheries management through the lens of the food system and in particular the local food system. The answer, for her, is therefore local fish. 'When it comes to most of our foods, the closer we are to the source of it, the more likely it is that it has been sustainably caught (or grown) and harvested. Local food is good not just because of food miles; it's about the amount of information you can gather and the face-to-face conversations we have with the people who are producing or catching it. People want to look their customer in the face and speak about what they do. It gives them a sense of responsibility.'

Niaz Dorry was interesting about fishing methods. 'No single method has a halo above its head,' she said. There had been big improvements made in many kinds – even in shrimping and other kinds of trawling that are notoriously wasteful. Fishing gear had been lightened dramatically and by-catch rates had been reduced almost to zero in some cases. So it wasn't a case of just using different fishing methods, in her opinion, but improving all of them. Even static gear, such as the gill nets that hang down in the sea, could be set in a way that was better or worse.

She wasn't so sure that monitoring and certification schemes, such as the MSC, were as good as they seemed. 'I don't have any confidence in short-term monitoring efforts,' she said. 'My confidence is in a scale of operation that is economical and economically sustainable for the ocean. The fishing industry is at a fork in the road and has been for almost ten years. We can either go the aqua-business way, or we can go the small-scale, community-based way.' She also felt that, whatever the intentions of the MSC, once you got into supplying the likes of

Walmart, it just couldn't be sustainable because they would require consistent supplies of particular species, rather than spreading out the load to sell what the smaller fishermen caught.

Community Supported Fishing is a brilliant way forward on
this tack, and there are now ten on the eastern seaboard of the
US. The Gloucester-based scheme, Cape Ann Fresh Catch, attracted 1,000 subscribers in its first season, which runs from
spring to autumn. Steve Parkes runs the scheme and drives his
fish van to sixteen pickup points, including Boston. He explains
that he is not so much selling the fish – which, after all, the customers have already bought – but selling a programme of eating
fish sustainably. The conversations of what exactly is sustainable
are 'ongoing', he says, and one of the main tasks is to help the
customer eat what is caught rather than what's on a shopping
list. For many, it is about learning the basics of fish cookery.
'Most people don't know how to deal with whole fish – we
have to teach them,' says Steve. He advises them to start by cooking the whole fish, perhaps with a simple marinade of olive oil,
lemon juice and parsley, and just putting it in the oven. 'About
99 times out of 100 they come back and say: It was awesome
and so easy to do.' After a few weeks, Steve then shows them
how to fillet the fish, cutting up half a dozen fish in the back of
the truck to show how it's done.

Niaz Dorry is a big fan of cooking fish on the bone rather
than always as fillets. As with meat, it keeps the flesh more juicy
and more flavourful. She cooks it simply, with lemon or lime
juice, olive oil, salt and pepper, and grills it, or bakes it, or makes
a stew using the whole fish and herbs and perhaps tamarind

paste. Her heritage is Iranian and she also has recipes using herbs, walnuts and the tiny sour berries called barberries that are a part of Middle Eastern cooking, as well as sumac, a powder that tenderizes and flavours the fish; or else she marinades it in goat's milk yoghurt. The key, again, is using what is caught by the fishermen rather than demanding the same species time after time. She reasons: 'If they are doing their best to be as selective as they possibly can, why can't we do our best to be a little less selective than we have been and really allow our diets to reflect the seasonality and complexity of the ocean?'

I hope the CSF movement will spread, and soon. It feels like a more engaged way for consumers to participate in finding part of a solution to the problems of the sea, and for the more sustainable fishermen to be enabled to make a living from their efforts. But I know it will require the efforts of people who can span all the different aspects: fishermen, consumers, regulators and retailers. As so often in these cases, it requires that people with very different perspectives should understand each other.

I am writing these words in my partner's cottage in Hastings, on the south coast of the UK, about five minutes' walk from the sea. On the shingle beach is a collection of tall, narrow, black buildings. The look is so strangely distinctive that you half-wonder if marine dragons are furled up inside like roosting umbrellas. These are where the fishermen traditionally hung their nets, though the nets these days lie out on the beach or are put into conventional sheds.

This is a fleet of around just 25 small boats. They don't have large fishing gear but just static nets that hang down in the water and with a mesh size that makes them reasonably selective about size and type of fish, in contrast to the heavy beam trawl nets that larger boats run along the seabed, scooping up everything.

The Hastings boats launch off the shingle beach and their comings and goings are central to the character and ebb and flow of the town, as are boats in all ports. When the sea is 'lumpy' they might not go out for days. In the right conditions you see them being heaved up the shingle on winches, with flocks of seagulls barking above. It's a scene that has remained essentially the same for the last six hundred years and is clearly recognizable from paintings by the artists the town has attracted over the centuries.

Now there is a modern slant to this continuing tradition. The Hastings fleet is MSC-certified for mackerel, herring and Dover sole. Near the beach, you can buy your fish from the fishmongers who have a range of seafood from here and further away, or from the 'boys ashore' who sell just a few kinds of fish from simple huts right on the shingle. These only have what has just been landed and perhaps couldn't be sold, for example because a crab had nipped off a small bit of Dover sole flesh. This local fish is easily the most delicious kind that I have ever bought and has that transient, sweet minerality that comes from being just out of the sea. I'll happily fight my way through the sleeting rain, as if on the deck of a ship, to get lunch from these huts and talk to the seller about the price of fish and anything else that comes up.

Part of the pleasure of buying from people who know their ingredients properly is that they can tell you how to cook the fish – or whatever it is – in a way that you'll never forget. Take dabs, one of the regular fish sold by the 'boys ashore' (and one of their favourites). These small flat fish are considered too small and fiddly to bother with by the mainstream and I had no idea what to do with one. I asked one seller, and he said, 'Dust the fish with flour and fry it in butter or oil until the flour goes brown.' What simpler recipe could you have? It works perfectly. Such help is a vivid and immediate reason for buying from the specialist rather than the supermarket.

The Good Catch organization, which aims to bring sustainable fish to the table, invited me to an event that brought chefs and restaurateurs from the southeast of England to the Hastings beach to meet some fishermen and talk about sustainability. Having lived near the fishermen and enjoyed their fish, I was interested to see the mechanics of how such local fish got to the marketplace on a wider scale and how easy it was for restaurants to sell it to their customers.

It turned out that 90 per cent of the fish isn't eaten in Hastings, for all its chip shops and restaurants. It isn't even sold in the southeast, despite the fact that Billingsgate market, the biggest wholesale market in the UK, is only a short drive away. Most of this beautiful fresh fish is taken away by lorries that drive along the south coast and then head off for nearby France. The ready French market pushes up the price of local fish and, whilst the fishmongers all still sell the beautiful local catch, apparently it can be cheaper for them to get fish landed at a port such as Grimsby; fish that's from hundreds of miles away and can be seven days old, instead of hours from the sea that is literally just outside the shops.

We went into a sorting room where a young fisherman was throwing Dovers graded by size into different boxes. A few were small but the vast majority of them were a decent size. He said three of the fishermen were in their early twenties, the rest were mostly in their fifties and three were in their seventies. The two we then met were in the middle group, had been fishing since they were sixteen and were fed up. They said the MSC certification hadn't meant they made any more money, in fact, though it clearly helps attract investment to the fleet and Hastings as a whole (and others say they have made more). It seemed a shame that the fish went to France rather than Billingsgate, where you would hope that the eco-certification would bring a special kudos and price in the home market.

Then we went into a new cooking demonstration room for a discussion amongst the group of thirty or so professionals trying to sell sustainable fish to their customers. The owner of an Italian restaurant in Marylebone said it was hard to convince the front-of-house to pass on the message and sell the sustainable fish. Customers wanted their usual choice, what they knew they liked, and that was that. It requires a proper push and conviction to make them change their minds, and goes against the idea that the customer is always right.

Some of the group had started to find ways through these problems. One chain of Mexican restaurants, Wahaca, makes a big noise about sustainability in its colourful news-sheet, menus and social networking. The message is backed up on the menu by the option of a catch of the day that is an economical choice. Similarly, the green fast food chain Leon makes home-made fish fingers from sustainable fish. Another restaurateur had given away small pieces of gurnard, a delicious, firm flaked fish with a good flavour. Once people had tried it, they felt confident about ordering it, he said.

Then we tasted some of the sustainable fish available. The sprats were crispy-fried and we guzzled them like seals. These are a particular type of small fish, as opposed to whitebait, which are the juveniles of different kinds of fish, and tasted richly oily and delicious. One of the locals said many people in the town used to go down to the sea with plastic bags when a shoal of these came close to the shore, and some still do. I remember having to leave the sea where I was bathing, a little further west along the Sussex coast, because it was suddenly rippling with these little fish. Now I see I could have grabbed my towel and used it as a makeshift 'net'. Sprats are now part of the seafood I enjoy in Hastings.

Another fish we tried was the above-mentioned gurnard, which is meaty and tastes a little of the prawns that the fish feeds on. Then the cuttlefish had a slightly more gluey texture than squid but was also good. In Cornwall, Chris Bean certainly found he could sell out of it with a bit of effort promoting it at his market stall.

The Good Catch event linked up different parts of the chain, but inevitably it was hard not to feel that familiar feeling of frustration about the problems of fish: here are people who have a common interest but who don't speak the same language.

Not all the fishermen see the point of the MSC, especially if they themselves aren't getting more money for their fish. They currently sell on a very small scale to good local restaurants, but not surprisingly are most interested in bulk, not in a few dozen Dover soles a week. The restaurateurs can find it hard to convince their customers to eat better fish. The customers who care wonder if they should be eating fish at all. The people marketing sustainability focus on putting across the right messages, but it is not their job to get the fish into places such as Billingsgate, even though it is a supreme example of a good UK food that is, alas, sold mostly in France.

Then on a larger scale, government is dragging its heels over creating marine reservations, and ceded rights to the rich fishing grounds off our shores to other countries in the EU in the 1970s, thus making it harder for everyone to engage the politics at a national level, let along a local one.

The official in charge of British fishing described managing North Sea cod stocks to Charles Clover in 1997 as walking backwards through the fog towards the cliff edge. At least now the fog is clearing a little, in patches; but it's hard not to feel a deep sense of anxiety about the whole situation, unless people from different sectors talk more to each other and governments act strongly on sustainability – and internationally, too, since fish swim around and boats move over the oceans.

Part of getting closer to fish is getting to know more about the human side of the equation: the fishermen. Whilst it is right to question fishing methods and to want improvements, there is an ugly hypocrisy in eating fish while at the same time being dismissively critical of the people who risk their lives to catch it. Fishing is a rich and lively part of our history and culture, and to enjoy that is part of cherishing seafood.

I spent a year travelling around the coastline of the UK talking to fishermen, fish restaurateurs and fishmongers to help compile a book of recipes and short essays to celebrate the *Best of British Fish*. The book was in aid of the Fishermen's Mission, a charity that helps those who have fallen into hardship and tragedy, with representatives or Mission Men who cover the UK's seventy-odd ports.

Two main impressions remain with me from this time. The first is how interesting it was to talk to the fishermen. Their time at sea gave most of them a different slant on life. They tend to be more philosophical than any other group of food producers I've met. Whilst farmers are down-to-earth, if you go below a boat then what you find are watery depths and the ever-present fact that existence is just a short cold plunge away from obliteration. The expanses of water, beautiful and dangerous in as many ways as there are days and even hours, seemed to crystallize a way of thinking. I did not come away with an overly romantic view of fishermen; some are perfectly capable of buccaneering self-interest. But the way they told a tale and their observations of the world and nature were often moving and special. Many had a strong sense of the environment – hardly surprising when they are surrounded by it and are vulnerable to the elements every time they fish.

The second impression I got from my time travelling around Britain's coast was the great diversity of fish in the sea and the many different ways people found to use them. The recipes gathered into the book spanned the fisherman's supper to the superchef's showstopper. There was a slow-cooked squid recipe from a Brighton fisherman called Ted Gillam, whose name goes back to the Domesday book and a very long line of fishermen. After a bit of initial frying, he chucks squid, tinned tomatoes, red wine, onion, garlic, basil and a bit of chilli powder into a pot and cooks it for a couple of hours. A fisherman turned chef in Looe uses local cider and cream as a sauce for the beautiful lemon sole they catch down there. In the northeast of England they are into wolf-fish, a white fish that uses its fearsome set of gnashers to eat shellfish, and so has a great taste. Mussels and laverbread (a seaweed paste) from Wales; dab-in-a-bun in Hastings; Scandinavian-cured mackerel to use up the summer's glut; Szechuan salt-and-pepper squid from a gastropub chef in Lancashire; potato and herring salad from Mike Smylie, a historian devoted to chronicling the rise and fall of this nutritious creature; 'haddock fluff', a dish from a fisherman's wife in Macduff; scallop and basil salad from a diver on the Isle of Skye: the many recipes were like a rich haul caught in a net cast over the great breadth of British fish.

This diversity was followed through to the stories and places ashore. In East Anglia I learned about fishermen's nicknames. These come about partly because so many have the same name in a trade that runs in families. Sheringham at one time had thirteen Mr Wests at sea, five of them sharing the first name

Henry. To tell them apart they all had nicknames: Downtide, Joyful, Doker, Teapot, Fiddy, Raleigh, Jacko, Paris, Oden, Squinter, Nuts, Custard and Tweet. I talked to some of the older Cornish fishermen about the language they developed to describe fishing spots in the days before satellite navigation. They would line up landmarks on shore and remember that the fishing was good at, say, church-spire-beyond-big-black-rock. The method epitomizes the practical poetry of the sea.

There was also, undeniably, a melancholic undertow to my journey. Scotland held the sight of fishing villages that just landed a few crabs, or langoustines that were mostly for export. It sometimes seemed to me that the richness of seafaring culture, so full of lively, salty anecdotes, faces and characters, was in danger of receding into the past. It does not have to be this way. There are around three thousand smaller boats (classified as under ten metres) in the British fleet. The British Government and the European Commission recently spent £5 million trying to decommission some. Around seventy went. You wonder if such money could be put into promoting the idea of eating local, sustainably caught fish instead. At present, 85 per cent of the British fleet is under ten metres, but they are allowed just 4 per cent of the quota of catch. These day boats, generally using sustainable fishing gear, are less favoured than the big boats, a situation that their organization, NUTFA (New Under Tens Fishermen's Association) is battling to alter.

On shore, supermarkets so often pay lip service to local food these days. Those near the coast could have a catch of the day and pay a decent price so that not all the fish would go for export. Small-scale processing units could be set up that would make it easier to get such fish into the catering trade as well as the retail.

We should rediscover our local and national pride at being a maritime nation instead of feeling anxious and guilty about fish. Save the fishermen and their skills as well as the fish! We need the fish caught in Hastings to be sold in the town's supermarkets and restaurants instead of going abroad. I remember going into a little sushi bar on the seafront and knowing immediately that their fish just wasn't going to be local. For the owner, a straight-forward supply chain was more important than having fish with that magical sparkle of freshness.

But moving forward isn't just about the small day boats but also the larger ones that are catching fish well and within sus-tainable limits. I met the crew of a Scottish boat that caught mackerel from a fishery that has MSC certification. But this sustainable status was in danger because the Faroe Islands and Icelandic boats were playing fast and loose with catch quotas. Not all fish is going to be caught by small boats and this boat landed a quality product. The fish are quickly chilled and frozen, preserving the qualities of the fish and making it a delicious, easy and cheap way to get your omega-3s.

The situation made me think once more about Charles Clover's point. The oceans are not there for a few to plunder; they are our commonwealth, our environmental capital, and if governance cannot sort out such matters then this needs to be reformed, and quickly.

The subject of fish turned out to be more opaque and complicated than almost anything else in this book. I certainly came away feeling that there has to be strong action by governments, but that needs public opinion to push it forward to action. In this regard, the supermarkets are a strong force for lobbying for improvements. But, in the end, the very best solutions are about making a proper connection with what you are eating, valuing it more and being more appreciative of what is essentially a wild food.

In the meantime, understanding the problems at least made me feel on firmer ground. In the light of the complications, and having talked to many parties, I evolved some broad-brush principles of how to eat more sustainable fish.

Thought One: Broaden your Tastes

It's all too easy to come back to the same fish again and again and these species get over-exploited. In the UK, just five species account for around 80 per cent of all seafood sold: cod, haddock, salmon, tuna and prawns. Such is the concentration that supermarkets refer to these as 'the big five'. As Niaz Dorry says, what's needed is a great deal more flexibility on the part of the consumer. In restaurants, the concerned chef who tries to serve less popular species may come up against the brick wall of the customer expecting to get what they want. If we can accept a 'catch of the day' and try other species, rather than wanting, say, cod all the time, then a big barrier is broken.

Fish vary a great deal in their appearance, texture and, to some extent, taste; but in the end it is basically 'fish'. From playing around with lesser-known species, I saw you could make fish pie with various firmish-textured white fish; fry any number in batter; cut up the fish small or thin for ceviche; coat it in polenta or breadcrumbs for frying; pie it, fry it, fishcake it, bake it. Why not go for what is caught rather than demanding the same from what is ultimately a shifting and uncertain resource?

Thought Two: Be Aware of the Catching Method
The MSC will look at any fishing method, so long as it keeps within its three principles that there are enough fish, not too many are taken and the whole process is monitored for increasing sustainability. They will even look at large-scale beam trawling. This is said to be improving. Some fishermen are now using lighter gear running on sledge-type runners instead of scraping the seabed; in same cases there are escape panels and square mesh panels so fewer immature fish get caught up as by-catch; and there may even be little cameras going down to check that they are, in the main, catching the right species. Trawlers, fishermen claim, go over the same areas, which are 'like a well-ploughed field'; they don't want to drag their expensive £20,000 nets over new, rocky ground because it ruins their gear as much as it ruins the ground.

The End of the Line author Charles Clover reckons the Americans are thirty years ahead and the Norwegians twenty years ahead of the UK in terms of using more sustainable technology. 'Europe is completely lumpen in dealing with technical measures,' he told me when we spoke. 'You can do a fantastic amount.' The Scottish fishermen are starting to do more and so are some of the Cornish, he says. 'You can't feed the world without trawling,' is the cry. There will always be trawling, for better or worse – but at least it can be better.

As an individual consumer, I am willing to buy into the MSC certification scheme because it involves standards and monitoring. As many people said to me during my research, 'It's what we've got.' Yet I am still concerned about trawling. It is always going to be a big sock dragged through the sea catching everything in its path. The single most affecting image I have of the wastefulness of fishing is that of fish being dumped out of a trawl net, much of it to be thrown back in the sea, dead or about to die.

When you can, look on labels and menus for fishing methods that are more finely targeted than the dragged trawl. 'Diver-caught' scallops are hand-plucked from the seabed as opposed to dredged, which scrapes the seabed. Gill and drift nets are left in the sea for a short while and have mesh sizes that only pick the mature fish the fisherman wants – this is what most day boats use. Handline fishing is carried out on a small scale; longline is more industrial. Both can bait hooks to catch particular species and should be less wasteful. 'Line caught,' however, can sound better than it is. Forget about a fisherman happily dangling a hook off a boat and hauling in his catch. In reality, it may be fifty miles of line going out into the sea, and the line can catch birds as well as fish. But here methods are also improving, as the MSC-certified hake fishery in South Africa showed – another example of how it helps to have an organization that studies the detail of individual fisheries and the methods they use.

Thought Three: Enjoy Shellfish

Of all the methods of capturing seafood, plucking static shellfish from the sea is the most straightforwardly sustainable. Mussels can be simply grown on ropes left in clean stretches of the sea where they feed on the plankton and nutrients in the water. Oysters are laid on trays to be washed and fed by tidal waters in the same way. I've been to see both being 'farmed' and felt confident that this was eco-aquaculture.

This really is working with nature. I was impressed when I met Ian MacKinnon, an inshore fisherman based in the squiggled shoreline of the west coast of Scotland. After studying agricultural economics and biology at Glasgow University, he found himself drawn to the sea and his childhood memories of fishing with his grandfather on the Hebridean island of Eigg. After a spell on the open seas, he set up a mussel farming business. In spring he puts out ten-metre ropes into a sea loch. The mussel spat floating in the water attach themselves and the ropes bloom with little mussels that feed by filtering on what floats to them in the water, swelling to maturity in two years. How much more natural can you get? Ian was a man at one with his surroundings, appreciating the light in the sky and harvesting a sustainable crop. He picks just what has been ordered and sells them through a fish merchant, Andy Race. They are the plumpest, tastiest mussels I've ever eaten. Ever since seeing this kind of sustainable, low-key form of aquaculture in action, I've felt happy to eat this kind of shellfish.

Thought Four: Go 'Oily'

At its eco-best this means eating more mackerel and herring. Fishing is about following a food chain. We follow the bass that follow the mackerel that follow the whitebait. At each stage the fish get more numerous and are more likely to be sustainable. Instead of just feasting on wild sea bass, delicious as it is, go for what the bass eats.

Fish such as herring and mackerel are known as pelagic fish, which means they swim higher up in the water partly because they are rich in the omega-3s that are so good for us (think of oil rising in water and you can picture the way herring and mackerel swim higher up than the flat fish that lie on the sea-bed). They swim in large, reasonably homogenous shoals and can be caught more cleanly with less by-catch. They are also very cheap in comparison to other fish, precisely because they are plentiful.

It is all very well in principle to 'go oily' but you do have to face up to the smell issue. Oily fish are best eaten very, very fresh. Some other fish, such as cod and skate, are best eaten a few days old. But the oils in oily fish go off rapidly and rancidly.

There are various ways round the freshness issue. Find a shop that has a good throughflow – and this is likely to be a good fishmonger – and look keenly to see if the mackerel is 'stiff-alive', as Cornish fishermen say, that is, still has rigor mortis, or is at least as fresh as possible. There is a gleam to really fresh fish, bright red gills, bright eyes, a sheen to the beautiful silvery skin. This is hard to do but, above everything else, worth the effort. It's all very well to decide to eat more mackerel, but if you go to a supermarket and buy an aging fish, then that's the end of that.

The alternative is to buy your fish ready-processed – smoked mackerel, rollmop herrings, kippers – and enjoy it that way. I like to toss smoked mackerel through pasta with some spinach or purple sprouting broccoli, for example, or eat it on oatcakes as a little pre-dinner snack.

If the mackerel is not the freshest – and to be honest, away from the sea it rarely is – then I use a Japanese method of simmering fillets in a mixture of sliced root ginger, soy sauce, mirin and sake that is strong enough to take away any fishiness.

Thought Five: Think about Farmed Fish

The other good oily fish are salmon and trout. In the face of dwindling wild stocks, farmed fish are being seen as the answer to the problem. Around half of all the fish we eat are farmed. Yet most of them are fed on fish from the sea. It's said to take, on average, 3kg of wild small fish to make 1kg of farmed large fish (although some fish farmers say it can be much less than this). Fish farming is often mentioned as 'the way forward' for the problems of the seas. But it is a false sort of solution on its own. We need to sort out the mess that causes dwindling stocks of wild fish and destroys the marine environment as a whole.

There are more sustainable ways of farming fish. The feed can be made from offcuts of fish destined for the human table, and this is the method used for organic farmed fish. Much work is being done to try to make fish feed more sustainable. A type of worm-farming is already being used to provide more sustainable fish food, and ways of growing algae for the same purpose are being developed. Some fish, such as tilapia, can eat vegetable matter, and this particular fish is useful because its firm, meaty fillets are good for kids and others who don't like to deal with bones. (I can't get very enthusiastic about the taste, however.)

The farmed fish industry says it is solving other problems associated with aquaculture. These are many. Alongside waste from fish farms, the overcrowded pens lead to disease, which is treated with antibiotics, which also pollute the marine environment. Sea lice from farmed fish attack the wild stock – this really is a problem – and escaped fish interbreed with the wild fish and lessen the quality of the gene pool. There are ways of preventing this. The farmed fish can be sited more carefully and looked after better. Some advocate that fish farming should be carried on in tanks that are separate from the sea. But at the end of the day, the problem of feed remains. The Monterey Bay Aquarium, which has a 'fish to avoid' list in the US, does not give any approval for farmed fish at all. An Aquaculture Stewardship Council, the farmed-fish counterpart of the Marine Stewardship Council, is shortly to be launched and this should help raise standards.

Andrew Mallison, whom I spoke to at the MSC, previously spent twelve-and-a-half years at Marks and Spencer, a retailer that prides itself on sustainable, quality food. He said the company spent three years developing a better form of fish farming, with less crowded pens (a problem for welfare and disease – though if they are too spaced out apparently the fish get aggressive towards each other), less pollution and more secure boundaries so there should be, in theory, fewer escaped fish, which dilutes the genetic make-up of the wild stock. He travelled to Asia and Latin America to develop better-farmed prawns that take into consideration worker welfare and the environment (the destruction of mangrove swamps in places such as Thailand and the Philippines for prawn farming is a scandal). 'It's a really valuable employment opportunity but it has to be done well,' he said.

This matters because we are all attracted to the 'big five' for good reasons – taste, habit and lack of bones. At the moment, I stand in front of the counter of my local posh supermarket and look at the MSC-certified wild Alaskan salmon. Then I look at the organic salmon, and finally at the more basic. In the end, I tend to eat half wild, half organic. And most of the time I try to eat something else altogether, following the principle of Thought One, 'Broaden Your Tastes.'

It matters a great deal that policy-makers don't think that fish farming can just replace wild fish and solve all the problems. Farmed fish themselves rely on wild fish and so the ecological consequences of both are intertwined.

Thought Six: Cherish the Local
At its heart, this means you make a connection with the origin of your fish and the 'who, where and how' of its catching. You do not have to be beside the sea in order to eat such fish. Some eco-minded restaurants chalk up the origin of their fish on a daily changing blackboard menu. The fishermen and suppliers, in turn, are making the restaurateurs more aware of where the fish comes from. One Cornish supplier, based near the treacherous

Lizard in Cornwall, sends invoices to her chefs naming the skipper of the boat – 'Caught by Wilfy off the Manacles' (a notorious group of rocks) – and, if applicable, the appalling weather conditions. The message is that the fish comes from somewhere and was caught by someone; it becomes more than an anonymous slab and gains an identity and value.

You could argue that local fish supplies are too small-scale and, for many, too remote to be practicable. But if we see fish as a precious and finite resource rather than a casually wasted commodity, then buying fish that comes from smaller local boats is one good way forward. And it can be done through online sales, sustainable restaurants and, with the greatest pleasure of all, on the coast.

WHAT TO EAT?

Easy. Try fish beyond the 'big five' (cod, haddock, salmon, prawns and tuna); look for the MSC's blue sticker on seafood and when eating out; find ways to eat oily fish; go to local fishmongers or find restaurants, cafés and chippies that sell local fish when you are at the seaside.

Worth the Effort. Cook a whole fish on the bone and take time to eat and appreciate it; find a good fishmonger and ask him or her for recipes; try mail-order fish from a quality fishmonger in a fishing port; get a copy of the Marine Conservation Society's red/amber/green list.

Hopes and Dreams. That the Marine and Aquaculture Stewardship

Councils maintain and drive up standards; that community supported fishing takes off; that governments get tough on those who abuse the oceans and their creatures; that there is more local governance of fishing and that supermarkets start to buy fish from their nearest port rather than it mostly being exported abroad; that the EU and international governments put sustainable fishing high on their agendas.

5

What is 'Kind' Meat?

Meat is not just another food. It's still, for many of us, at the centre of a plate – it's sausage and mash, not mash and sausage. Meat is the food we honour guests with, the highlight of feasts and a family treat. Adults in their sixties talk of how, in their childhood, a roast chicken used to be a birthdays-and-Easter sort of meal. When I was young, a trip to the butchers in the 1970s was still the most expensive and important part of shopping; the queue slowly approaching a man with a cleaver, a big-handed secular God, despatching life, death and rump steak wrapped in smooth folds of greaseproof paper.

But modern meat production – factory farming, you could call it – has made meat into a much cheaper, everyday food. As a consequence, whilst you don't need that much meat – a piece the size of a pack of cards at a meal would suffice in nutritional terms – we now eat a great deal; 50 per cent more than we did in the late sixties, when I was born. I had thought of myself as a moderate meat-eater but when I looked a little harder I realized it is quite easy to eat meat three times a day: bacon for breakfast, a ham sandwich for lunch, a meaty stir-fry or some chops for supper. Apparently, the amount of meat eaten in the UK divided by the total population equates to 8 cows, 36 sheep,

36 pigs and 550 chickens and other birds per person in a life-time. Imagine that small farm of animals outside your front door – and that's just for you.

There are many reasons why we eat so much meat these days, not just price. Meat has deep associations. The carver at the domestic table was traditionally the head of the household and meat on the table was a symbol of prosperity; when you could afford meat, you would buy it, which is why consumption is going up so much in developing countries such as China. But there's another explanation for its place on the modern table. In today's busy world, convenience is king and meat is simple to prepare. You don't have to do very much to make fresh meat delicious. Anyone can grill a chop. Vegetable-based dishes, in contrast, take a great deal more preparation.

And so this powerful, convenient food, with good nutrition and strong associations, is now much more widely available, and of course we eat more of it. We do so, most of all, for its taste. The glossy steak, the savoury scent of the leg of lamb with its gravy, the aromatic depth of a Thai chicken soup, the break-fast bacon sandwich: the very thought makes me, as a meat-eater, salivate.

I wonder whether meat had a special status in the past also because people lived much closer to the animals, either in the countryside, or even in towns and cities where people kept pigs. It was a bigger deal to kill a creature, and the resulting meal was therefore more of an occasion.

In Britain, our links with the countryside were much more

suddenly and radically broken by the industrial revolution than in any other country in Europe. Sociologist Stephen Mennell, in his comparison of French and British eating, *All Manners of Food*, shows just how quickly the British moved to the city during the industrial revolution; our society was essentially transformed within a couple of generations. In other countries such as Italy and Portugal, many more people have retained a link with rural relatives or a family smallholding and tend to have a realistic understanding of how animals are kept.

Most of us, now urban and suburban, have a more complicated relationship to our fellow creatures. We tend to think of them as wildlife or pets, not food. When images of battery chickens became widely disseminated in the UK, in news footage and through campaigns, consumers switched in large numbers to free-range eggs; around half of all fresh eggs sold in the UK today are higher welfare. But in the case of meat, which is more expensive, there is a tension between our desire to be kind to animals and our unwillingness to pay more. The animals become expedient meat units instead of sentient creatures.

Furthermore, we often don't know how the animals are raised and, distanced from the realities of farming, are too squeamish to find out. Nobody wants to see pictures of animals suffering; no wonder we do not want to look into those guilty dark sheds. After all, knowing more might lead us to not want to eat meat at all.

'Nothing in life is to be feared. It is only to be understood,' Marie Curie said. It's a sound principle, but as I embarked on writing a book about chickens and the chicken industry, at the back of my mind was this same uncomfortable question: would I be able to eat the meat at the end? People talked of 'happy chickens' but could such meat, ultimately, be kind? A pithy vegan friend remarked that eating animals 'just didn't seem very polite'. I felt, or perhaps hoped, that there could be a way of eating meat that was acceptable. But I wasn't sure. It was time to discover which side of the fence I was on.

These days, the respected animal charity Compassion in World Farming walks on the bright side, its emphasis and images as much on happy animals as on the cruelties in the dark sheds. The idea is that people want to be turned on to the good as much as turned off by the bad. Both are motivating.

My chicken odyssey took ten years, and it started with a shock. In my mid-twenties, I was curious to see how chickens were produced and a contact got me into a chicken shed. The man who ran it seemed like a decent enough fellow. Yet he was clearly uncomfortable about the way he was producing the birds. The economics were so tough that to make any money at all he had to follow the industry norms. These are, then as now, super-logical: rear as many birds as possible to get maximum growth in minimum time.

That shed was a weird place, one that was so far apart from my experience that the phrase 'planet chicken' came into my mind (and became the title of the book). A vast swathe of semi-automated matter stretched out in front of me, shuffling a little. Many birds were down on the ground looking like they could barely stand. The most basic welfare problem with chickens reared for meat, as opposed to eggs, is that their genetics have been super-tweaked so they can grow as much as possible as fast as possible. The industry calls this 'efficient', but I learnt that 3–5 per cent of the birds could die because they grew too fast.

I honestly believe if any human not inured to the ways of factory farming went into one of those crowded, windowless sheds and discovered what the system did to the birds, here as well as in the slaughterhouse, they quite simply would not serve this type of chicken at their table. It wasn't that it was feather-torn pandemonium; there was a weird quietness to the place. What chilled me was the way living creatures had been turned into mere economic units.

But what's the alternative? What is a good chicken? I went to see the different kinds of production: the basic; the better than basic; the free-range; the organic; and the smaller groups on what you might call traditional farms.

Overall, it was encouraging, and in some cases inspiring, to see birds kept in more natural conditions. Higher welfare systems, such as free-range and organic, and even some well-managed shed-reared birds, mean that the super-turbocharged type of bird is not used, or at least the birds are 'grown' more slowly instead of being exploited to the limit. Far fewer go 'off their legs', as the phrase goes, or die from sudden death syndrome – heart failure due to over-fast growth. The properly farmed bird, where real consideration is given to its biology and nature, is a different sort of creature from the factory chicken both in life and on the table.

My experiences made me think harder about my

initial concept of what was 'kind'. Is it a relative or an absolute quality? I felt a growing conviction that changes could be made to all systems to make them better (or in the case of the basic, less bad). The UK poultry industry certainly argues that improvements are being made all the time for basic factory bird production: that the animals' legs have been bred to be stronger than they used to be; that fewer drugs are used these days (the routine feeding of birds with antibiotics for faster growth has stopped in the UK); that the birds are now allowed more space and are given artificial light that dims at night and increases at dawn, rather than a twenty-four-hour stretch of non-stop eating and growing. This does make a bit of a difference and it's important that such changes are made, especially given the vast number of chickens we eat. A small difference to many, you could argue, adds up to a big difference.

But in the end, the improvements to industrial indoor systems still feel like a matter of inching forward rather than a radical switch to a real consideration of the individual chicken as a creature. The challenge is to work out exactly what this would amount to. You often hear it said 'They wouldn't thrive if they weren't happy' from apologists of factory systems. But it is perfectly possible to fatten up a creature for the table whilst it suffers, and existing systems allow for a certain percentage of 'wastage', so not all thrive.

There are a number of progressive Dr Dolittle scientists who are trying to listen to the animals and work out what makes a chicken a chicken, in order to design ways of farming that take into account their natural instincts. Alongside crucial improvements to intensive systems, they know that free-range systems could certainly still be improved. The birds don't go out much if they are sited in a barren field without much going on, and become more stressed and prone to feather-pecking. Some producers have planted trees to give them some cover, and this does make a difference; the birds did, after all, evolve from jungle fowl. Paying attention to their nature is important.

But systems aren't everything; the operator or farmer matters, too. Some of the birds that it felt all right to eat, in the end, were not organic, or even free-range, but they were carefully tended, all the same.

When I lived in Lewes, East Sussex, at our local farmers' market I met Michael Vines, who runs Ersham Farm, a patch of country life on the outskirts of urban Hailsham. His chickens were double the price of factory farmed but half the price of top-notch organic. His stall had pictures that showed how five hundred or so birds were kept in small, light- and straw-filled barns.

I went to see the birds on the farm. It felt like a good place where there was a proper regard for the birds, and they took longer to grow because their feed was less high in protein and so their genetics were not pushed to the limit. You could properly call this a farm and not a factory. The stockmanship was skilled and personal; it was at a scale in which Michael could know what was happening to his birds. He was not a man flicking switches in a shed of 40,000 semi-automated units; he really was a farmer with a flock.

What impressed me was what a difference scale made to the

whole enterprise, especially on the killing day. This was the crux of what made me feel that Ersham Farm was better than some large free-range industrial systems. Killing day was on a Monday and I went along to watch. The birds were taken a matter of metres from their barn and calmly and quietly despatched by a slaughterman who came to do the job once a week. He did not have to do this work all day and every day. Like the day-boat fishermen I'd come across, Michael and his farm represented the value of local or small-scale production. You can have a connection with a place and a person that gives you a different level of trust and knowledge.

At the end of writing my book about chickens, I felt that I could continue to eat meat, but it had to be done decently. On the whole, unless I knew and trusted the producer or the butcher, it would be a Soil Association certified organic chicken, which is by far the best, as systems go, in terms of welfare. The organic birds I saw were leading a far more natural life, living for twice as long, or more, than the turbo-charged factory creatures. Free-range is also good, if done well. Best of all, however, would be to make a proper connection with a farm and to find people I trusted, rather than just a system.

I'd seen with chicken that there were different shades of 'kindness' and that the best farmers respected the nature of their animals. I wanted to look at other meats to see whether the better ways of farming exemplified this principle and could offer not just value for money, but values for money.

Christmas is the one time of year when more people

routinely go out of their way to visit a butcher to get a special bird. My first quest was to find out what lay behind the most celebratory of poultry, the turkey.

The turkey still exists as a wild bird in its native America, as I discovered when a couple startled me by running out onto a road I was driving along in rural Massachusetts. The bird was domesticated for meat by the Aztecs, who used their feathers for elaborate and magnificent ceremonial gear and spread the streets with crushed eggshells as a festive thank-you for their fowl. Turkeys were brought to Europe by the conquistadors and soon became popular. With their glamorous tail feathers, expanding snoods and wobbling wattles and caruncles, they were much admired for their looks, and the meat was regarded as a dish fit for kings and celebratory meals. Elizabeth I owned a salt-cellar of a turkey cock encrusted with gold and pearls, and George II kept a flock of 3,000 wild turkeys in Richmond Park.

In the nineteenth century, breeders focused on producing birds with more meat. Then in the twentieth century the inexorable application of science put pressure on the turkey just as it did on the chicken. These days, most turkeys are 'grown' like chickens, in windowless barns with concentrated feeds. Again, the genetics are super-charged and the body has been changed in a way that is visually even more grotesque. The modern turkey is genetically geared towards a huge breast, to provide the white meat people like. Their bodies are so inflated that they cannot even breed by themselves. Reproduction throughout almost the entire system, including nearly all free-range and organic birds, is carried out by artificial insemination. One of the worst consequences of modern turkey farming is that, kept in low artificial light, the birds can develop eye problems, with some even becoming blind, according to the RSPCA. It is just as well that nobody sees the head of their turkey on the Christmas table.

I had managed to avoid cooking the Christmas feast for the first forty years of my life, but now it fell to me. It seemed a good opportunity to first meet my turkey.

The founding principle of Sheepdrove Organic Farm is first to look at the nature of its animals and then to farm accordingly. It is run by Peter and Juliet Kindersley, who are using the proceeds from the sale of Peter's publishing house, Dorling Kindersley, to develop a better way of livestock farming. Sheepdrove was starting to rear what are called rare breed or 'heritage' turkeys. These are genetically closer to the wild turkeys in the US and are the kind that would have been eaten by the Victorians. Juliet Kindersley is in charge of the birds and took me to see the flock. An artist, she has her own views on farming: that it should respect the basic nature of the creature. It was the second year they had farmed heritage birds and she was excited by how active they were, not only free-range on the label but really exploring the field, chasing insects, hunting for food and even flying a little, which is unimaginable for a big turkey. The Kindersleys were planting a good many herbs and interesting plants on their organic fields to give the birds a variety of forage, with the view that this helped the health of the bird.

The day of my visit was a misty, wet Sunday, but through the damp veil of November you could see the birds' colours: reddish and a lovely grey and black, the males with their peculiar livid-red snoods. As we approached, Juliet called one of their three main cries, the 'Hello, how are you?' call. 'Turkeys are so sociable,' she said. 'They love human beings. They immediately come towards you.' And they did. They clearly have a flocking instinct and it was fun to watch and hear them move and call. You felt the pleasure and engagement that belongs to all real livestock farmers; one that any pet owner would recognize. The turkey herdsman was a young hippie residing in a colourfully painted bus near his charges. In contrast, it must be dispiriting to work in those dark, barren sheds, where the only movement is the heavings of a crowd, not the flocking patterns of animals. Juliet's view was that buying good meat was good for everyone – bird, farmer and consumer. 'I feel passionately that if you support your local community and your local farmer and growers, your farmers' market and local shops, it is very good for your self-esteem,' she said. 'You can see you are making a difference.'

When it came to my Christmas dinner, the Sheepdrove turkey was very different from a big busty one: longer and sleeker rather than hyper-inflated. There was a lot of dark meat and all of it very tasty and completely juicy. It took less time to cook than a big bird and the strong bones made sensational stock. I felt proud to put it on the table.

Heritage turkey breeding turns out to be a small but interesting movement. In the US, Slow Food has been promoting heritage turkeys. In the UK, a Turkey Club has been running for a decade and now has 180 members. In the last six years there has been a shift towards the older types of birds, with people farming them on a small, local-food scale with some as pets; one of the breeders, Pat Taylor of Rutland Organic Poultry, has a vegan customer who keeps her birds for the garden. Even at six weeks, the young males raise their display feathers. No wonder turkeys once strutted their stuff in aristocratic parkland alongside peacocks.

I cooked one of Pat Taylor's turkeys the following Christmas and it was a magnificent roast that came bronzed and handsome from the oven. It fed eight on Christmas day, ten for a Boxing Day fricassée, two lunches for five in a Thai turkey noodle soup and a couple of days of turkey sandwiches. At around £3 a portion, it was certainly much more than a Bernard Matthews' 'bootiful' bird, but it seemed like a fair price to pay on a special occasion for a meal that really was beautiful.

I wanted to see how turkeys were being produced on a large scale at a lower price, so I visited Mark Gorton at Traditional Norfolk Poultry. The company had been set up twenty years earlier and was now the largest speciality turkey company in the UK. That year, the company's farmers were rearing 90,000 birds. The birds were mostly sold in a number of large supermarkets. At agricultural college, Gorton wanted to earn some extra money and got twelve bronze free-range turkeys. They gave the bird perches because, well, birds like to perch. 'We just thought it would be nice,' he says. 'People said it would give them bruises on their breasts. It's a load of rubbish.' From then on he scaled up, and helped write the turkey standards for the Freedom Food label. This was set up by the RSPCA, an animal charity that is now addressing the biggest animal cruelty issue of all, in terms of numbers: factory farming.

Mark's birds are kept in light, airy, straw-filled sheds. Once they reach an age when they have 'feathered up' and are sufficiently hardy, they can go outside (not all Freedom Food turkeys are free-range). Around the shed were straw bales and bits of plastic on string for diversion. It was on a larger and less natural scale than the Kindersleys or Pat Taylor at Rutland Organic Poultry, but decently done all the same. Mark was also experimenting with heritage breeds and selling them through supermarkets. He was enthusiastic about the quality, and the birds flew off the shelves, as it were. All his birds were slower-growing and this made them much tastier. A 'fast-farmed' bird is killed once it reaches the right weight for the table, but it will still be young and relatively tasteless. Maturity brings a nice covering of fat. 'A nice steak has marbling in it and the fat makes it cook and eat well,' said Mark. 'It's the same for a turkey.' What he looks for in the shop is a bird with a nice buttery-white colour, showing the deposits of fat on the breast and thighs which will self-baste the meat as it cooks.

It was interesting that better turkey farming could be carried out on some scale. Sheepdrove and Rutland had even more natural systems of production, I felt better about their lives and the meat was more special and, yes, the turkeys cost more. Freedom Food does make better meat more accessible. Then it is a step on to buy organic or small-scale humanely reared birds. The advice, in the end, is to buy the best you can afford, and if you've made a connection with the farm you'll really understand what you are paying for, which is important when a bird costs £70 or more.

Alongside chickens and turkeys, the pig is another meat animal with a natural and social history greatly at odds with modern production methods. This sad state of affairs is all the worse because we have such long and strong connections with the pig and its pork. William Cobbett, the nineteenth-century rural reformer, wrote admiringly of this creature and how 'a good cottage had a pig'. Pork used to be the real 'roast beef' of the English. Whilst beef was beyond most pockets, many households could afford to keep a pig, feeding it on scraps. Even today, in deeply rural parts of Europe (including a wave of British neo-peasants), a pig is killed and some parts are eaten fresh, while the rest is preserved for eating throughout the year, even if just to flavour a dish with a few cubes of bacon or a piece of sausage. Those of us who live urban lives can have pork in a surprising number of meals, from a breakfast bacon sandwich through to a lunchtime ham roll and onwards. This happens because salted meat, from the farmhouse tradition of preserving the meat for the year, is now embedded in our diet.

The pig is the most engagingly social of all farm animals and the easiest to relate to. Piglets in a field playfully chase around with each other, and Winston Churchill observed: 'Cats look down on you; dogs look up to you; but pigs look you in the eye as equals.'

So much worse, then, is the descent from such a life to the factory farm. We have a picture of the start of factory farming

from Upton Sinclair, the American novelist, who used his research in a meat-packing company in Chicago to write his campaigning novel *The Jungle* (1906). Many of the descriptions of
the abattoir are truly gruesome; this is, literally, muckraking re-
portage. One of the most disturbing and poignant scenes is not
about blood and guts. It comes as the main character, Jurgis
Rudkus, watches a river of pigs patiently toil up to the top of a
tall factory building to meet their machine-bound destiny. Rudkus had dressed many a carcass in his native Lithuania. But this
was on a smallholding, not in an industrial context. He finds the
large production unit almost fascinating in its businesslike manner. 'And yet somehow the most matter-of-fact person could
not help thinking of the hogs,' writes Sinclair. '[T]hey were so
innocent, they came so very trustingly; and they were so very
human in their protests – and so perfectly within their rights!'

Sinclair could see clearly what was happening because he
stood on the cusp of change. A hundred years on, I spoke to a
former pig buyer for a supermarket who described the sounds
of the animals squealing in the slaughterhouse as part of an inner
circle of Hell. But this situation is now 'normal' and unseen.
Some producers now use gas to kill the pigs. Consumers dislike
this idea, but it is an example of how our cultural squeamishness
is not for the good of the animals. Slaughterhouses, however, can
choose between a better, more expensive kind of gas and a
cheaper one. Corners can still be cut.

Modern pork meat-packing plants can be boggling in their
size. Smithfield, the US pork giant, is said to slaughter 33,000
pigs a day at its Tar Heel plant in North Carolina. I looked at the

site on Google Earth and it was so big that it was hard to get a handle on its size. There isn't a single animal to be seen: all is done behind closed doors. The company is now setting up business in Poland, the better to access the European market. Factory farming is a global phenomenon and the methods and 'advances' have spread quickly because they are about producing meat as cheaply as possible. You may think Tar Heel and its ilk are a long way away, but their products may well sit on your plate, as the bacon or ham alongside your free-range egg.

What does this mean to the animals? It means the sow, in many countries, is kept penned up in a restrictive sow stall for each four-and-a-half-month pregnancy, and confined to a narrow farrowing crate to feed the piglets for three weeks before starting the whole process again. During this whole time she cannot even turn around. The sow stall is to be banned in Europe by 2013, though not for the first month of pregnancy, and is already illegal in the UK and illegal or being phased out in other countries, including some US states, New Zealand and Australia. It should be illegal everywhere.

As for the offspring, the majority of modern pigs are kept indoors, at best allowed to nestle down in straw, and at worst kept on barren metal slats. You can see footage of this online: go to YouTube and watch *Pig Business*, a brave documentary about the expansion of the pig industry. It is hard to watch such footage and not want to cry; the mammalian pig is close to instinctive human sympathies. Once I had connected these images to what was on my plate, I found it hard to buy or eat such meat.

In Britain, we like to think our basic animal husbandry is of a higher quality. Some of the worst excesses of the industrial pig systems have been banned. We now have many more outdoor-bred pigs, when the sows are allowed to range outdoors; the piglets are reared indoors, at best on straw. Then there are outdoor-reared pigs, which Compassion in World Farming says means the piglets spend approximately half their life outside, though this can vary. Both are positive steps forward in terms of welfare. CIWF thinks free-range, when the pigs can be outside all the time, is best of all.

But there are no welfare barriers to trade. As British farm welfare has improved, British shoppers have gone for the cheaper options, and now half our meat is imported. It is estimated that 70 per cent of the nearly 1 million tonnes of imported pig meat we eat in the UK is not raised to this country's welfare standards. It is even difficult to tell if the pork is properly British, since imports can be labelled with a Union Jack just because they have been packed or processed in the UK. There is a new voluntary labelling scheme that aims to stop this misleading packaging, but how effective this will be remains to be seen.

Even if the meat is British, and therefore should be better in welfare terms than imported, it is still not a guarantee of the best welfare. Compassion in World Farming urges four levels of a more meaningful kind of labelling: intensive indoor; extensive indoor; free-range; and 'premium' free-range. This would certainly have covered the chickens I'd come across, in a broad-brush manner. Yet my feeling about labelling is that you can then go one step further by discovering where to get meat from an individual who bothers.

★

One such 'real meat' farmer is Tim Wilson of the Ginger Pig, a Yorkshire-based company with four shops in London. The eponymous ginger pig is a Tamworth, a traditional British breed with copper-orange bristles. These were Tim's first pigs when he came back to farming in his mid-thirties. He had grown up on a typical mixed farm in Yorkshire that produced chickens, grew some crops, had a cow for milk, and also kept some pigs, like many farms did. 'If something failed, then something else made money,' he says. It all had a tidy circularity. The crops were sold or fed to the animals, and the animal manure fertilized the crops. The surplus was sold and the farmer started each year without debts. But now, Tim explained, farmers are specialists selling into commodity markets and are always trying to get the 'product' to grow faster and yield more. In other words, pigs have become units. He thinks such people aren't really farmers any more but scientists who take advice from scientific advisers. 'Some of them come to talk to me and I don't understand them,' he says. 'I've got a thousand pigs and I'm listening to them and I don't know a single word they are on about. That's where farming goes berserk. It takes an animal and tries to make it into something else.'

Tim didn't go into the family farm for a very simple reason. Much livestock production involves selling on animals for fattening elsewhere, and this was something that Tim didn't want to do. 'I enjoy keeping animals but I will not sell live animals,' he said. 'At some point, a lorry's going to come and take them away. And it does worry me how those animals are then treated. I've no trouble getting them killed; but if you breed them, they're your responsibility.'

Tim came back to farming by accident. A property developer, he one day bought a farm that was completely run-down but still full of livestock. When the farmer moved, the animals went. 'It was so sad,' he says. 'The duck pond in the yard became just a mucky hole.' Living on the farm, he had to have some animals, and bought his first lot of ginger pigs. One day, a retired pork butcher in the village cast his eye over the field and said, 'Your pigs want to be done.' They were seven months old and starting to mate, as brothers and sisters. 'I made them into sausages and it sort of caught on,' says Tim, with Yorkshire brevity.

One of the tenets of the Ginger Pig is to use traditional breeds that were developed in British farming's nineteenth-century heyday. They have a great deal of character: alongside the ginger Tamworths are the snub-snouted Middle Whites, the pink-and-black Gloucester Old Spots and the black Berkshires with their chubby faces. They are not being bred for looks but for the unhurried way they grow, enabling them to develop a layer of fat. Modern pigs have been bred lean because that is the preference of 'the housewife' (as a surprising number of farmers still call the shopper). But this means the meat becomes dry and cardboardy when cooked. Many people have quietly stopped cooking pork for the very good reason that it is often disappointing. You don't have to eat all the fat on the plate, but it is important in cooking because it imparts overall flavour and succulence.

★

I was interested to taste the difference between standard modern pork and the meat from a traditional breed. First I went to my local butcher, a down-to-earth place in a row of basic shops, and bought a Gloucester Old Spot chop. Then I went to a super-market and bought a packet containing two chops from free-range pigs of a modern breed. The supermarket packaging gave good 'blurb' about how the pigs could rootle around and bed down in deep straw and generally live the life of Riley. The butcher's chop had no packaging. There was no information in the shop and the butcher wasn't in to tell me its tale. The single Old Spot chop cost £2.60 and the packet of two chops from the supermarket cost £3.30.

At home, I cut off the rind of the Old Spot chop (this had already been done on the supermarket ones) and put it on the scales. To my surprise, it was exactly the same weight as the two supermarket chops together. The latter looked much better value because it came as two portions, and we shop for how many we are serving rather than by weight. The Old Spot, in one piece, looked like one large portion. The appearance and texture of the two meats were very different. The Old Spot was a dark rosy-red and the fat was creamy and dry to the touch. The supermarket chops were paler, and the fat was slippery and greasy.

I cooked the chops over a medium-low heat for twelve min-utes or so, turning them over once, then crisping up the fat by propping them up against the side of the frying pan with my wooden spoon. Then the chops were on a plate, side by side, with mashed potato, carrots, gravy and Bramley apple sauce. The contrast was quite striking. The supermarket chops came from pigs with apparently good welfare. They looked good and, from the packet copy, they sounded great. The Gloucester Old Spot chop didn't have marketing copy and nor did it need any. It was, quite simply, in a completely different league in terms of taste: deeper, more savoury, with softer, more luscious fat that was almost pearly in your mouth. The other pork was, in comparison, distinctly ordinary.

So there it was, a tale of two chops. And the better one was cheaper. But you had to know about the different kinds of pork, go to the butcher and bother to cut the rind off (ten seconds' work with a sharp knife). It came from the sort of traditional breed that is impossible to rear intensively so I knew that, to some extent, it would have led a natural life. Whether it was farmed well would depend upon the farmer, and I didn't know who that was. As far as cost went, the traditional chop was cheaper – but not in terms of portion size. I have to be honest and say it was so good that you really wanted to eat the whole chop. Rather than cutting it in two, I scoffed the lot and licked the plate.

I asked Tim Wilson whether such traditional pork could catch on, since it certainly made sense on the plate. Whilst his own shops were doing well, he was sceptical. 'The supermarkets like pork lean and the farmer gets his money back quickly,' he said. There is a demand for proper pork, but it is perceived as expensive. Tim's response is that you can buy better meat at a lower price if you are canny. At his stall in Borough Market, he advises customers on a budget to buy bacon off-cuts for their bacon sandwiches rather than prime back bacon. You can slow-roast shoulder, or even the hand and spring (the end of the front leg). You can simmer a leg in milk, as the Spanish and Italians do. Take the bone out of the shoulder, wrap it in soft fat and cook it slowly, rather than worrying about crackling, he said. He likes it with mashed potato, spiced red cabbage and thick onion sauce. Then the next day, it's good cold, with a swipe of mustard.

Would the story of chicken, turkey and pork turn out to be true for beef? This is the meat with the highest status in the British kitchen; think of such classics as a juicy rump steak, a cold beef sandwich, steak-and-kidney pie (and pudding), and, of course, a beautiful joint of ruby-centered roast beef, be it sirloin, juicy rib or the cheaper topside. We have such time-honoured recipes because of a great heritage of good beef animals. Britain, with its lush green grass, suits grazing beasts. Grass is marvellous stuff as feed, producing meat that is higher in vitamin E and the desirable omega-3 fatty acids than when the animals are grain-fed. Taste panels have detected more flavour as well.

Native breeds, such as Aberdeen Angus and Hereford, can thrive on a grass-based diet and were bred to grow slowly on this, gradually layering up the fat that keeps them warm outside. In the oven, this internal marbling of fat self-bastes the meat as it cooks, giving a beautifully juicy result. But since the 1970s, farmers have favoured the Continental breeds, such as Limousin and Charolais, which are larger, leaner, grow more quickly and will grow well when fed on grain rather than grass. Beef lovers think the taste inferior, however, not least because they are grown so quickly for the burger and the ready-meal – another example of how fast food links in with fast farming.

I don't eat beef very often but when I do it is with a great deal of anticipation – and also some trepidation: you don't always know whether it will be good or not. Many a steak or joint proves to be disappointingly dry, tough and tasteless. I wanted to find out why, what was the best beef to eat and whether, on the whole, it was 'kind'. Was better taste in this case linked to a more natural way of farming?

The best book on meat on my bookshelf is Hugh Fearnley-Whittingstall's *The River Cottage Meat Book*, and I turned to it first for some clues. There are two main systems for producing beef in the UK. First is the traditional way, which is rearing beef breeds in the fields. These are known as suckler herds because the young are kept with their mothers for six months or more. The cattle then either go on to be finished with a more cereal-based diet (when they are known as store cattle), or left outside on grass, depending on the time of year and the breed.

Then there are the fast-growing dairy-cross beef cattle. These are the males from the dairy herd. Dairy cattle and beef cattle are different breeds for different jobs. Dairy cows – most commonly the black-and-white Holsteins you see in the fields – have high milk yields but don't produce so much meat. They keep producing calves in order to produce milk. To produce dairy-cross offspring they are mated with a beef-breed bull. The calves are taken off the mother (we want her milk) and the males are often fed concentrates in order to grow quickly so they can be slaughtered young for beef. To replace the milking cows, the best females are mated with a dairy-breed bull. The females go on to replace their mothers, whilst the males are either kept for veal or killed at birth, the poignantly named 'bobby calves'.

There is a fair amount of slower-growing grass-fed meat from beef breeds on the supermarket shelves. But the shops don't like to specify the type, unless they have a premium line. So if you buy ordinary stewing beef in a supermarket, or a cheap steak, it could be pretty good or pretty poor.

Hugh Fearnley-Whittingstall makes the point that good, extensive farming is being squandered after the animals are sold. You don't necessarily know if beef is grass-fed or cereal-fed, whether it is dairy meat or from a specialist beef breed. Then, crucially, meat is often not hung for long enough to deliver its maximum potential. Hanging is the process by which enzymes soften the meat, making it more tender and tastier. Ideally, beef will be hung for twenty-one days or more. The paradox behind the point of hanging meat is that the more moisture in the meat you cook, the drier it will be to eat. This is because the moisture evaporates in the heat, leaving the meat muscles more stringy. Hanging, or 'dry-ageing', can lose up to 20 per cent of the moisture, and so an aged steak weighs a fifth less than an unaged one. But will the customer want to pay a fifth more? Not if they are buying beef just as a standard commodity. However, if you appreciate meat and want to really enjoy beef as a treat, then you will want your meat hung.

Meat-lovers believe well-hung meat is less affected by freezing because it has less liquid to turn into ice and change the texture and juiciness of the final dish. Some people buy a big meat box from a farm that they know, and enjoy eating it over time. This is an option well worth considering if you want to make a link with a particular farm and its animals. Most of us, however, don't have the necessary storage space. It is a good thought, however, that if you go to a butcher or a farm shop you like for some fresh meat, you can buy a few extra steaks for the freezer.

To find the best steak, I ate my way through a range of rumps. Rump is a good test for steak. It can be terrific value – cheaper than sirloin and far cheaper than fillet, but still tasty and toothsome, yet tender enough, if hung well. But if it is not good, it can be tough and tasteless. My selection was this: supermarket standard; supermarket premium; organic meat box and butcher's.

The supermarket standard rump steak was 30 per cent cheaper than the premium one. The latter tried to make itself look better value by being divided into 6 vacuum-packed portions. This is a convenient form of packaging, allowing the meat to be frozen easily and transported and sold in easy portions. Unfortunately it also means fluid leaches out of the meat. Meat-lovers are not fans of the vac-pac.

Tasting these two against each other was revealing. The cheaper rump steak was far juicier and more tender, as well as being cheaper. It was the plainest steak on the block – no claims, no bumf – and yet it was really good. The supermarket premium steak was a real disappointment. It was a bit tasteless and lacked juicy oomph.

Then I tasted the organic meat-box steak against the butch-er's. The butcher's rump steak was Aberdeen Angus, an old-fashioned breed; the organic one was also from a traditional breed. The methods of farming were similar – grass-fed animals with a bit of grain in the winter – and so was the price. In this case, they were both delicious, but the butcher's steak was more tender. It showed me that, in the case of beef, organic was not in itself a guarantee of better quality.

I had been surprised that the supermarket standard steak was so good – though perhaps I struck lucky. As Fearnley-Whittingstall says, you can't be sure what you are eating. Overall, there is a good amount of decent beef farming in this country. But alas, the quality doesn't always continue to the plate, and after all, that's what it's meant to be about.

That was all very well; but was the meat 'kind'? On the whole, like sheep, cattle are still extensively reared. Beef production in the UK is less industrialized than chicken and pork. Kindness is also about how naturally the animals are kept. With cattle, this is partly how they fit into the countryside.

To understand more, I went to Yorkshire to meet some of the farmers involved in a pioneering project called Limestone Country Beef. This is a modern take on traditional farming methods. It showed me how intimately the beef of Britain is linked to the countryside that I love to walk in, and it gave me another way to appreciate my beef.

The Yorkshire Dales are one of the most beautiful parts of England, with their craggy limestone uplands, dry-stone walls and big horizons. The land used to be grazed by sheep and hardy native-breed cattle. The cattle tugged up the coarse grasses and tougher plants with their long tongues, while the sheep nibbled away with their teeth. This dual-action grazing gave space for wildflowers to flourish. Then sheep farmers began to receive subsidies: the more sheep farmers kept, the more they earned. Continental cattle breeds began to appear. They could be grown more quickly by wintering indoors and they didn't eat the rough highland pastures. The native beef went off the shelves and out of the fields. Hordes of sheep took to the hills, picking out all the delicate plants and leaving the coarser ones. The limestone upland soon became tussocky, unkempt scrubland with fewer flowers and less wildlife.

The push to reverse this trend came from conservationists. Natural England and the Yorkshire Dales National Park Authority took five years to pull together a group of fifteen farmers to form a Limestone Country Beef group. The idea was to return native breeds to more than 1,000 hectares of the Dales in such a way as to help bring wildlife back to the hillsides. The beef would be marketed as meat that had a direct relevance to this particularly beautiful area.

I joined one of the Limestone Country farmers, Neil Heseltine, to see how it looked on the ground. He had taken on the family farm and had seen that government subsidies for farming were increasingly linked to the environment. With the energy of a man in his thirties, he wanted to seize an opportunity to make a change. 'We've done our farming at the expense of the environment since the war, but there' s no reason why the two shouldn't go in harness,' he said bluntly. 'It's the way we should be looking.'

The day I visited, Neil, his father and uncle were moving a herd of Belted Galloways from one pasture to another. Instead of loading them onto a lorry and driving them from one valley to another, they were walking the cattle along an old drovers' road. This was the shortest route and ultimately the least effort. The Belties looked like Dales zebras as they were herded through the massy, limestone landscape, their black and white stripes a striking graphic image in the drizzly mist. The whole scene worked together – the cattle living off and improving the land; and the farmer connecting to a trend for local, quality food and going back to an old farming method that worked again, in a new way.

As for the conservationists, they were already delighted with the outcome. One of the most famous sights of this countryside is the limestone pavement, with big square slabs, or clints, separated by deep grikes, some fifteen feet deep. The sheep used to shave off the top, but now ferns are putting their heads over the parapet. 'It's starting to look like a fabulous wildflower rockery rather than just bare rocks,' said Paul Evans, the conservationist heading the project with Natural England. The butchers I spoke to were really enthusiastic about the beef. It was tender yet full of 'beefiness'. The butchers took care to hang this special beef properly. One of them, Colin Robinson in Grassington, was using some of the cheaper cuts to make a Limestone Beef pastrami. The experience also showed me that making a connection to the meat you eat does improve your appreciation and makes it more of a treat.

The Limestone Country Beef farmers are no longer acting as a marketing group – apparently the interests of the farmers was too diverse – but there are still plenty of native breed cattle in the area. Neil is now thinking of selling the hides as well as the meat. 'They're a beautiful product and most hides sold here come in from South America,' he says.

One of the major stumbling blocks for such better beef farmers is that in order to make their enterprise viable, they need to sell the whole carcass. There is a seller's market for the prime cuts such as sirloin, fillet and other more tender, quick-cooking parts. But it is a buyers' market for the tougher cuts. In the quest to eat less-but-better meat, it is well worth learning how to cook these cheaper cuts because it means you can eat top quality beef at a reasonable price.

Canny chefs have been at the forefront of showing how to make the most from such meat. Whether it is down to the influence of the more informal gastropubs, the credit crunch or just restaurateurs shaking off stuffy custom, over the past few years eating out has become more affordable and based on classic home-cooked dishes rather than 'cheffy' food, with the whiff of too many fussy fingers poking around our plate. This is good news. Food is more fashion-led than you'd think and such chefs are style-setters.

Great Queen Street near London's Covent Garden is one of several places that can afford better quality meat because it does its own butchery and uses all parts of the animal. On Monday mornings, the carcasses of half a cow, two sheep and a pig can turn up at the door to be cut up. The restaurant has a good reputation for meat dishes – the Hereford beef they serve is outstanding. Yet the chef and co-owner, Tom Norrington-Davies, is the opposite of the stereotypical cleaver-wielding macho chef who throws his chops around. 'I've never really been comfortable with the meatiness of the restaurant trade,' he said with an unfussed candour, as we sat down on a Tuesday lunchtime in January, when the restaurant was full to bursting. His partner is vegetarian and that is how they eat at home. As a chef, however, Tom likes to have meat in his palette, but wants to do it in as sound a way as possible.

Tom's feeling about meat production was similar to my conclusions about fish and poultry: size matters. If you deal directly with a farmer or with a butcher who sources from small producers, you are likely to get a better deal all round, and so is the animal. The only way Tom can afford to do this is by working with the whole beast. I found much to learn from his approach, particularly his willingness to take what was there rather than ordering the norm.

Getting to grips with a side of beef took quite a while. Tom admits that to start with, he dreaded it each time. But the farmer, a playwright who had taken on his family farm in Wales, would patiently explain again and again how it was done. The reward of all this work, and Tom's effort not to be squeamish, is that the beef in Great Queen Street is cherished. Each part finds its place. The rib of beef or steak with chips are both excellent; so are the less expensive dishes using up the tougher cuts, the salt beef, the braises and the mince pie in a suet pastry with a pickled walnut on top.

Eating out at such places inspired me to go back to the pâtés and stews and *bon marché* dishes that are from a time-honoured kitchen tradition. A great deal is said about food that is 'quick and easy'. Another style is 'slow and easy'. I worked my way through ox cheek, which is ultra-beefy and good value; chicken liver pâté; pork spare ribs and lamb liver dusted with flour and cumin. In a meat box, I found myself with a 'hand' of pork, a cheaper cut that Tim at the Ginger Pig had mentioned. This cost less than a fiver. I found a recipe on the Internet by the food writer Mathew Fort that told me how to slow roast it with cider vinegar. Delicious.

Slow and easy is, in fact, a way of cooking that does need a little attention. You have to ensure the meat doesn't dry out and you have to get the seasoning right. But as I stand in the kitchen, amidst wafts of savoury steam from the pot, I can feel the influence of Tom's respect for his ingredients. If you are going to eat meat, do it justice; honour that animal. You get more affordable 'good' meat as your reward.

If finding a way to eat 'kind' meat means going back to more naturally produced food, then the most obvious next step is to eat more wild meat. I'd also reached this conclusion in looking at what we evolved to eat.

Game is not always purely the 'beast of the field, the bird of the air', with the freedom and natural way of life that you might imagine. Pheasant and partridges are often reared in pens rather than breeding in the wild. I ate some especially succulent pigeons at a posh restaurant and was told the secret ingredient was the fact that the birds' wings were clipped so they couldn't fly. Perhaps this could be done well, but it didn't sound great; an instance where the good-tasting meat wasn't necessarily natural.

However, most game does have an outdoor life and lives naturally until taken for the pot. Plenty of it is plentiful. Indeed, there is a 'culling' aspect to some game. Rabbits and pigeons can decimate crops and deer certainly need to be culled in order to keep a healthy breeding stock.

Following the seasons for game takes you deep into the changes in the countryside. One gamekeeper told me that pigeons are delicious in the autumn when they feed on acorns. Rabbits are also best in the autumn when the forage is drier. An experienced shot and cook, Valentine Warner, told me they taste hormonal in the spring and summer – quite apart from the fact they are looking after their bunnies. You can also buy farmed rabbits, from either China or France, but I would be cautious about the conditions they are kept in. How can you condemn caging up a chicken and not a rabbit? I'd personally rather take my chances with the wild, although many chefs prefer the farmed in terms of tenderness and consistency.

Game is a challenge to most cooks and eaters. Industrial meat tends to be boneless, and comes in uniform portions that bear no resemblance to the original animal. Game birds and rabbit are generally cooked and served on the bone. You need to pay so much attention with your knife and fork that it can feel more like surgery than dinner. By far the simplest game for the beginner is venison, since it is more akin to beef or lamb in terms of size and cuts. However, you have to be careful the meat doesn't dry out as it cooks. Overall, I felt I needed some help to get to grips with this less familiar type of food.

The best value and most interesting cookery courses, for me, are the ones based on or near a farm. These often involve a talk by a farmer or gamekeeper, perhaps even a visit to where the animals live, followed by a cookery demonstration and lunch. I went on a Suffolk Food Safari day course about wild meat led by Robert Gooch of the Wild Meat Company. This was hands-on, big style. Each of us was handed a butcher-sharp knife and then, slightly to my surprise, a whole haunch of venison. This is a back leg that is the size of a dog. But it was an opportunity to learn about the different muscles and the craft of butchery. It was hard not to feel like Hannibal Lecter on the Generation Game. At the same time, it gave me a new level of respect for the meat.

Robert explained how many chefs and game-fans like to eat the smaller deer, such as roe and fallow, because of their closer, fine-textured meat. The little muntjac deer, escapees from parklands that now live in the wild, also have their fans, but are hard to come across – they are so small that most game dealers don't consider them worth selling.

Tom Norrington-Davies at Great Queen Street has written a book on game that has plenty of Eastern and South Asian recipes as well as classic British dishes. He is interesting about what really is 'wild'. His preference is for eating, to put it undelectably, 'vermin', in other words the rabbits, pigeons and deer that thrive naturally in the wild without being reared for shoots, and that need controlling. He recommends pigeon breasts as a quick fry for starters, or braised venison or rabbit as easy dishes for beginners. At our lunch I ate rabbit leg braised in cider: a dense yet unfatty meat with lots of flavour.

But how easy is it to get hold of rabbit? Tom is right to say that you can get game at the click of an Internet button, but it certainly costs more this way. I was used to getting rabbit inexpensively from my local butcher in Sussex, where one of their farmers brought them in from his 'rough shoot'. Paying £4.50 for a rabbit that could feed two or maybe three was well and good, but if you add on a £10 delivery charge it starts to get quite steep. I phoned my local butcher. Yes, they had rabbits – though not right today as the ground was too frozen from the snow – and yes, pigeon, partridge, pheasant and venison. Just phone on the Tuesday and they'd get it from their game dealers on the Wednesday. I bought one from my local farmers' market and smuggled it into the house past teenage boys who are happily slaughtering zombies on the Xbox but might not want to look at the death that was dinner. It stayed in my freezer for months because it would need such active PR to get it on the table. Such are the factors that stop good ideas becoming good deeds.

All my explorations with meat were leading me to a particular conclusion. After falling into the habit of buying some meat at a supermarket, it was time to go back to the specialist, the butcher's shop and the farmers' market. It felt right to make some kind of effort for meat. It helped, again, to make it more special. Tom Norrington-Davies commented at our lunch that perhaps there should be a bit of a drama about getting hold of food; that there should be a bit of 'jeopardy' about getting dinner on the table. His comment made me think back to the Paleo Diet and the way we evolved, hunting down a small quantity of high-quality meat and eating plenty of greens alongside it. Yes, there is a great deal of emphasis on the 'quick and easy' – and that's perfectly understandable. But is it right for everything to be convenient, and for convenience to be placed above every other quality? Perhaps life is about striving and is all the more satisfying for that, in the end. Perhaps it is good to get back in touch with your inner hunter-gatherer.

This resolution is not always carried through. But I've become more aware of falling into the trap of convenience, and every time I do make the effort I feel, more and more, that it is worthwhile.

The elephant in the room, when you come to talk about ethical meat-eating, is the fact that the animal has to be killed. All the good meat producers I talked to had followed their animals through to the end and felt that it could be done decently, and I'd seen it done well, myself. But this can be the worst part of an otherwise ethically farmed animal's life. Organic and free-range chickens, especially those farmed on a larger scale, can go to exactly the same abattoirs as the intensively farmed ones.

One of the chilling parts of depictions of meat-packing plants, be it *The Jungle* or the campaigning film *Food Inc.*, is the way that workers are almost units as much as the animals. The accident rates are especially high in this trade, not just because of the sharp tools but also because of the speeding up of production and the killing line. It also means that workers are under a great deal of pressure in a business that must be, to some extent, brutalizing.

On the other hand, larger operations can be well-regulated. I spoke to one organic meat producer whose take on abattoirs was that the small ones could be good and the large ones could also be fine, because their size meant proper regulations needed to be in place. He'd found another medium-sized one more sinister: a place that was so rough you really felt you had to (literally) watch your back. 'You've got the two ends of the spectrum that are just about satisfactory,' he said. 'The ones in the middle I'd question.'

Big or small, it's a job that must be done, and accepting that is one of the hardest parts of thinking that meat can be 'kind'. This is why one of the most courageous people in food today is the welfare scientist Temple Grandin. A woman with high-functioning autism, she is one of the very few people who manages to work within a field that most people who care about animals would find impossible to stomach. Grandin's moderations, such as calming devices for cattle going into the slaughterhouses, have led to improvements on a large scale. I saw her give a talk at an animal welfare conference where she got an overwhelmingly positive round of applause from an audience that would, for the most part, be against killing animals at all. It made me see how someone who confronts a highly uncomfortable issue is kinder than those who pretend it isn't happening.

For myself, the killing part of meat production underpins a basic preference for buying meat from smaller producers. Many of these prefer – insist – on their animals going to a smaller abattoir that will take in small numbers of animals. The good small abattoir is a crucial link in the chain of ethical meat production because it is on this scale that they can, potentially, care the most. And it is one constantly under threat because they do not offer economies of scale. Tim Wilson of the Ginger Pig has recently got planning permission for an abattoir because he is anxious about the future of the current one he uses. At the moment his pigs travel twenty miles to a small plant in York. It is a place that kills 140 pigs a week, as opposed to the 40,000 at the nearby bacon factory. 'How would I know that they were my pigs coming out?' he asks.

Eating meat is a tricky business. Can you have 'kind' meat? Yes, but only if you give meat its due care. This is a challenge in our rushed lives. Kindness is about striving to act with consideration in daily detail. Asking questions, making the effort to go to a butcher, eating meat less often but giving it more attention, finding out about the animal and the farmer – all these are part of knowing and doing.

There is always a paradox in eating meat; you are killing the animal you care about. I said to Tom Norrington-Davies: I feel that I, too, am an animal, and one that eats meat. Yes, he said; but I am a human animal and do I behave in a way that is humane?

Meat requires such self-questioning, and it is right that it should. It's a check on those of us who would like to continue to eat meat, but believe we should do so in a 'kind' way. Yes, it is harder. Yes, it is more expensive, though there are ways round this. And yes, it is ultimately more rewarding. It's true: meat is certainly not just another food.

WHAT TO EAT?
Easy. Eat less but better meat; go for free-range or organic; explore wild meat; make the most of cheap cuts; shop at a butcher's and not just the supermarket.

Worth the Effort. Don't just trust a label but find out about meat without packaging; ask questions at a farmers' market; buy meat online from a traditional or organic producer; support rare-breed meat producers; visit a farm.

Hopes and Dreams. That meat becomes more of a cherished treat rather than a thrice-daily convenience; that we don't just fall for 'greenwash' when it comes to the welfare of farm animals; that the EU will put animal welfare as a legitimate trade barrier and take pride in treating meat creatures well.

6

Can I Eat to Avoid Heart Disease and Cancer?

For what I sincerely hope will be the first half of my life, I've been fortunate enough to hardly think about my health. At the age of forty, it started to creep into my mind. I started to get the occasional chest pain, and when I stooped suddenly there would sometimes be a creasing ache in my left side, as if a tube had been twisted beyond its stretch. On top of this came a general lack of energy. I could no longer run for the bus. Generally I cycle rather than drive, but it was now at such a trundling pace that I had the odd conversation with a passer-by.

Somewhat reluctantly, I started to look more closely at how my health and well-being might be connected to the plate and the glass. Like any food writer, my table is often full and my cup overflowing. I think butter is one of the secrets of good food and good times deserve a drink. I 'know', like anyone else, that both saturated fats and too much alcohol are meant to be a problem. But how far is that true? And how much is too much?

I started with one particular anxiety. Statistics show heart disease to be the biggest health concern for both men and women. Considering my diet and relative lack of exercise, heart disease could well be on my horizon; and perhaps that horizon wasn't so very distant.

Then I spent a year writing for a cancer charity, Maggie's Cancer Caring Centres, and met many people with the disease. I understood better what it meant to face the crisis of a life-threatening diagnosis and woke up to the fact that breast cancer was really very common (now 1 in 8 women). When I'd drunk too much, I'd notice my breasts aching slightly the next day. Breast cancer rates have soared over the last thirty years. Sure, this can be partly explained by ageing populations and better detection and, sure, we are better at treating it and more people live for longer with cancer. But the fact remains that it is the number one cancer in the UK.

All this was sobering – not least because statistics feel somewhat pointless when you see the disease close up. If you have breast cancer – or know someone with it – then the figure is not one in eight; it is one in one.

Yet there was a counterforce as far as my thinking about health and food was concerned. I'd come to feel an overarching irritation about the Naysayers taking over my plate. What is called healthy eating can make all sorts of delicious foods curiously unappealing. This is partly from the way you are almost told to 'take' carrots, tomatoes, salad leaves and so on like pills rather than just eat and enjoy a meal. And there's a general sense of 'What do I have to give up now?' rather than something more positive.

When I looked at healthy eating dishes in leaflets and cookbooks, they were often very different from what I would normally eat. Cuisines evolve over a long time, developing a great deal of wisdom about health as well as taste along the way. I didn't want to be transported, suddenly, to Planet Healthy Eating just because some group of people called nutritionists told me to. Did they really have better answers? A remark by the convivial writer John Mortimer passes through my mind when yet another finger is wagged over my plate: 'I've always believed that no pleasure is worth giving up for six months in a geriatric home in Weston-super-Mare.'

On the other hand, I felt my body to be no longer what it was. I watched those I now called 'young' (at least it wasn't 'the young' – yet) dancing at parties and gigs, bouncing up and down as if their bodies were made of rubber. Meanwhile my every cell seemed slower. Sometimes I like the stillness that time has brought; yet this sense of gravity also weighed me down.

So there was a concrete and immediate reason for examining what I ate, in terms of health: I wanted my oomph back. The only way I could imagine changing my diet was by finding credible advice that made me feel better and didn't impinge on my love of food. I was after vitality – but not if it meant misery at the table.

First, how strong is the evidence for what you should and shouldn't be eating?

Professor Walter Willett of Harvard Medical School has spent his distinguished career analysing what we should eat. His book, *Eat, Drink and Be Healthy* (2001) seemed like a good place to start. Willett has spent decades analysing the epidemiological evidence gathered since the mid-1970s from 121,000 nurses in the US. He thinks that more than 80 per cent of coronary heart disease, 70 per cent of strokes, 70 per cent of some cancers and 90 per cent of type-2 diabetes may be avoided by careful attention to diet and lifestyle. Sounds like pretty good odds. Furthermore, he gives broadly the same advice for all these diseases. It's a powerful point that by paying attention to your well-being you may be protecting yourself from many forms of ill health. Over the years, Willett and other colleagues have changed the way they eat and drink after seeing the results of their own large-scale study. How?

Before I listened to what Professor Willett had to say, I wanted to know more about the quality of the evidence. Willett goes some way towards explaining why the advice about what to eat seems so contradictory. 'For nutrition research, the rhythm is more a cha–cha – two steps forward and one step back – than a straight-ahead march,' he admits in his book's introduction. This underlined my understanding, raised by Michael Pollan, that newspapers pick up on a piece of research and trumpet it as the best new finding when it is, in fact, merely the latest. In other words, these pieces of research are not views from the top of the mountain but steps upon a path that may yet have switchbacks.

Yet some findings are stronger than others. Whenever you read a big headline full of fear or hope, you have to bear in mind the hierarchy of scientific evidence.

The gold standard is the intervention study. This is when one group of people is given a certain kind of food or diet, and the results can be measured against a 'control' group of people who do not have that intervention. However, these studies are often impossible to carry out effectively, in part because people may not stick to their prescribed diet for year after year.

The next level of evidence comes from what are called 'cohort studies', when the food eaten by a large sample of people is studied retrospectively alongside their health. This is the sort of epidemiological work that Willett and his team are involved in. There are many variables, such as exercise and other elements of lifestyle, which are meant to be taken into account when working out whether, for example, a high-fat diet makes you more likely to have a heart attack. All the same, the results show associations of one particular kind of food or diet with ill health are not cast-iron proof. Food and eating are notoriously complex to study. Many studies rely on diet questionnaires and diaries that can be imperfect. People may forget what they really ate, or exaggerate the 'good' and downplay the 'bad'. Such studies can give good clues and point up trends but are not, in the end, completely solid proof.

Then you have small-scale experiments that are done in laboratories, sometimes with animals. These may give clues, but are a long way from the realities of how humans actually eat. They tend to isolate one element in food, such as a vitamin, rather than looking at an overall diet and lifestyle. A test-tube experiment or even an animal experiment are nothing like the complexity of a human's body and diet. The conclusions can often be disproven when the experiment goes up to the level of proof of an intervention study. Yet when you see a headline reading 'Fat causes cancer,' it may well have been a result from mice in a laboratory.

★

So summing up the best evidence he could find, what does Willett say? I was surprised at how far his advice differed from the public health messages of the time.

In an attempt to simplify matters, over the years governments have produced various graphics such as pyramids and plates. In 1992, the United States Department of Agriculture produced a Food Guide pyramid as part of its public health work. Walter Willett and the Harvard School of Public Health in response produced a Healthy Eating Pyramid that was strikingly different. My eye was drawn to the Food Guide pyramid's warning that we should not eat much fat, advising us to use fats 'sparingly'. Willett's point is that not all fats are bad; indeed, some fats, such as olive oil and other vegetable oils, seem to be positively protective and we should try to eat more of them, with the proviso that you don't want to put on too much weight. Good news! Particularly to avoid, however, are the trans fats found in fast food and baked goods. I decided that I wanted to look specifically at the differences between all these fats.

The second major point of difference is that this USDA pyramid advised you to base each meal on carbohydrates. Walter Willett's point is that you need to be more particular about what kind of carbohydrate you are eating. Refined carbohydrates, such as baked goods like biscuits and cakes, lead to blood-sugar 'spikes' that can make you more hungry more quickly by interfering with the way you metabolize food, with the result that you put on weight more quickly. This is the whole g.i. issue that I'd studied when looking into the best breakfast.

The third point of disagreement was the recommendation to

eat plenty of dairy products – two to three servings a day, according to the USDA pyramid. Willett points out that dairy products are a relatively expensive option and we can get calcium from other sources. Plants have a surprising amount of calcium, for example. (I would find out later, when talking to him, that he has other concerns about consuming an excessive quantity of dairy produce.)

Willett argues that, in general, we need to choose our proteins carefully, choosing more fish and vegetable protein such as beans and not consuming just red meat and dairy. Lean meat such as chicken and game are a good way to go. Ideally, we should eat nuts and beans one to three times daily and eat red meat 'sparingly'.

Then there is what goes beyond the plate. There was no specific guidance on weight, exercise, alcohol and vitamins on the original USDA food pyramid. Willett says that keeping a good weight is the single most important factor (apart from not smoking) in helping your health. Keeping relatively fit is important, and a drink a day, for most people, is positively good. Interestingly, he also thinks a multi-vitamin supplement is a good idea for insurance for the vitamins that are hard to get in even a good diet.

Just about the only point of total agreement between Willett's healthy pyramid and the 1990s USDA pyramid is the recommendation to eat lots of fruit and vegetables – though he disagrees with the government's 'target' of three to five servings of vegetables and two to four servings of fruit, saying rather that you should have vegetables 'in abundance'.

As far as the original pyramid went, Willet did not pull his punches in his book. It was based on shaky scientific grounds that had been eroded. He wrote: 'At best, the USDA Pyramid offers wishy-washy, scientifically unfounded advice on an absolutely vital topic – what to eat. At worst the misinformation contributes to overweight, poor health, and unnecessary early deaths.'

The American government has now changed its public health policy to be more in line with Willett's advice. USDA's 2011 MyPlate, an update on the pyramid, recommends that half the plate is fruit and vegetables and that you should consume at least half your grains as wholegrains. The scientists and the public health message-makers are now moving towards more of a consensus. But looking at how they got there deepened my suspicion that what is recommended is not necessarily the final answer.

Eat, Drink and Be Healthy was published a decade ago, and I talked to Professor Willett on the phone to see what had changed since then. 'The book is not yet fully written about diet and health,' he admitted. 'There's still a lot to be learnt. But there's quite a bit more agreement than there was a few years ago.' The broad agreements could be summarized thus: sugary drinks – bad; wholegrains better than refined. There is quite a bit of agreement on fruit and vegetables. They are now thought to be less protective against cancer than once believed; but they are still good to eat.

What about fats? There's 'good agreement', he said, that we

should keep saturated fats low, but some confusion as to what to replace them with. He said the evidence for a total low-fat diet wasn't all that strong, even though it became part of a public health message. 'It was part of the low-fat idea that anything that wasn't fat was good for you and people loaded up on sugar and refined starch,' he said. What happened was a simplification, designed to make a healthy diet look straightforward, that led to unhealthy solutions – broadly, that we swapped fat for carbohydrates (low-fat yoghurts that are high in sugar, for example). Such foods, it turned out, have made us plumper and less healthy than the fats had in the first place.

Walter Willett's own diet sounded like the hardcore end of 'healthy eating'. In the morning, he has a mixture of wholegrains with fruit and nuts. His lunch is based on bread or cooked wholegrains. For dinner he might have no carbohydrates, but salad and fish. He tries to avoid salt as much as possible. The good news is that he likes a couple of glasses of wine, usually red. Like some other scientists I've spoken to over the years, he does still take a multi-vitamin. A really good diet can have everything, but they see it as an insurance policy for good health.

One of Willett's current lines of enquiry was disturbing. He was looking into dairy products and in particular the amount consumed by young adults. His concern, broadly speaking, is that growth spurts, powered by the likes of milk and cheese, may have consequences in later life in terms of cancer. 'It is very complex, but it's pretty clear that consuming high amounts of dairy products throughout life is not normal behaviour and we are only starting to get the implications of that,' he said.

Aggressive prostate cancer in men and possibly ovarian and breast cancer in women may be linked to milk and other forms of dairy produce. What the exact mechanism may be is not known, but investigating it is a priority.

In the meantime, it is hard not to think of the teenagers all over the developed world who drink pints and pints of milk, splashing it on sugary cereal as a snack, drinking it with sugary, flavoured powders and then having more as cheese – cheese on toast, in sandwiches and eaten as hunks. Then I thought of my fridge and the way yoghurt, milk and butter were always there, and quite often cream as well. I saw again how dairy has become a basic convenience food of our time. If there are worries about it, you'd want to know. Yet is this a scare story, since the theory is as yet unproven?

Whatever the current state of evidence, Willett's words certainly got me thinking. We didn't evolve with a great amount of dairy and I could well believe that it may well have got out of proportion in our diet. I decided to be a touch more watchful of the amount I had. I certainly wouldn't ban dairy foods from the kitchen. No cheese or yoghurt – unthinkable! These are good, delicious, nourishing foods with a great deal of culture (and healthy bacterial cultures) behind them. But reassessing the overall amount to eat felt like a good step, not least to get greater diversity into my diet, which was the most basic lesson I'd learnt so far in my quest to eat well. If you are eating less meat, it is all too easy to replace it with dairy.

There are other reasons not to go overboard on dairy produce. The same ethical questions of welfare very much apply to dairy cows as to meat animals and there are also, I discovered, environmental concerns as well. So for a variety of reasons more powerful than a question mark over the health aspect, I stopped eating cheese all the time as a default snack or quick lunch. But I still enjoy it, and perhaps more so now that I eat less. I traded up slightly on cheese, and buy those that have more taste and are for appreciating rather than gobbling. It's all too easy to hack a quarter off a block of Cheddar if it doesn't taste (or cost) that much.

The angels – as well as the devil – are always in the detail. I wanted to understand more about fats and wholegrains, how they could be useful in my kitchen and relate to my health.

Fats have been demonized in the last couple of decades and low-fat foods have become mainstream. To understand Walter Willett's advice better, I went to a talk on fats, the British Nutrition Foundation's annual lecture that was given in 2009 by Tom Sanders, a nutrition professor at King's College London and an expert, in particular, on how diet is connected to the risk of coronary heart disease.

Professor Sanders wasn't especially skinny, which I somehow found reassuring. Either he wasn't practising what he preached or else – and this is what I hoped – he felt confident that it was all right to have a slight paunch, as long as you are eating the right foods. Of course, you can talk the talk without walking the walk (or munching the lunch). Yet Sanders looked comfortable in his skin. Furthermore, he was interested in solid proof and was a man who ate in the real world. Whilst Walter Willett sang the praises of nuts, Sanders acknowledged that whilst they were fine in moderation, that was rarely the case. 'Nuts are very more-ish,' he said. 'One nut leads to another.' The problem is that eating too many nuts can mean putting on weight. I remember his words when my snack handful of dried fruit and nuts turns into three or four.

On the screen behind Sanders were the chemical formulae for a series of fats, or fatty acids to be more technically correct. Broadly, these come in one of three categories. Saturated fats are the kind found largely in butter, lard, dairy produce and red meats. These are solid at room temperatures. Then come the monounsaturated fats that predominate in olive oil, avocados and nuts. These remain liquid as pure oils, released from food. Finally, the polyunsaturates, or PUFAs (polyunsaturated fatty acids), which can become solid in cold temperatures – think of how olive oil goes opaque and thick in the fridge. It came as a surprise to me that most fats are combinations of many types of fatty acids. Butter is mostly saturated fats but is also 16 per cent monounsaturates, olive oil is 13 per cent saturated fatty acids and fish oil is 21 per cent saturated fatty acids. Following one element, as you do in nutritionism, is a false move: foods are complex.

One encouraging message Sanders gave is that it is a myth to think that fats make you fat. It is all too easy to imagine the fat from shiny chips or slathers of butter going straight to your wobbling thighs. But no: the evidence for linking fat and obesity is 'very thin', he said. In the Women's Health Initiative, the gold standard intervention study in the US, fat intake was lowered, but it made no difference to mortality and the people who followed the low-fat diet ended up weighing just 400g less. Big deal. You wouldn't be very pleased if you deprived yourself of luscious fats for years and ended up only slightly lighter that you were to begin with. Of course, if you eat too much fat, as with too much of anything else, you will get fat. But I'd already learnt in my Best Breakfast research that fat could help you eat less by making you feel fuller.

This sounded like good news, but then I also heard that the Women's Health Initiative findings about diet and fat remain controversial. Scientists advocating a low-fat diet in regard to cancer, such as Dean Ornish, say that the diet wasn't low enough in fat to make a difference. Hmmmm.

Sanders emphasized that with all the anti-fat messages going out, we shouldn't forget the fact that fats are not just good for us but essential. This was first suspected by a husband-and-wife nutrition team. George and Mildred Burr (those who remember 1970s UK sitcoms will appreciate this pairing of names) fed rats on a fat-free diet, then noticed something called 'steamy beaker affect'; the rats' tails got saturated with water that seeped through their poor membranes and was sweated out into the glass rat-room. All our cell membranes need a bit of waxy fat to stop dehydration. Fat is important at a cellular level. When I drizzle my olive oil, I reflect that it is going to taste good and top up my cells.

Sanders had other good news. The stearic acid that is the main saturated fat in chocolate is not as bad as that in animal fat. So a square of chocolate after lunch or in times of need is no bad thing. If plant-derived fats are all right, fish fats are best of all because of their omega-3 content. Sanders joked that he had spent some time eating 3g of fish oil a day and his wife said he smelt like a mackerel and the cat kept sidling up to him. Nevertheless, his advice was that fish, in particular, is important to eat and you should try to have two portions a week, at least one of them oily.

Much as I wanted to, I couldn't ignore that Sanders was generally down on saturated fats. He thinks you should replace animal fats with vegetable oils, choose low-fat dairy products and favour lean meat. But his clearest nutritional message as regards 'bad' fats, like Willett's, is that trans fats are especially bad, giving you 27 per cent more chance of having a heart attack.

I knew from other research I'd done that trans fats are much worse than saturated fats. They are one of the scandals of the food industry and a classic example of misfired nutritional advice. They are an invented fat that can be stored at room temperature for a long time and so are of great convenience to manufacturers and fast food outlets. Made of vegetable fats, they were, initially, seen as a 'healthy' replacement for animal fats. But the body can't process this new food properly and, what's more, it actively prevents you from metabolizing good fats. For decades now, they have been under suspicion. Enlightened legislators in places such as California and Denmark have even banned trans fats. But they are still used in many processed and deep-fried foods elsewhere in the world, not least in the UK.

The big players in the food industry in the UK are at last phasing out these bad fats, but the tardiness of their action is not impressive. Of course, making a change to a processed food is extremely costly. But the trans fat story confirms my feeling that the food industry acts more slowly than you would like on health matters. A food factory is not like your parents. And they are still being used by plenty of fast food outlets and food manufacturers, since withdrawal is voluntary. This is also another interesting example of the way government intervention and advice works in the UK, and how blunt statistics can be. The UK government's line is that the 'average' person eats trans fats within a 'safe' amount. Their main point is that these fats should be labelled and that industry should voluntarily reduce or eliminate them. But there is still a small proportion of people who eat a great deal of trans fats in such foods as take-aways and pies. Such people tend not to look on labels – and there aren't labels on most of these foods in the first place. If the UK government just outlawed the use of trans fats, as others have, it is likely there would be a substantial saving on the nation's health bill.

One of the most welcome pieces of news about fats in Professor Sanders's talk was the advice to eat olive oil. The olive is the symbol of the healthy Mediterranean diet. There is, praise be, a correlation between taste and healthfulness. The freshest extra virgin and virgin olive oils, the simply pressed oil of the fruit, contain the most phytonutrients, which are molecules that may be helpful but unlike vitamins and minerals haven't got defined benefits. Lower-quality oils are heated, treated and deodorized, leaving fewer of these goodies and less flavour. A taste indication of healthfulness is the hit you get at the back of your throat with a number of good olive oils. The Italians call this pepperiness *pizzica*, and it's the result of antioxidant polyphenols. These decrease over time. Whilst it is true that all olive oil is good, because of the basic nature of its fats, it is best of all to consume cold-pressed virgin olive oil that is as fresh as possible. Such very fresh oils are harder to get hold of, however. You tend to get them through contacts and from good delicatessens.

One place where I tried the fresh oil was at a meal based on the new crop at a pop-up restaurant run by Lori di Mori and Jason Lowe in Dalston, East London. I love the sense of abundance that you get from any harvest, and the meal celebrated that year's new olive oil in dish after dish. There was a slick of gold on top of a chestnut soup, mushrooms rich with Tuscan oil and big platefuls of kale waiting to be anointed with the bright green bottlefuls on each table. They have such meals in Italy, a celebration of the good that has returned for another year. The message is this: don't hoard your oil like some sort of boutique elixir, but enjoy it now.

I began to explore the range of flavours in good olive oil. The Spanish produce a golden oil, partly because of the heat of their climate. The Portuguese tend to leave the olives for longer between picking and milling, which gives a distinctive flavour. Tuscan oils are peppery and bright green because they use fruits that are just turning from green towards black. This is thought by some gourmets to be the best time to pick the olives, though the ripe, black fruits produce more oil. A London importer of quality oils, Charles Carey of The Oil Merchant, says that, on the other hand, French oils from black olives can be described as sweeter than other kinds. He thinks the 'grassy' Greek oils, especially from places such as Crete, can be undervalued (in other words, a bargain); I started finding these in supermarkets and they were good value. As for the Italian oils, apparently a number are from North African olives but are packaged in Italy and termed Italian, with a mark-up. The properly branded single-estate bottles are the best quality in terms of taste but, again, all olive oil is good in terms of health.

I wondered if it was strange to use olive oil when living in a northern European country. But oils are transported by ship, not the environmentally problematic aeroplanes. Moreover, olives and their oil couldn't be a more time-honoured food. 'A taste older than meat, older than wine. A taste as old as cold water,' is how Lawrence Durrell describes it in his novel *Prospero's Cell*, based on his time in Corfu. Britain's associations with the Mediterranean go way back. Aldous Huxley, in a lyrical essay on the olive, argued that the English have a yearning for the Mediterranean that goes back to the French element flowing in our national bloodstream. We are, he said, Germans who have partly 'gone Latin'. Perhaps the way we've taken to olive oil is not so strange but a rather more ingrained part of our national culture. In any case, I find olive oil easy and pleasurable to eat in many ways, whether drizzled on toast and tomatoes in my own version of the Catalan breakfast, *pa amb tomaquet*, or swirled on top of soups, or put into mayonnaise to eat with fish, or used as a basic cooking medium. I like the way olive oil makes healthy food more delicious and less puritanical.

★

Another food dilemma relating to fats is the choice between semi-skimmed and whole milk. Many cite this as a good 'healthy swap'. But when I looked closer, the public health messages about this seemed to be about putting on weight, and there are other ways to watch this. Full-fat milk has more flavour and lusciousness, and if it is organic it is likely to have more of the beneficial omega-3s, vitamin E and beta-carotene, perhaps because the cows have a different sort of grazing than non-organic, generally including red clover. In such milk the fat is an integral part of the goodness.

There was also something a touch parsimonious about the 'no sats' brigade. No wonder that my eye lit upon a newspaper headline that said 'Saturated fat may not always be harmful.' Hardly the most ringing endorsement, admittedly, but one to follow up.

The words referred to a survey of all the epidemiological evidence linking saturated fat and heart disease that had been published in the *American Journal of Clinical Nutrition* in 2010. I waded through the academic language, which is always such a contrast to the over-confident summaries of the headlines they spawn. The findings, broadly, were that there had been associations between diets that were very high in fat and heart disease, but the picture may well be more complex than at first assumed. Replacing saturated fats with monounsaturates had an 'unclear' affect on heart disease. Replacing them with polyunsaturates seemed to be a small help. However, replacing them with refined carbohydrates, such as sugars, could be harmful and 'more research was needed on this aspect', the usual end to scientific studies: we don't know everything but this is the next step needed. Rather than focusing just on replacing saturated fats, we should focus on eating more seafood, whole grains, fruit and vegetables and decreasing the intake of salt and trans fats, the paper said.

The studies on this subject were not ultimately conclusive and certainly not agreed by everyone. Many scientists are still adamant that it is a good idea to eat a low-fat diet, especially to avoid cancer, and so this study didn't send me any deeper into the butter-dish. But it made me see again how the principal of a varied and balanced diet still held and – hallelujah! – I felt that this variety had room for (some) butter. Can I eat cheese and full-fat milk? Yes, but I personally don't think at every meal, though for many reasons other than just health.

There were now plenty of warnings that refined carbohydrates may be a type of food to be wary of, not just for heart disease but for health in general. The crucial point, according to Walter Willett, is that you should eat wholegrains rather than processed carbohydrates. People who habitually eat wholegrains have lower rates of heart disease than those who don't. Why should this be? 'When you eat wholegrains, you get more fibre and more micronutrients like folic acid, magnesium, and vitamin E,' he says. Whilst admitting that it may be almost impossible to isolate the pieces of the puzzle as to why exactly they are good, his overall advice is to eat wholegrain cereals and wholegrain breads; that wholewheat pasta can be delicious; to bake with wholewheat flour; and to pester chefs to use more wholegrains. Some of this sounded doable, some of it sounded dubious (wholewheat pasta?) and some of it was plain 'pie-in-the-sky' – and a drab-brown pie, at that. I couldn't imagine, for example, going into my local curry house and asking for brown rice instead of white. If I were a chef, my response would be 'My gaff, my rules.'

I wanted to know exactly what a wholegrain was, and whether some grains were whole-ier than others. It isn't always obvious. Couscous, for example, is made from wheat that has been coarsely milled and has therefore lost its outer bran. Some of it is more refined than others; you need to look for wholewheat couscous, which is just as easy to cook and doesn't feel at all claggy. But because more of the wheat grain is intact, both types are still nutritionally 'better' than pasta. Popcorn, seen as junk food because it is sold (at vast expense) covered in salt and butter or sugar in cinemas, is a useful wholegrain if eaten with more sparing seasoning. Oats are wholegrains, even if pulverized into instant porridge.

A breakthrough came when I realized that I didn't have to be a wholegrain puritan. Over the years, I've come to like the flavour of brown rice with some dishes but I still prefer white with a curry, for example; it almost feels like a different kind of food. But you don't need to go all the way, even with rice. I discovered this at the Japan Centre in London's Piccadilly.

I got an inkling that this was an unusual place when I noticed that they used Sheepdrove Farm chicken, from one of the best organic farms in the country, in their inexpensive noodle soup. This led me to talk to the owner, who said he managed to serve this kind of chicken by using up the cheaper legs. He was clearly attentive to quality. Another example was that the shop had a rice polisher, which meant you could choose how you wanted your rice in shades from brown to pearly white. A number of Japanese consumers go for a semi-brown rice, which has perhaps 20 per cent of the outside bran left on. Purists say you should have the brownest of the brown, but I just wouldn't eat this all the time and I liked this slight shift from the very white to slightly brown. I also found that pasta could be found in half-and-half forms, and I sometimes eat this, though I couldn't initially get into the hardcore wholewheat type.

Then I edited a recipe for wholewheat pasta with an onion and anchovy sauce produced by the über-cool Polpo, a Venetian bar in Soho. Its Bigoli in Salsa uses brown spaghetti dressed in a sauce of onions cooked long, slow and melting in olive oil. You mash down some good omega-3 anchovies and toss the pasta in the sauce. Simple, delicious and – yes – healthy. This wasn't some edict from a healthy eating manual just … good food. Through this route, I have come to like wholewheat pasta in certain rustic dishes, but only really spaghetti and not the larger pieces of pasta.

I started to explore other grains. People rave about quinoa (prounced 'keen-wah') because it has a high protein content and can be used to replace meat. I found it unexciting at first and slightly weird; when cooked, it spills its guts and looks like squiggled frogspawn. But then I had another go, and by chance ate some with a bowl of leftover chicken korma. The grain absorbed the sauce better than rice and I came to appreciate its juiciness and texture. A recipe by a food writer friend, Diana Henry, persuaded me to toast the grain first by putting it in a dry pan over heat for a few minutes. In the recipe, she then mixes it with fried onion, ground cumin, leaf coriander, lime juice, chilli and roasted peppers (Diana is a 'more is more' kind of gal). Her tip is that you shouldn't put too much water with quinoa (slightly over double volume to weight). This explained why I'd found it a touch soggy and tasteless on my first go.

The lesson I learnt is that it takes time and attention to enjoy wholegrains and to make the most of them as the subtle canvas for more vivid culinary colours. It is all too easy to buy a bag and then hide it away in the dark recess of a cupboard. You need to put an unfamiliar grain in a storage jar in a place where you can see it, and make the effort to use it once a fortnight, at least, while getting to know its ways. By doing this, I also began to enjoy wild rice, which is more expensive than some grains but deliciously nutty.

Wholewheat Japanese noodles, such as soba, were easy to get into and a natural part of a cuisine that is generally healthy. Barley also became part of my kitchen. I find it simple to slip a couple of spoonfuls into soups and stews, and I also cook it with a well-flavoured stock to make a rough kind of risotto, either with vegetables or as the base for a piece of fish or meat. Spelt can be used in the same way.

I also experimented by using half-and-half brown and white flour in baking and found this could work well, unless I was making something elegant like a Victoria sponge. On the whole, I make cakes that are full of nourishment as much as sugar – fruit cakes and cakes containing grated vegetables, such as courgette and chocolate cake and carrot cake. Such tea-time fillers can take a mixture of flours. The half-brown and half-white mixture made biscuits more satisfying and a crumble topping more tasty. I had come to see that wholegrains fill you up, add flavour and mean you get a bit more from your food.

When it came to cancer, my first port of call was the 2007 World Cancer Research Fund report into food and cancer, a summary of expert advice. The report's main advice is this: eat more fruit and vegetables, and more vegetable protein such as you get in grains and pulses – or, as the report puts it, 'Eat mostly foods of plant origin'; limit red meat and avoid processed meat (such as sausages, bacon and salami); don't drink too much – for women this is one drink a day; cut down on salt to 5g a day; and, finally, dietary supplements are not recommended.

First, is this achievable? I looked first at the message about fruit and vegetables. The report recommends eating 400g fruit and vegetables (excluding potatoes) per day. A portion is 80g: an apple, orange or banana; two plums; a tablespoon of dried fruit; two serving spoons of cooked vegetables; a dessert bowl of salad. A portion of juice is 150ml, but only one a day counts as it doesn't contain the fibre that is thought to be part of what is beneficial. I noticed that the advice is not really 'Eat five-a-day' but 'Eat *at least* five-a-day.' It certainly seemed possible to eat this much, and it prompted me to try to have salads at meals and fruit as snacks.

The WCRF recommends having no more than 500g of cooked red meat in a week (700–750g before cooking). This is around 70g a day. A slice of ham is 23g, a slice of beef 45g, a thick slice of lamb 90g and a small steak is 100g. You could still have four meaty dinners a week and be within the health guidelines, but you'd have to think hard about portion size. This size of steak is a third of one of those sold in my local pub's steak night.

The biggest concern about red meat is its association with colorectal cancers, the third most common type of cancer in the UK after breast and lung cancer, and on the rise around the world due, it is thought, to the Western diet, not least to the high consumption of red and processed meat. One of the problems may be something called haem-iron. This gives red meat its colour and has been shown to damage the lining of the colon, though, once again, it is not known exactly how this works and we don't know, yet, who is or isn't susceptible to the problem. It may be that in years to come a genetic test will let you know. In the meantime, the health advice is the same for everyone.

It is especially challenging that the WCRF report says that 'very little if any' of the meat should be processed. That's a hard one to swallow if you like your bacon sarnie, have chorizo as a convenient fridge stand-by and sometimes have a ham sandwich for lunch. One of the tricks to eating less meat and more vegetables is to use a little highly flavoured salted meat; for example, basing part of the flavour of a risotto on a little chopped bacon. The panel decided that red meat does have nutritional benefits, but since processed red meats, such as bacon, raise the same concerns plus extra ones, particularly because of the nitrites in cured meat, you are better off eating red meat and no processed meat.

My personal conclusion from the report, for now, is that it is all right to eat some red meat – but certainly not every day – and some (but less) processed meats (tasty, salty meats such as chorizo help me to eat less meat overall), but I did decide to cut down. This decision is also based on the fundamental principal I had picked up from my quest: that it is good to eat a diverse diet. It is as much about eating more plant foods as about eating less meat.

The WCRF is more encouraging on the subject of fat: 'In general, the Panel judges that there is only limited evidence suggesting that diets relatively high in fats and oils are in themselves a cause of any cancer.' This rows back from earlier reports, it adds. Being overweight is a problem; but this is the concern, not fat in the diet.

The report's guidance on fruit and vegetables appears, however, to be less cheering than you might hope. The studies since the mid-90s were 'somewhat less impressive' than previously. The advice to eat them was now 'probable' rather than 'convincing'. Yet the report also says that some types of vegetables and fruits probably *do* protect against a number of cancers, and the lack of evidence on pulses, nuts, seeds and most herbs and spices 'reflects the small amount of epidemiological evidence'. In other words, their benefits are not disproven, just not proven.

What is thought to be so special about fruit and veg? Sometimes a particular kind of food – generally a rare and expensive one – is hailed as a 'superfood' to be taken like a magic pill. Despite some reservations, I do quite like the idea of superfoods. My own psychology – and I think this is common – is that I'm generally more interested in what I can eat more of rather than cutting back. It just feels much more positive.

Two cancer researchers, Professor Richard Béliveau and Dr Denis Gingras, based at the University of Montreal, list eleven key types of 'good' foods in their book *Food to Fight Cancers*. These are: cabbage and other cruciferous vegetables such as broccoli and Brussels sprouts; garlic, onions and other alliums such as leeks and chives; soybean products such as tofu; turmeric; green tea; berries; oily fish rich in omega-3s; tomatoes; citrus fruits; chocolate and wine. I wanted to know more about how each might be good in my day-to-day diet.

There are also quite a few useful specifics in *The Prostate Care Cookbook* partly written by Margaret Rayman, Professor of Nutritional Medicine at the University of Surrey. This cookbook lays out, first of all, why food may be useful against cancer. Like Béliveau and Gingras, she says antioxidants, such as you find in high quantities in certain fruits and vegetables, can reduce the damage to cells and reduce the inflammation that is a risk for cancer. Such foods can improve your immune response and prevent damage to DNA. They can prevent the formation of new blood vessels that feed the rogue cells. This process is known as angiogenesis and is one of the current focuses of attention in the food and cancer world. Food can also reduce the invasion of tumour cells into the surrounding tissue; change the behaviour of genes; increase the rate at which compounds are detoxified and removed form the body; and, finally, modify the behaviour of hormones, such as those that cause cancer. It's quite a list.

This is all at a molecular level. There are cruder ways fruit and vegetables might help. I peered at a picture, produced by a scanning electron microscope in an extreme close-up, of the inside of a bowel where the cancerous cells were starting to creep through the colon wall into the rest of the body. It is argued that having good bowel movements by eating plenty of fibre, as you do with fruit and vegetables, means that such cancer cells are less likely to grow on the wall of your bowel; they are scraped away, as if by a road-sweeping truck.

However, all too often small studies are disproved once an expensive, randomized controlled study is carried out, and this was the case with colon cancer and fibre. But then again, what kind of fibre was eaten and did it improve the health of the participants in other ways? Such a study doesn't negate the fact that fruit and vegetables are likely to be good for you, as well as good to eat.

The theories on food and cancer stress that food isn't a magic bullet to zap the grown tumour. Drugs are clearly the most powerful weapons against cancer once it develops. What they stress is that a good day-to-day diet may keep you well at a cellular level, before, during and after cancer. It is eating the nutrients that wash into your cells all the time that may be good, like the 'interior sea' I had read about in Crawford and Marsh's *The Driving Force*. It is about making soups, salads, vegetable dishes and fruit part of your normal everyday food. I found that an approachable and empowering idea. Most of all, I found it a delicious one.

★

Superfoods often seem to be expensive berries. In fact, some of the healthiest foods are plentiful and cheap, such as cabbages. These belong to a family known as cruciferous vegetables because they get their name from the cross at the base of the plant. This is one reason you tell that a Brussels sprout is related to cauliflower, kale and spring greens. You also know because of the cabbagey smell you detect when cutting them or – perish the thought – in overcooking. The smell of these vegetables is both a sign of bad cooking and a clue as to their healthfulness. The sulphurous smell comes from a substance called sulforaphane, and this is thought to protect against cancer. Scientists have also isolated another element thought to be protective, called glucosiolates. These are highly soluble in water. Ideally, you eat cruciferous vegtables raw, or if not, steam them or cook in a soup as lightly as possible. The vegetables need to be chewed to break open the cells and allow the molecules to be metabolized, so give the vegetables a good chew – not difficult if they are raw. Broccoli is by far the best source of sulforaphane and Brussels spouts are also good. As it happens, I'd recently edited a raw sprout salad recipe by the chef Valentine Warner, which used thinly cut sprouts with goat's cheese. Intrigued, I made the dish and it was delicious – a revelation about how to eat sprouts. There are many, many ways to eat sprouts, offsetting their bitterness with cream, sweet fried onions, chestnuts, honey – many more interesting ways than plain old boiled. Taking an interest makes them more interesting.

Garlic, onions and other members of the allium family, such as leeks, shallots and chives, also have a strong smell that indicates potency. Garlic has at least twenty compounds that studies have shown to have anti-cancer properties. To get the most benefit you should crush or chop the cloves slightly in advance of cooking – 5–10 minutes – in order for the active ingredients to get going. It doesn't amount to a great increase, but all the same it has become my assumed routine to chop the garlic first and then get on with the rest of my kitchen prep.

Soybeans and their products are a slightly more controversial food as far as cancer goes. There is some concern that their oestrogens may not be good for post-menopausal women and women who have had breast cancer. Yet it has also been shown to be good to eat 50g of soybean foods a day. Although supplements are sold, it was the whole bean that was used in experiments. There has been a vogue for selling soybeans as beans. But I rather take my cue from how they are eaten in East Asia, where they tend to eat them as fermented or traditionally processed foods. I like tofu for its juicy bounciness and the way it takes up other flavours. It is good as an alternative protein to meat and, coming from the noodle generation, I have fun experimenting in my Anglo-amateur way with Japanese flavourings. My current favourites are the yuzu products, flavoured with a fragrant Japanese citrus fruit, and a Japanese seven-spice mixture that combines two kinds of chilli with orange peel, black and white sesame seeds, ginger and seaweed. It is a simple enough matter to put some cubed tofu in a bowl in the fridge with some crushed garlic, yuzu powder or seven-spice, soy sauce and sesame oil and then toss it through some soba noodles. That said, I felt more certain of converting my partner than his teenage boys.

Turmeric is part of the Indian ayurvedic tradition of healthy eating and was for many centuries consumed in the Okinawa region of Japan in the form of ucchin tea. The habit was forgotten for a time, but has now been revived. In this part of Japan, there are 77 centenarians per 100,000 population. This compares with 15 in the UK and 10 in the US. I didn't fancy the tea (and am not entirely sure about being 100) but did move the turmeric into a more prominent part of my spice box, always remember to put it in curries and dals and now also use it sometimes in marinades for fish. The main active ingredient is curcumin. If you believe that bright colours indicate plant power, then the bright ochre of turmeric is an obvious marker for health (as well as a shirt-stainer for over-enthusiastic curry eaters). The active part of it works better if eaten with black pepper, so I began to include that in curries along with chilli pepper.

It is easy for me to drink a pot of green tea every day as it has become one of my favourite drinks. Since I like the taste, I am only too happy to hear that it may be healthful. The drink has many elements specific to green rather than black tea. Both are made from the same plant, but black tea is fermented and then dried whereas green tea is closer to the original leaf. Not everyone likes the taste. A friend once quipped that green tea has two tastes: pond-water or pond-water with fish in it. They can be bitter fish, too, if you brew it in the wrong way.

I learnt a great deal from talking to two tea experts in London, Alex Fraser of East Teas and Tim d'Offay of Postcard Teas. The key to enjoying green tea is a simple one; brew it for longer at a lower temperature. There are specific temperatures that are best for each tea, but in a rough-and-ready way, I put one-third cold water and two-thirds just-boiled water in the pot or cup to get the right sort of temperature for extracting the goodness and the very wide variety of good tastes from the leaf.

It's not just the taste or the healthfulness that I like; brewing a pot of tea is a calming routine. I'm with the Buddhists who say there are four day-to-day ways to contentment: sitting still, being beside running water, watching fish and drinking tea. There's a burbling fishtank in our kitchen, so I could combine all of these for a quadruple dose of well-being. But of course I take time out to make the tea and then dash back to my computer with my teapot.

The vivid colours of berries – cranberries, blueberries, raspberries, strawberries – are an indicator of healthfulness. Many of the elements of food that are meant to be beneficial are linked to bright colours, which is why the advice is to try to 'eat a rainbow'. The pecking order in berries (and other fruits) in terms of antioxidants is: wild blueberries, cranberries, blackberries, raspberries, strawberries, then apples, cherries, plums, avocadoes, pears, oranges, red grapes and grapefruit. Antioxidants are just one part of the story. There are also many other phytonutrients in fruits and vegetables.

I edited a food booklet for Maggie's written by a health educationist and nutritionist, Kellie Anderson, and subsequently found a number of good recipes on her blog, foodtoglow. For the Maggie's food book, Kellie compiled a useful table listing many of the possible elements that are helpful in food. To take just one, ellagic acid, she says it is a very promising compound that, in animal studies, inhibits the growth of breast, colon and oesophagal cancer cells. Unlike healthy cells, cancer cells 'forget' to die, but in the presence of ellagic acid, they remember. Human studies of this acid have been fast-tracked in the US. In the meantime, the main researchers recommend eating a serving of berries every day. Blueberries contain the highest concentration of this phytonutrient. Other sources include strawberries, cranberries, raspberries, walnuts, pecans and pomegranates. There are many ways of eating more of these – put them on yoghurt, have a fruit salad, snack on them from a bowl in the fridge, use them in Middle Eastern dishes that call for fruit and nuts.

Kellie's recipes are certainly not of the puritanical 'healthy eating' ilk, but full of flavours, colour and freshness. Whilst she is certainly in the 'not-too-much-fat' camp, her stance is that a healthy diet is as much what you include as what you exclude, an overall positive approach to the subject. She is helpful about how best to prepare fruit and vegetables. Vitamins are either water- or fat-soluble, she says. The water-soluble ones need to be eaten every day as they are used or excreted. Most of these are best got from eaten raw or lightly cooked food. Fat-soluble vitamins, such as A, D, E and K, are made more available to you when cooked and stay in the fat in your body, so need to be eaten less often. The advice for watercress, for example, is that it's good to eat raw for its B vitamins and vitamin C, and then good also to sometimes have as a soup for the fat-soluble vitamin K (good for blood clotting), beta-carotene (that becomes vitamin A) and some vitamin E. Either way, even if you are destroying some vitamins you are enhancing others.

*

Going back to Béliveau and Gingras's *Foods to Fight Cancer* list, grapefruit is one of many citrus fruits that are thought to be helpful against cancer. They have an anti-inflammatory action amongst other elements. Grapefruit is so biochemically powerful that it interferes with how drugs are broken down by enzymes and metabolized. People taking statins to lower their cholesterol are told not to drink grapefruit juice nor eat the whole fruit. For those not on these medications, you wonder what else it does in a positive way; the grapefruit is clearly an especially potent form of citrus. It is not the only one. Oranges have 200 different compounds, including 60 polyphenols and a molecule that used to be called vitamin P for its action on capillary blood vessels.

But you have to be careful about getting excited about specific elements in foods. The limonene found in citrus peel, for example, is thought possibly to inhibit tumour growth. Kellie says, however, that you probably need higher amounts than you could feasibly eat for it to be effective, although she thinks organic, unwaxed citrus peel may still be good to include in salad dressings and cooking, not least for taste.

Tomatoes are dealt with at some length in the *Prostate Care Cookbook* because of their suggested protective nature against this particular form of the disease. It is the lycopene in tomatoes that is thought to be good. This becomes far more biochemically available if the tomatoes are cooked and especially with some olive oil. The book's authors recommend some sort of tomato sauce twice a week. Even tomato ketchup is good, at least in terms of lycopene.

Chocolate has a hefty dose of polyphenols, but you need to have 40g of chocolate with 70 per cent cocoa solids to get the possible health benefits. I tend to break off a square from the bar in my fridge when I'm having a post-lunch energy dip. But that is about 10g or so. A piece that is 40g contains 208 calories – a tenth of what I should eat in a day and a bit more than I would want to eat of an intense-tasting bar. Still, having a square or two of chocolate is better for you than a sweet, and much more delicious.

Researching an article on blackcurrants, I took the chance to ask one of the scientists involved in crop growing and research about how micronutrients in blackcurrants might work to make you healthier. Dr Derek Stewart is head of plant products and food quality at the James Hutton Institute, the centre of plant research in Scotland. He has done a survey of twenty fruits to make a superfruit wheel showing how this mighty British berry is top of the crops as a health food, justifying the slogan 'better than blueberries'. It is not just that blackcurrants have a big whack of vitamin C – six berries have the same amount as a large lemon – but they contain many other components. The good news is that these bioactive substances, such as anthocyanins, survive heating and processing, although some (but not all) vitamin C is destroyed. The research was funded by blackcurrant growers, sure, but whatever their bias, they have proved a point.

How do micronutrients work? Dr Stewart said it wasn't easy to know how they acted in the body; this was still part of the 'mystery of life'. We don't really know quite how the body takes these things in. It is thought, however, that they in some way prime the body's own defence mechanisms, giving the enzymes that help in the body's clean-up system a bit of a gee-up. In these phrases I could hear the scientist finding a simple way to describe a hugely complex biological process. I felt grateful that he'd boiled down his thoughts without, I hoped, losing the heart of the argument.

There is, however, a problem: that people don't eat blackcurrants at all because they are too tart. I had some fun trying blackcurrants in various dishes – a Kir trifle (or a Ribena trifle for the kids), a delicious Simon Hopkinson blackcurrant and port jelly, a sauce with duck, smoothies – but it is a stronger-tasting fruit than most, and I wondered whether there has been a general blanding-down of the palate which has resulted in such a berry, however good it is to eat and for your body, falling away from the table.

Right at the end of our conversation, as so often happens in interviews, Dr Stewart said something that was an interesting reality check. The important thing, he said, was to drip-feed them into your body over the long term. Then he said that the benefits of micronutrients are likely to be much greater if received at an early age – it may be that the ages of five to ten years are best of all, and also the teenage years. In other words, by the time you get to the age when you seriously start to think on such matters – i.e. middle age – you are working with an older system and the benefits, whilst still there, would probably not be so great. This comment didn't make me feel like giving up the fruit and veg. But it did make me want to look harder at the topic of how you get children, in particular, to eat their 'five-a-day'.

The 'dosage' of these phytonutrients is an interesting question, and nowhere more so than in the subject of vitamin D and whether we should take it as a supplement.

On the whole, I have felt sceptical about vitamin pills. There was a great deal of excitement in the 1980s and early 1990s when it looked as if the vitamins in particular foods were protective against cancer. I remember asking nutrition professors whether they took the pills. Off the record, some said they did, but they were all a bit sheepish about it because the case wasn't proven. And some were very sceptical. Professor John Garrow, the outspoken nutrition professor at the University of London, called vitamin C 'very expensive urine', because you can easily get enough from food, and the rest is excreted.

At this time, there was a buzz about antioxidants – particularly vitamins A, C and E, conveniently with their own 'ACE' brand tag. But the proof of the pudding is in whether such vitamin pills make a difference on the gold standard of scientific proof: randomized case-controlled studies. The results have surprised many scientists. Not only can such vitamin pills make no difference, but they can be actively harmful. It seems you can have too much of a good thing. Most scientists now believe that diets rich in certain foods seem to be protective, but not pills. Plants and humans are hugely complex biochemical entities. Most of the research is in isolating particular elements to see how they work in a lab. The epidemiological evidence is based on the association that long-living people tend to eat plenty of fruit and vegetables. We don't know why that is, or even that this is the exact reason. But whilst the evidence is not the strongest possible, it offers, at least, a positive pointer in what may well be the right direction.

I had noticed, however, that Walter Willett still took a multi-vitamin. And one vitamin, in particular, is currently causing a big stir. Interest in vitamin D arose in connection with bone strength and the fact that a shortage is linked to the bowed legs of rickets. This is because it affects how we absorb calcium. But scientists around the world are excited by the fact that vitamin D seems to be linked with cellular health. Some believe that it may be protective against up to seventeen types of cancer, coronary heart disease, multiple sclerosis ... well, so many afflictions that it might replace antioxidants as the latest magic bullet.

Vitamin D is known as the sunshine vitamin, because most of it is made when we expose plenty of skin to the high summer sun. Around fifteen to twenty minutes of midday sunbathing provides a good whack. Your body to some extent stores this up, like some form of sun-fat for dark, lean times. Naturally this is controversial because sunbathing can also cause skin cancer. There is also the argument that you should be able to get everything you need from food.

Yet there isn't enough vitamin D in most foods for most people to get what scientists believe is a healthy amount. The main food sources of vitamin D are oily fish (yet another reason to eat them), with herring and mackerel having the highest levels. Meat has more vitamin D potential than is commonly thought, because it has the vitamin in what is called an 'intermediate form' that can then be made into the 'full monty'. But even so it is hard to get enough through what you eat. So either you sunbathe, carefully, or you eat masses of oily fish – far too much to be feasible. Or else you have to go down the supplement route.

There is a stronger case for taking a vitamin D supplement than any other vitamin, if you live in a northern country such as the UK. We have an especially low amount of vitamin D in our blood – six out of ten people don't have enough – because we have so much cloud cover, weak sun and a buttoned-up way of dressing. The UK is on a high latitude, even though it is considered to have a mild climate because of the Gulf Stream's softening maritime influence. Interestingly, rickets used to be known as 'The English Disease'.

I found a strong advocate for vitamin D in Oliver Gillie, a former newspaper health correspondent who has become such an expert on the subject that he is now an academic. After many years of study, he is convinced vitamin D is an important missing element of our diet. When asked about the best way to eat vitamin D, he didn't focus on the food but instead advocated shirtless or bikini-clad lunches in the open air. 'You have to have sunshine, you can't really get it from food,' he says. 'Look at your shadow and when it's shorter than you, you're in business and you can start taking your clothes off.'

Fortification of common foods is one way to go. In the US,

milk and orange juice both have vitamin D added. But some people don't want such additives, others don't like to sunbathe, and most don't want to eat oily fish every day. The answer, therefore, comes in the form of a supplement. Gillie takes 5,000IU of vitamin D a day, as does his wife, and his teenage sons take 3,000IU.

This is where it all becomes controversial. Vitamin D fans think official advice lags badly behind the science. The scientific overview is that not enough gold-standard intervention trials have been done to prove the point, though they admit that there are many other results that seem like positive pointers. The problem is that vitamin D is very inexpensive to make so there isn't enough profit in it for a pharmaceutical company to fund the sort of trials that would prove the point. However, in 2009 there was a significant intervention study on post-menopausal women in Nebraska that showed they were at least 60 per cent less likely to get cancer if they took a supplement of 1,100IU a day with some extra calcium.

The quantity of vitamin D generally advised is between 1,000 and 2,000IU and the health insurance company BUPA recently recommended 2,000IU. The health 'mood music' is tuning in to vitamin D. Cancer Research UK has changed its stance against sunbathing with a Sun Smart campaign to encourage safe sunbathing. But there is still no backing for vitamin D supplements, and Oliver Gillie says the sunbathing advice is generally woefully inadequate if you are really serious about topping up your vitamin D. On the other hand, there are still concerns about skin cancer, and as far as supplements are concerned, there is said to be a risk of vitamin D toxicity, although Gillie says trials show that taking as much as 10,000IU a day can be done safely. The latest US government advice is that up to 4,000IU can be taken safely by adults.

So what to do? On the one hand, I believe that good nutrition is best found in wholefoods. They contain many hundreds of micronutrients that undoubtedly work together in ways that we don't understand. The evidence connecting food and health is down to overall diets and wholefoods, not pills. I am at once sceptical and a touch anxious about taking one element in a large amount in the form of a pill. On the other hand, there is the evidence that, especially at the end of winter, many people have a low amount of vitamin D in their blood. Having learnt how long it is stored in the body, I am going to enjoy lunch outside in the sun whenever I can, and garden and walk in shorts and a T-shirt, though without burning. It is yet another reason for trying to eat oily fish. But I am considering taking vitamin D as a supplement, especially in the winter. My only problem is that when you take pills it does help to be a proper believer – the placebo effect is as high as 30 per cent in trials – and I am probably not certain enough to get this boost. So let's hope, if I do take a supplement, it really does work in its own right.

I was further on in knowing what to eat but still uncertain about what (or what not) to drink. Wine is an essentially civilized part of a meal; it opens up your tastebuds, relaxes, cheers and is convivial. Yet there is much tut-tutting about units of alcohol. A book on how to drink for health by a professor at the William

Harvey Research Institute in London caught my eye. I read Roger Corder's *The Wine Diet* and went to hear him talk.

The Wine Professor in his diet gives a more rounded picture to health than most books, which tend to focus messianically on one point. Diet and lifestyle are the keys to good health, not just wine, he says. Nonetheless, he notes that many chronic conditions, and not just heart disease, share underlying symptoms. One important one is how well your blood vessels and capillaries function. He quotes Sir William Osler, the nineteenth-century Canadian physician cited as one of the founders of modern medicine: 'A man is as old as his arteries.' More than a century on, Corder reckons the key to good cardiac health is to keep the cardiovascular system healthy and to achieve this by the way you live. We each have 100,000 miles of blood vessels in our bodies, and each vessel has a lining called an endothelium. Stresses such as pollution and a poor diet can damage these. To counteract this, Corder prescribes the polyphenols that are plentiful in traditionally made red wine, particularly one kind of polyphenol, the procyanidins. These he can measure, and on this basis can recommend particular kinds of wine that are good to drink.

Throughout my research, I had come across many instances of the way in which production details make a difference to the end result. This was certainly true of the procyanidins in wine, which are found in the skins and pips. Wines made from small red grapes, left to macerate for a reasonable length of time, will have more procyanidins than wines rushed through in modern production methods. Polyphenols tend to be astringent, and modern wine production veers towards easy-drinking gluggers rather than wines with more structure and tannins to counter-balance the lush fruit. Professor Corder's advice took me to more traditionally made wines, and these are rewarding in all sorts of ways. They are wines more likely to be drunk with food, and there is a big difference, in terms of health, between knocking back glassfuls and drinking one or two as part of a meal.

Red wine is high in these polyphenols, but they are present in other foods such as apples, berries and dark chocolate, although modern production methods have also made the latter less healthy than it could be, not least by adding sugar. You didn't want to eat too much of chocolate and get fat, Corder warns, but 25–30g of good dark chocolate is the procyanidin equivalent of a 125ml glass of good red wine, and has about 150 calories, nearly double that of the wine.

During the talk, Professor Corder referred to the way gender difference is important for the advice about drinking. To give just one example, whilst most evidence says that moderate wine drinking – this is surprisingly high at a quarter to half a bottle – was positively beneficial for your heart, just two drinks a day increased your risk of getting breast cancer by just over 20 per cent. He thought a diet rich in fruit and vegetables may be sufficient to counteract this risk, but all the same it was a big caveat to the good news about wine, as far as I was concerned.

I liked the idea of drinking better if I was going to drink less. Professor Corder, clearly a man who enjoyed and explored wine, has linked up with a wine supplier to produce a half-case of wines rich in polyphenols. They are in the range of £10–£14 a bottle, and so for reasons other than tannins, I at least aim to enjoy no more than a glass or two with supper. The wines range from those from Madiran and Cahors in the southwest of France (look for wines with the Tannat grape), to the Douro in Portugal, and from Italy, Barolos and Barbarescos and other wines made from the tannic Nebbilolo grape. Corder also recommends Sardinian wines, and has visited the island where a common greeting is 'A kent' annos' – 'To one hundred years.'

Over the past fifteen years – as long as health and food issues have been some sort of part of my work and life as a food writer – I have felt an increasing sense of frustration over how to deal with the diet and health advice.

For a start, to be told first one thing and then another undermines your confidence. The public health advice is always so definite, but on what basis? To take just one example: we were told to cut down on eggs and seafood because they were high in cholesterol. Then it was said that such forms of dietary cholesterol didn't really count as far as blood cholesterol went. Now some experts question whether blood cholesterol itself is the most important link to heart disease – and even if it is, suggest that it may be caused principally by a diet high in refined carbohydrates rather than saturated fats.

By chance, I saw not one but two doctors at my GP surgery when I went there to get advice about heart disease and cholesterol. I was sufficiently anxious about my chest pains to get some sort of steer, and I had been told that a general health check was available to the over-forties. One of the doctors – who originally trained as a nutritionist – said that cholesterol levels weren't the be-all and end-all of good health, and even if my cholesterol was high (it turned out to be fine), did I really want to go onto medication for decades? When my results came in, this doctor wasn't available. The other doctor at the surgery gave me a stern look when I asked about the issue, said high cholesterol was bad news for a woman after menopause, and was a touch annoyed that I had had a test at all. Whilst not wanting to stretch resources and join the ranks of the 'worried well', I still didn't like being ticked off for wanting to know more about the health of my heart (though of course I sat there meekly and said 'Thank you, doctor'). I left confused: did cholesterol matter or didn't it? Not as much as we are led to believe, it seems – but nobody is entirely sure.

You can't help thinking that dietary advice is often, inevitably, a touch broad-brush. It may be good for some people to cut down on salt, say, but does that mean everyone else has to suffer bland food? The worries about salt come from studying the figures for large populations and are not applicable to every individual. Apparently most people have a perfectly good mechanism for excreting the salt they don't need; just some have a potential problem.

As I was cooking supper one evening, I happened to hear a radio programme on the salt debate which confused me even more. A review paper of the science had just said that the case for cutting back on salt was 'not proven'. This was challenged by the anti-salt scientists, who said salt did matter. Yet another scientist said it didn't matter if you looked at what was 'statistically significant' – but this didn't mean it didn't matter. Aaaaggggghhhh!

I stood there, stirring my pot and thought: Well, I'm not a scientist and can't entirely understand all this. I tried to take my cue from common sense. Over-salted food makes me feel unpleasantly thirsty and it is true that our cave-dwelling ancestors didn't tip it onto every plate but ate what was available in nature. If I eat fresh rather than processed food, then at least I control my salt intake – most of the salt we eat is in processed foods; bread, yes, but even more so in ready-meals and snacks. Good home-cooked food has plenty of flavour without having to be boosted by too much salt. It is also true that if you are light with the salt, or cut back on it, your tastebuds soon adapt. Your food is subtler and, after all, you may be feeding people for whom salt is a serious issue.

Then you can make an adjustment by looking at the type of salt you use. Sea salt has more flavour and you tend to use it more sparingly. Out of interest, I used my digital scales to weigh out what the recommended maximum amount of salt (6g) looked like for both flaked sea salt and standard salt. The sea salt looked like a far bigger heap and would last far longer than the powdery stuff. It was certainly a great deal more than you would consume in a day if you cooked your own food.

All in all, I have seen enough conflicting and imprecise public health messages to at least question what I'm told to do rather than following each headline to the letter and zig-zagging all over the place. This does not mean, however, that I don't listen.

Talking to Walter Willett finally gave me some sort of a breakthrough in the way I thought about the subject of health advice as regards food. Clearly, nobody can be totally and utterly certain of what we should or shouldn't eat. The biochemistry of food and of our own bodies is extraordinarily complex and as yet imperfectly understood. That being the case, I could look at the advice, see how it fitted into my own way of eating and make my own decisions based on what made me feel good and what seemed likely to be true.

And there *is* some sort of consensus about what is most likely to be good to eat, and this has been known for some time. It helps to have this in as few words as possible. Nutrition Professor Marion Nestle has written a book called *What to Eat* (like this book, but without the question mark). Her basic advice boils down to ten words: 'Eat less, move more, eat lots of fruits and vegetables.' She adds to this: 'Go easy on junk foods.' Michael Pollan's dictum amounts to broadly the same message, and he manages it in just seven words: 'Eat food, not too much, mostly plants.'

Both these are based on the evidence as it relates to overall diet and lifestyle, not one particular nutrient. The way forward can – Hallelujah! – be based on delicious, real food.

Can you design a specific diet that means you will avoid heart disease and cancer? There are far too many other elements in play – genes, exercise, environment and so on – to say a resounding 'Yes.' Many of the elements to do with such conditions are nothing to do with food. It may well be about *how* you eat as well as what you eat. There is one theory that the French Paradox (that people in southwest France eat fatty foods and drink lots, but have comparatively low levels of heart disease) can be explained by the fact that they take time to eat lunch together; sociability and relaxation seem to be good for your health. The role that stress plays in disease may well be another piece of the puzzle. What an irony it would be if all the anxiety about food was worse for you than the food itself!

But there are some clear pointers as to what is likely to be best, and I am with Pollan and Nestle on keeping it broad whilst taking an interest in and enjoying the foods that may well be good in every way.

Beyond this, many cancer medics say that there is one particular big fish to fry (or steam) in terms of health and food. Healthiness may be, in the end, not just about how long you take over lunch or the tiny quantities of micronutrients in fruit and vegetables; it may be about the somewhat larger quantities of flesh and fat that sit not on your plate but on your tummy.

WHAT TO EAT?

Easy. Enjoy olive oil; explore different kinds of wholegrains; eat outside in summer; have plenty of fruit and veg in a wide variety of colours; drink a pot of green tea a day.

Worth the Effort. Sit down and take time over meals; find new season's olive oil; have a bowl of salad or a soup with lunch and supper; drink less but better red wine; again, find ways to eat oily fish; explore other cheap 'superfoods'; (perhaps) take a vitamin D supplement in winter.

Hopes and Dreams. That we don't get stressed about contradictory dietary advice but will find a way forward that suits what the individual likes to eat; that there will be a proper shift in thinking about eating good food rather than prescriptive 'healthy eating'; that home cooking, using fresh ingredients, is seen as being right at the heart of food and health; that governments around the world agree to an international ban on trans fats; that fruits and vegetables will be subsidized and made more accessible.

7

Does Any Diet Work?

Around the time that I became more aware of my health, weight began to spread over my stomach. In the past, my waist went in and out, fluctuating with changes in lifestyle. Living in a hill town and walking every day in the summer, I got thinner; when happily holed up in a pub during winter, a little beer belly arrived courtesy of Harvey's award-winning ales. As a food writer, you are surrounded by food. But these seasonal changes and the dash of being alive seemed to keep the kilos at bay. Dieting was not on my agenda.

I went in, I went out … Then I noticed, like so many in their forties, that the movement was one way. I saw my belly move just slightly separately from the rest of me as I walked from shower to bedroom. I looked down and thought: So this is it – middle-aged spread. There was a certain discomfort sitting in particular ways and I had a little less bounce. My clothes moved up a size. How did that happen?

At a certain point I wanted to measure the situation. It wasn't quite as simple as buying a set of scales. Apparently I had to find out whether I was the right weight for my height through a Body Mass Index (BMI). My height is 5 feet 2 inches or 157 centimetres, my weight at this point 65 kilogrammes. According to the graph put on the Internet by the National Health Service, I had a BMI of 26.2 This was officially overweight. As a woman, above a BMI of 25 you are 'overweight' or, even less attractively, 'pre-obese'. My 'maximum healthy weight' was apparently 63kg. But was this the best weight? The risk graph I looked at showed that the risk of diabetes, hypertension (a precursor for stroke) and coronary heart disease all go up in a steady line with your weight, and then heart disease soars after BMI 27.5. But the shocking fact was that all of them start to rise after a BMI of just 22.

I also knew that a high BMI is linked to a higher risk of some of the most common cancers, including breast and prostate, respectively the most common female and male cancers. There are various theories about why this may be the case, such as that being overweight alters the hormones in your blood and this can promote the growth of rogue cells. I was told by a spokesman for the World Cancer Research Fund that it was better to be close to a BMI 20 or so. To get to a BMI of 22, say, I would have to weigh 55 kg and lose 10kg (1½ stone). Losing that amount of weight would be a very big deal. I wouldn't feel myself, quite literally. And I wasn't entirely sure about the BMI measurements. Surely body type makes a difference? In my case it wasn't to do with 'big bones' as much as curves. In my kinder moments, I would say I have an hour-glass shape. But over the past year or two, in all honesty it has become rather more of a pint-glass.

I went to the BBC's Health pages and read an article by a doctor. Apparently your BMI is now no longer seen as the be-all and end-all. Waist measurement is a better indication of whether you are more at risk of ill health (and an untimely death). A woman's waist should not be more than 80cm (or 32 inches). Apparently it was my hip-to-waist ratio that mattered most and weight stored around the tummy is the problem. Abdominal fat is more 'metabolically active' than fat stored elsewhere. I was told to divide my waist measurement by my hips. If the ratio was more than 0.8, then as a woman I was an 'apple' shape and that was bad.

First of all, I had to find my waist – perhaps an early indication that all was not well. The correct place is halfway between your lowest rib and your hip bone, and you have to breathe out as you measure, no cheating. I had to poke around a bit to find my bottom rib. My waist was 38 inches – six whole inches bigger than it should be. It seemed like a great deal. I suppose if you 'pinch an inch' all the way around your middle, it adds up. My hope was that my sturdy hips would mean I was technically in proportion. My hips were 43 inches. The ratio between the two was 0.88. I was an apple.

Surely, I thought, *surely* weight and waist aren't everything. I thought of my Scottish great-aunts and grandmother, all comfortably foursquare, who had lived to a good age. I knew them when they were post-menopausal, and perhaps that made a difference. But looking at old family photographs, when they were younger, they still carried some inches.

And no, weight isn't everything, and nor is body type. Yet another study was published in the *Lancet* in 2011. It measured the connection between heart disease and obesity amongst 220,000 adults. It showed that obesity (a BMI above 30) was a risk factor, but not body shape. Did it matter if you were merely a bit plump? The website of the British Heart Foundation said that being *either* overweight *or* obese was 'very likely' to increase the risk of heart disease. I wasn't off the hook. And the cancer people are pretty strong on weight being an issue.

Beyond this, the BBC website had told me to be aware of lack of exercise (half a tick), a poor diet (what exactly did that mean?), smoking (negative) and alcohol (big tick). Perhaps I wouldn't live as long as my forebears.

Reluctantly, though perhaps with some of the smugness of the incipient self-improver, I decided that I probably did need to lose some weight, though not 10 kilos. It wasn't about looks and it wasn't even, really, about future health. It was mostly because I knew I felt better in my day-to-day life when I was carrying a bit less. Whatever the reason, it seemed pointless to go on a crash diet. I wanted, if possible, to lose weight in such a way that got the basic building blocks of my diet on a better footing.

Healthy eating, I had discovered, is not as set in stone as you might think, but there is a basic consensus. You could summarize it as the following: eat a diet that has variety and balance; cut back as much as possible on processed foods; eat plenty of fruit and vegetables; don't drink too much; don't eat too much red and processed meat; don't be overweight. Beyond this was another idea, related to the last two: eat the right fats in the right quantity. By this, health pundits tend to mean not too many saturated fats and certainly no trans fats.

The general medical line is that a healthy diet like this allows you to achieve and maintain a healthy weight. It sounds plausible. If you eat less fat and drink less alcohol and have lots of fruit and vegetables instead of lots of red meat and cakes and biscuits, you are effectively on a diet (so long as your portions are all right). It sounded as though this strategy might work in the long run if I could do it.

I had, thus far, been a diet refusenik. This is, in part, because I am a diet book refusenik. I do own a stack, picked up over the years, generally in January. The Wellcome Trust in London has a vast collection of 700 diet books, a number of them bestsellers. If any of them really worked, this pile would be considerably smaller. But whilst the prose slips down easily enough, the advice is ultimately indigestible. Whatever the theme – no fat/high fat, just grapefruit, just cabbage, just juices – they have a basic style in common: an evangelical certainty combined with a complete lack of realism.

Recipe books have a certain spell-like quality – combining egg yolks and oil to make mayonnaise springs to mind – but diet books really are hocus-pocus. Read any one and you feel absolutely certain that this is The Answer. But by the time you've flicked on to the six-week eating plan, belief falls away. It's completely simple, each one promises: just give up everything you like eating and have *this* instead. Picking one off my shelf at random I find a list of recipes such as Power Shakes made with protein powder as meal replacements; pasta made with soya flour; a pudding made by mixing sugar-free lemon-flavoured jelly crystals with tomato juice; and dishes with garlic powder and onion powder, as if meals were the flavourings from a packet of crisps (but without the crisps).

This is why diet bibles annoy me so much. They have evolved recipes and a meta-language about food that have nothing to do with breakfast, lunch, dinner and all points in between and rarely engage in the pleasures and reality of eating. Instead, in an insidious way, they promote a bad attitude towards the table. The idea is that food is mostly there to affect how you look rather than giving you energy, companionship and happiness. A number of women I know see food, essentially, as 'the enemy', to be beaten down and avoided, with endless tactics and obsessive plotting. This misses the point in so many ways – not least that food is there primarily to keep you alive and give you health and energy. The really worrying part is that dieters are often those who are in charge of children's food, and an inhibited attitude to food can be passed on like mother's milk. People get upset about eating disorders such as anorexia, but widespread yo-yo dieting is a far bigger problem because of its scale.

Yet there is a great deal of pressure to be thin, from both without and within. Sure, you can try to make an effort to avoid paying attention to celebrity pap and the endless pictures of bodies that have had time and money and effort poured into making them look the right way for a camera. But adverts and articles featuring Photoshopped bodies are *everywhere*. And then what about films and television?

I found myself appraising people in the street. Being slim wasn't really so great, I thought. It mainly seems to happen to people in their teens and twenties. I had earned my belly; it was proof of all the good food I had eaten and my convivial times around the table. It was the ballast of my knowledge, picked up in forkfuls over the years. Perhaps the underlying impulse behind dieting is a wish to be young again; you want to have the slenderness of your youth. If so, there's more than a touch of poignant futility to the whole enterprise.

And yet … I had begun to see how weight might affect how long I would live and, rather more importantly, how much energy I had every day. For the first time in my life, I started to look seriously at going on a diet.

The authors of some of the most recent diet books have come up with recipes that at least relate to real food. But there is still a theme. Carbohydrates are now the big issue. Following on from the Atkins Diet, the latest diets say that you can eat whatever you like (more or less) – so long as you cut out or severely restrict the carbs. No bread, no rice, no pasta, no root vegetables, not much fruit, if any, and certainly no bananas or grapes, which have sugars that apparently go quickly to your tum.

The mechanics of carbohydrates and weight sounded interesting and I wanted to know more. But I had some initial reservations, to say the least. I was sceptical about anything that would put me off eating fruit, which gives me pleasure and is full of micronutrients and fibre. In this and other ways, such diets go directly against the consensus about what is a healthy diet and, more importantly, what feels natural to eat. A sandwich without the bread? A burger without the bun? Pasta without the pasta? Carbohydrates form the base of most dishes, not least because they are less expensive than protein. They provide us with quick and good energy. The books talk disapprovingly of the 'sugar rush' you get from carbohydrates, but after all you are eating food precisely in order to give you energy.

Yet I knew a number of people who kept saying that low-carb diets were different: they worked. The couple who run my local bookshop shed stones on the low-carb Atkins Diet. I got talking to them as I bought a couple of diet books (it was January). Our conversation showed me why such dieters often come in pairs. Low-carb is a different way of eating, and would be hard to do alone within a household. But whilst there wasn't much choice when they went out to eat, they said it was easy at home. Talking further, their low-carb diet seemed as restrictive as a calorie-controlled diet, just in a different way, but it had certainly worked for them.

Diets are notorious for not working. Could low-carb diets – Atkins et al. – be bucking the trend? If so, how? And whilst they might work for a few weeks, or a few months, do they work long-term?

Because diet books are so bizarrely over-certain – evangelical, in a word – I first wanted to get to grips with some fundamentals to understand what was really going on. The anti-carb brigade's case for what causes weight loss and weight gain rests on the idea that a calorie is not just a calorie: it depends on how we digest and use that calorie. Richard Wrangham makes a similar point in his book about evolution and food. His point is that we get more calories from cooked than raw food: the value in food is different depending on how it is prepared and digested. But what is a calorie? And what is digestion, for that matter?

The science of eating was my favourite part of biology lessons when I was at school. The cross-section of a human body reveals a fairground ride of loop-the-loops and gurgling, pumping tubes and organs that your food slides down like a slow-mo helter-skelter. Squirting ducts spray out strangely named chemicals, and something called a pancreas is involved – what was that? I was more familiar with the liver, which turned up at lunch on a plate with onions and mashed potato. The school-dinner livers had repulsive tubes. I could now imagine that these might have a function.

Then your food goes into the small intestine and colon that are, we were told, miles long and with an absorbent area as big as a football pitch. How did all this fit into my middle? And how strange to have parts of your body that you can't picture as you can your head, shoulders, knees and toes, and that all this is going on inside, without your active knowledge or control.

Of course you don't think about your digestion; it would be far too self-conscious. Navel gazing is bad enough without staring within as well. You only pay attention to your innards when there is a problem. But why shouldn't they be interesting – especially if a better understanding could help me lose some weight?

I began to imagine a plate of food as it went through the fun-park of this inner world, step by step.

The forkfuls go into my mouth, and saliva immediately starts to make them into something other than food, breaking down the starches, along with my grinding teeth. This is pre-digestion; no nutrients are absorbed. I remembered the notorious 'chew-spit' diet of certain celebrities in the 1990s, the ultimate in consumer decadence – to not consume. More constructively, the nineteenth-century American dietary guru Horace Fletcher, known as the Great Masticator, instructed his disciples to chew each mouthful thirty-two times to get the most from their food.

There is some point in keeping food in your mouth for longer, but for me that is as much to do with taste as digestion. As you chew and breathe, the flavour molecules are released and drawn, by breathing, into your nose where your smell receptors are located. Strange to say, the taste of food happens mostly in your nose, although the tongue has the basic receptors to distinguish salty, sweet, sour and so on.

Eating a little more slowly and consciously made me taste more and also appreciate texture – the cool, juicy slipperiness of mango, the succulence of pork belly – just as wine lovers appreciate the haunting viscosity of a good wine that holds traces of a place and its grapes. Taking more time at the table helped me look more at the food I was eating and its colours and shapes, to enjoy it sensually on the plate as well as the palate.

You really do get more from food by using your tongue, I thought as I chewed (at somewhat less than Horace Fletcher's quota). When I began to flex my tongue muscles a little more, I realized how much I had become a gobbler. An American farmer once tried to explain what had gone wrong with American food culture. 'The problem is there's an attitude to food that is gobble and squat,' he had said. He may have said 'squat and gobble', but that's not how I remember it, perhaps because his basic point was to describe a very bare-boned functionality to the whole process of eating, and the phrase stuck in my head. Once eating becomes so functional, you stop appreciating and enjoying your food. Instead, you gulp it down. Squat, gobble, squat. 'Gourmet' has connotations of snobbery and self-indulgence, but simply to appreciate food is a good way of eating. You eat more slowly, appreciate what you have, eat a bit less and get more altogether from your plateful. Relaxing is good for your health and well-being. This is all about eating well, not just about weight loss or, dread phrase, 'healthy eating'.

Eating more slowly is a little like being a child again. When I started to eat regularly with young children once more, they seemed so incredibly slow. Why don't they just sit down and chomp and get on with it, I wondered? Why does it take such a long time? I read up on the subject and realized that a child has much more sensitive sense organs and hence some of the faddiness and suspicion of new foods. Cooking at home, I learnt that my partner's 11-year-old didn't much like cooked vegetables, except tomatoes, which *had* to be cooked. It became easy to know what to put on his plate when I realized it was a matter of texture – that he loved crunchy carrots and crisp peppers and juicy cucumbers but hated – really hated – certain vegetables that had been cooked, especially the slithery creatures he called 'evil cucumbers' (courgettes). I learnt from him to relish the crisp juiciness of an apple once again, and to understand that what may seem fussiness in kids is also appreciation of texture.

★

The food goes in, and then your body – that is, you, as I keep having to remind myself about this alien space within – takes over, trying to extract the most nutrition possible. Even before you start to eat, your body prepares to digest. The mere smell of sweet food apparently makes your carb-digesting hormones start to squirt. The whole process happens within what is known as the alimentary tract. All animals have one – even a prawn does. I knew this from being advised in cookbooks to remove the dark thread curving over the back; this is the prawn's last meal, in effect. Our digestive system is particularly sophisticated and efficient, so we make the most of the calories and nutrition in food, as Richard Wrangham points out in his discussion about human evolution.

The food reaches the stomach. This is said to 'pump and pummel' the food to break it down in 'peristaltic waves', words that suggest such violent churning that I can hardly believe it is going on without my feeling it. Your stomach is said to churn in horror, but in fact it does so the whole time during digestion. I know a bit about how a stomach moves because I have seen inside one. A mischievous doctor acquaintance, knowing I was a food writer, invited me to his hospital to get more closely acquainted with what happens after the plate. I found myself in medical overalls watching an endoscopy, when they put a little camera down the oesophagus and into the stomach. The picture on the screen enables the doctors to investigate and work on your insides. I am ashamed to say that the sight of livid, slicked internals combined with the rasping of the poor patient and the sound and smell of the whole operation was too much for me – stomach-churning, in fact. No wonder we don't want to know too much. These days, there is footage from endoscopies on the appropriately named 'YouTube', but I wouldn't recommend viewing them before supper.

The main point about the stomach, as far as dieting is concerned, is that it reacts quite differently to different kinds of foods. Fats are not water-soluble and need to be emulsified before being digested. They therefore need to spend longer in your stomach being broken down. This means that your stomach feels fuller for longer, and you don't get the stomach rumbles that signal 'More please!' Protein also takes longer to go through. If you have a snack, it will keep you fuller for longer if it includes a bit of protein. A low-fat meal, of whatever size, just means you soon feel hungry again and then you eat more, or at the very least sit there thinking about your stomach.

It also makes a difference if the food in your stomach is a bit lumpy rather than just fine particles. If it needs to be broken down more, then it stays in your stomach for longer. This is not to say you should bolt down great gobbets – the eat-like-a-dog diet – but it does mean that processed foods with their easy-to-eatness are going to fill you up less in a physical sense. Fast is the word, quick is the action.

Once your food has been broken down to a slurry, it is now all about absorption into the body. Some 90 per cent of this happens in the small intestine and the large intestine, or colon. In the colon, microbes work on the remnants of your food to extract more nutrition. Some other creatures do this by simply eating their faeces, as a rabbit does, but we – or our microbes – do it 'in-house'.

The whole process is said to take a few days to happen completely, but my observations of large, gulped-down pieces of spinach and beetroot show that most of it is much quicker – a matter of here today, gone tomorrow. This may be to do with the fact that I eat lots of fruit and vegetables, providing plenty of roughage to keep the show on the road.

Some 70 per cent of our immune system is thought to be connected to the alimentary tract, a fact that becomes very obvious when you have food poisoning and feel so hopelessly floppy and prone to other bugs. There has been renewed attention to gut health in recent years from the pro- and prebiotics industry, which is now a £100bn-a-year market. Probiotics and prebiotics work in different ways. Probiotics are microbes that help you digest what you have eaten and prebiotics are there to help the beneficial microbes that are already in your gut. Apparently we are mostly microbial, excreting our own weight in bacteria every year, and the health of your gut bugs matters.

I went along to a talk that two digestion experts gave to a group of health writers, who – almost inevitably – get funding from the pro- and prebiotics industry. A recent EU ruling had said that the health claims for some of the commercial probiotic products were unproven. However, they can still be said to have the status of 'can't do any harm and may do some good'. A couple of types in particular, the experts said, might be effective and could have implications for bowel and stomach cancer, food poisoning and bone health. It was also possible they might help with blood cholesterol and through this perhaps heart disease.

I came away thinking that if I had taken antibiotics then I would consider taking such products to build up my gut flora again, but not otherwise, on present evidence. Obtaining prebiotics is a matter of eating slippery foods such as onions and okra, which is easy enough and cheaper than pills.

More broadly, I knew from the Oxford Symposium of Food and Cooking on fermented foods (see chapter 3), and from my researches into evolution and food, that we live in symbiosis with microbes, and this is an aspect of eating to be valued, if not necessarily to be popped as pills or eaten in little pots. The food scientist Harold McGee thinks his father's life was partly saved by yoghurt when he fell ill in India and was given a helping to get back on his feet. Villages have extraordinary yoghurt cultures that have been kept going for years, he said, and one of these helped rebuild his father's gut health.

Now I knew a little bit more about my inner space, I wanted to know more about what to put inside, and to address the biggest debate in the diet world: whether you should cut down on a particular type of food or just reduce your total calories.

Supporters of low-carb diets say the key is cutting out or severely restricting carbohydrates for one reason: a mechanism called 'ketosis'. Dr Atkins, the low-carb guru, was the man who popularized this concept. A cardiac doctor with a weight problem – he put on nearly 23kg in his early thirties – he delved into the medical literature and realized that it would be possible to eat many of the foods he loved, such as butter, cream, cheese and meat, and still lose weight.

The theory goes like this. Our usual energy source is glucose, which comes from eating carbohydrates, be it a baked potato or a Mars Bar. But if you severely restrict carbohydrates, to 60g or less a day (a slice of bread is about 12–15g carbs, an egg-sized potato is 10g), the body has to switch to another energy source: stored fat. Ketosis is a mechanism that goes back to our evolution as hunter-gatherers, who had to survive times of feast and famine. If you are a woman, the process of ketosis starts earlier than if you are a man – after one or two days' dieting, rather that three or four. This is thought to be down to the realpolitik of evolution: a man's sperm is profligate and can further his genes far and wide, so you need fewer men. It is more important that a woman survives with her fewer eggs.

Greatly restricting carbs means you are soon in a state of ketosis, or 'burning fat'. This means there is a rise in the blood of ketones, acidic chemicals that are released as part of fat metabolism, which accounts for the 'peardrop' breath of ketogenic dieters. Ketones are appetite suppressants, and, along with the fact that fat and protein take longer to digest and keep you feeling fuller for longer, it is feasible that low-carb diets are low-calorie diets in another guise. There is only so much meat and other animal protein you can eat.

It sounds a bit dog-like, stuffing yourself with animal protein. Such diets go totally against current healthy eating advice, which is to base your meals on wholefood carbohydrates. Doctors mutter dark warnings about low-carb diets, saying they make your body acidic, potentially leaching calcium and minerals from your body and leading to kidney problems. The diets often encourage people to eat more saturated fats and therefore could increase the risk of heart disease and cancer (even if you are thinner). Some make you restrict or abstain from vitamin-rich foods such as fruits and some vegetables. Atkins's original diet was pretty hardcore on fruit and even restrictive on vegetables, although the latest versions of the diet have loosened up.

Yet proponents of low-carb diets, including some NHS obesity specialists, argue that low-carb diets are safe and that the medical objections are theoretical and not proven. Carb-counting is an effective way of losing weight, they say, and the government is doing dieters a disservice by encouraging the overweight and obese to eat grains and potatoes since it is these, they argue, that may be the problem in the first place.

When I read Gary Taubes's iconoclastic book about carbohydrates, *The Diet Delusion*, I realized I had walked into a really interesting controversy that could have much greater implications for my health than simply shedding some kilos.

Taubes is a science journalist whose *modus operandi* is to look at accepted public health advice and then to go back to the original evidence that it is based upon in order to see if it really holds up. His conclusion about healthy eating and dieting is that the evidence for low-fat diets is extremely flimsy. For him, and for a small but adamant group of scientists, the finger should be pointed not at fat at all but at carbohydrates. It is the bun, not the burger, that can make us fat; the chips, not the sausages.

To understand this, Taubes goes into the biochemistry of the body and in particular what makes us fat in the first place. He cites some fascinating experiments, both on animals and on humans, that provide pointers. First of all, it is clear that a great deal is genetic. We all know people who can eat like a horse but remain the size of a foal. In one 1960s experiment, an endocrinologist called Ethan Sims fed convicts at Vermont State Prison ever-growing meals, increasing their calorie consumption to 4,000 a day. Then he upped it to 5,000, then to 7,000, then 10,000. All in all, the inmates had thirty weeks of this punishing piggery. Of the eight convicts, two put on a lot of weight easily, but six didn't. Sims's conclusion was that our bodies adapt to over-nutrition in different ways. Professor John Garrow, the lean professor of obesity whom I had talked to in the past about vitamin pills, tried to put on weight by eating an extra 1,200 calories a day. He found it incredibly difficult, finally managing the task through eating copious chocolate biscuits (an experiment copied during countless office tea-breaks around the world).

It also seems that certain parts of our body are prone to putting on weight. In one famous case, reported in 1908, a 12-year-old girl was given a skin graft from her abdomen to repair the burned back of her hand. When she reached her thirties, she had become fat. This included not just her thighs and stomach but, in a bizarre twist, the skin on the back of her hand. She needed an operation to remove the big fat pads.

All this made me think how awful – almost tragic – it is that so many women want to be a particular shape and spend so much energy trying to have a small bottom, say, when this was just meant to be, at least to some degree. In the meantime, we set up a hopeless and negative relationship with food. You may want to be Kate Moss but end up as Queen Canute.

So there is a genetic predisposition both to putting on weight and to where this happens . Many think that weight gain is partly a result of your metabolism becoming less active once you are past your physical peak, which I am afraid is the twenties. It's also not unusual to become less active as you get older. Perhaps you drive a car rather than bicycling; perhaps you sit at home watching television rather than going out dancing. Yet we keep eating the same amount – or even more – even though our bodies no longer require the same number of calories. This is what leads to the infamous 'middle-age spread'.

But it is clearly not just about age. I remember watching a softball game of overweight 12-year-olds in the US and thinking: Wow, these are the *sporty* ones, as they wobbled between bases.

Taubes, in fact, turns this sequence around. His theory is that eating too many carbohydrates, and processed ones in particular, lies behind weight gain at all ages and behind the modern obesity epidemic. He points out, as many have, that during the very time we were encouraged by health messages to go onto low-fat diets, we got fatter. One of the problems was that people switched from fatty foods to processed carbs such as bread and low-fat but sugary cereals. These were meant to be 'good'. But such foods make you release insulin – the mere smell (or even thought) of sugar or any carbohydrate-rich food is enough to trigger this. Taubes says that insulin causes calories, excess or not, to be locked up in the fat tissue and it tells our body not to burn that fat. If we eat too many carbohydrates too often – all that snacking – then we are going to put on fat, even if we are actively trying to eat less and exercise more. 'It's not metabolism that changes, leading to an increase in fat storage, but the hormonal environment determining fat storage that changes,' he says.

Taubes points out that cutting down on carbs is nothing new in the world of dieting. It used to be standard knowledge that if you wanted to lose weight then you cut down on spuds. Vronsky in *Anna Karenina* cuts down on the potatoes but not the steak to get to a better weight for his horse race. But we seem to have forgotten this time-honoured trick of trimming back, and, as I had discovered in my Best Breakfast research, the industrial carpet of carbs rolls out all too easily into breakfast, lunch, tea, supper and all points in between.

So I tried eating mostly protein. Breakfast was ham and eggs; lunch was cheese or an omelette, or a cheesy omelette, and a vast salad; dinner a steak or other piece of meat or fish, and three kinds of veg. But it didn't last long – just a couple of days. First of all, I found myself becoming bad-tempered and my attention span would suddenly crash. Beyond this, it was too weird and too expensive. I didn't feel happy stuffing myself with all those animals. I thought about food the whole time, and not in a good way. Eating this much protein didn't feel right from an environmental point of view; I had read about the carbon footprint of meat. Yes, I could see how such a diet might help you lose weight. But for me it wasn't possible in the short term, let alone the long. It wasn't hunger that stopped me following the diet, but there were plenty of other reasons. Not least of these was that the diet felt so unbalanced. The anti-*carbonistas* might have a point, but they had surely gone too far in the other direction.

Yet whilst I didn't feel the need to cut out carbohydrates altogether, simply being more aware of the role they played in weight gain meant I ate fewer. Instead of having four potatoes, I had two; instead of a big plateful of pasta, I had a smaller portion with a bit more sauce. My biggest discovery was that it wasn't necessary to always have carbohydrates at night, or very few. All I was doing was going to sleep, and that doesn't take much energy. But I did have – and need – bread and other carbohydrates such as porridge for breakfast. After all, this is when you want energy, and fast. When I had just ham and a poached egg, my energy dipped and I became tetchy by mid-morning. I also need carbohydrates for lunch to keep me going.

As for puddings, cakes and biscuits, these aren't my particular bent but my carb-awareness meant they became more explicitly a treat – and all the nicer for this. When it comes to any way of eating, there is in any case a 80:20 principle that seems to me fairly sound: you do what you should for about 80 per cent of the time and otherwise do what you want. This conveniently ties (roughly) into weekdays and weekends. Baking was for weekends – well, mostly.

After several months of eating more carefully like this and slightly adjusting my diet I noticed that I had shed a kilo. Furthermore, the slight chest pains I had been getting had gone.

★

Intrigued, I then talked to a few of the medics who were advocating low-carb diets for weight loss.

The most outspoken was Richard Feinman, director of the Nutrition and Metabolism Society in the US. Feinman is a radical because he is going against the standard government advice, which is to lose weight through a standard 'healthy diet' – low fat, wholefood carbs. He thinks that low-carb diets have a big role to play. 'If you don't have a weight problem and no risk of diabetes and heart disease then eat whatever you eat,' he said. 'If you do have any of those factors, a low-carb diet should be the "default diet", the first one you try.' He told me what he had recently told an obesity conference: 'If you want to lose weight, don't eat; if you have to eat, don't eat carbs; if you have to eat carbs, eat low g.i. [glycaemic index] carbs.'

Feinman immediately questioned me about my own experience of lower-carb diets. I had lost some weight but couldn't be sure if it was down to lower carbs or lower calories. You have to learn to evaluate things for yourself, he said. Observing your own experience is science, too, and this is often forgotten in a country (he was speaking of the the US) where people want to have an MRI scan to tell them whether they are healthy or not. It was a good point. Of course, constantly testing your body can make you cranky. But why not try something out sensibly, without the blind faith of a follower of a diet guru, and assess what works for you through tweaks to your diet, from your own likes and dislikes? Eating is so individual and so are our bodies, to some degree.

Feinman thinks the evidence that supports Atkins-style diets has not been given proper airtime. It is difficult to get such work published at all because it goes against the accepted 'healthy eating' dogma. There is no evidence that ketogenic diets are harmful to the standard dieter, he said, and he was frustrated that concerns over kidney problems are repeated again and again when they are not proven. On the contrary, he said ketogenic diets are now thought to be beneficial and are being investigated for their therapeutic application. People with diabetes may have problems with their kidneys, but this arises from the condition itself, and low-carb diets have been shown to help people control this, he argued.

Low-carb diets are high-veg diets, in Feinman's opinion. 'Suppose your dinner is steak and potatoes and broccoli. If you take out the potatoes, are you going to put in another steak? Its much more likely you'll eat more broccoli.'

There have now been studies comparing low-carb diets with low-fat ones. One of these was cited by Tom Sanders in his lecture on fats as evidence that in the end weight loss is all about calories. Led by Frank Sacks at the Harvard School of Public Health and published in the *New England Journal of Medicine* in 2009, the study followed some 800 dieters. The main conclusion was that cutting calories worked, whatever type of nutrient was lowered. Feinman was highly critic of this particular study, saying that there was poor adherence to the diet. Other low-*carbonistas* say the diet wasn't low-carb enough to work properly in any case. When you see such studies from their perspective, you can see how the evidence may be a bit skewed.

Another study, published in the *Journal of American Medicine*

Association in 2007, followed 300 women for twelve months on four different diets. Its findings showed the Atkins Diet to be the most successful and the best for the blood cholesterol profile. I watched an Internet clip of the study's leader, Christopher Gardner, who said he had issues with the diet. The figure was an average – the diet had worked well for some and not for others – and he didn't know if it would work in the long term. Then he speculated that it could be the simplicity of the diet that made it effective; simply cut down, or cut out, carbs. Since these provide about 45–55 per cent of the average American's calories, cutting them down would have a big impact. Satiety also seemed to be a factor. He wondered if this was the secret of the diet: you feel fuller on fats and proteins. Here was another indication that fats had a role to play in a good diet – even for weight loss.

There have been other studies, says Feinman, that show low-carb diets work. The strongest evidence comes from short-term studies, he admits, but that doesn't mean to say they couldn't work over time.

Finally, I spoke to Iain Broom, an obesity consultant now retired from Aberdeen Royal Infirmary, who has a particular interest in ketogenic diets. He was less combative than his American colleagues but felt strongly that low-carbohydrate diets could be very useful if patients couldn't lose weight with the standard government-recommended approach – low fat, 'healthy eating'. He had seen many seriously obese patients whose problem was eating too many carbohydrates, and so it made sense to cut down on these.

Broom's diet allows one piece of fruit and day; no potatoes, rice or pasta; and controlled amounts of other root vegetables because they contain a lot of starch. Lots of green leafy vegetables are allowed, but no bananas and no grapes. Tomatoes are a fruit, and two or three cherry tomatoes or one large one are permitted. Then he had some more orthodox advice. 'No cakes,' he said. 'These are things that are not natural to us in the first place. Man is a hunter-gatherer who would have eaten berries and meat but not agricultural products.' We were back to the Paleo Diet again.

Getting towards half of all men in England are now overweight and 22 per cent are obese. The number of women overweight is 33 per cent of the population and 24 per cent are obese. The obesity figures have roughly doubled since the mid-1980s. The grim fact is that these figures may be altered back again by an epidemic of type-2 diabetes and children dying before their parents, said Professor Broom. Doctors were now seeing type-2 diabetes in people in their early teens.

I asked what caused obesity. Professor Broom didn't put it down to one single factor, such as carbohydrates. He said: 'There are complex environmental factors, the food industry, the way we eat, the way we live. Globalization and the free market economy seem to have an effect, stress, job security, and the way people work.' In other words, the problem could be caused by such habits as eating on the hoof instead of sitting down to meals, rather than just by what we are eating.

Could these other factors be important for weight loss? It feels far too simplistic to say 'eat less' when there are many reasons, psychological and environmental as well as physical, that lead us to eat too much in the first place.

I wanted to get away from the narrow focus on nutrients and see the bigger picture. One of the major theories about weight gain is that we live in a world that puts food in our path at every step. A phrase for this was coined in Australia in the 1990s: that we live in an 'obesogenic' society.

Walk out of the door – or rather rush out of it in haste, late and over-busy and without breakfast – and there is the coffee shop by the train station with pastries and milky lattes. Get to work and there is the vending machine and the biscuit-break. Flick through a magazine or look at the television and the adverts are for tempting processed foods, sold as part of a lifestyle package. One of Michael Pollan's dictums in his excellent guide, *Food Rules: An Eater's Manual*, is 'avoid foods you see advertised on television'. More than two-thirds of food advertising is devoted to processed foods and alcohol, he says.

Sit down in the canteen or take a break from your home computer and there is the nice olive-oily Italian bread, cheeses, the quick slices of salami that are there ready for fridge snacking. After work, the glass of chilled white wine is your mind's commute back to being yourself again. Drinking makes you hungry for reasons not yet fully understood. You have some crisps, or nuts; then some more. At the restaurant, the bread comes on the table. It is much nicer with butter. You talk and slather and munch and sip. Why not a starter? Then the main course comes with buttery potatoes and fills the plate. The pudding is shared since it is so rich, each mouthful eaten with great pleasure. It's only half the pudding, but the pudding is quite big. You are not hungry, but each course somehow renews your appetite. Perhaps you pick at a bit of cheese. A chocolate comes with coffee.

The point is not that we are greedy-guts but that unless you make a very conscious effort not to eat too much in what is, undoubtedly, an obesogenic world, you may well end up doing so. In a world of plenty and plentiful choices, many of them designed to please you with fat and sugar, we become overweight by default.

Now this may sound like a feeble excuse for poor willpower, but when I started to look at the mechanisms of overeating I could see all too clearly that this was the case, and I wondered why I wasn't far fatter.

I went to a talk given to the Guild of Food Writers by Andrew Hill, a psychology professor at the Institute of Health Sciences, University of Leeds. As an opening gambit, he asked how many times we made food and drink decisions in any single day. The audience was composed of people who think about food all the time, both as a living and a way of life. I mentally totted up what I had decided to eat the day before – what kind of honey to put on my toast; cheese or ham with my soup; what vegetables to have with the chops I had eaten for supper; whether to have some yoghurt afterwards or plums and cream – and came up with the number 24. The true answer, with the bizarre precision of a scientific study, was 226.7. When I thought about it, there are many, many points during the day when you decide what to eat and, crucially, how much. All of us drastically underestimated the number of decisions by a great margin because most are unconscious. And these unconscious decisions can all too easily lead us to eat too much in our obesogenic world.

I began to look at the work of psychologists who are discovering why we eat what we eat. One celebrated scientist, Paul Rozin, has studied the difference between how people eat in McDonald's in America and Paris. In the US, the portion sizes were a staggering 25 per cent bigger than in France. Admittedly, there is a 'doggy-bag' culture in the US – but surely not in fast food joints where the food comes in a form of doggy-bag in the first place? Such large portions are unimaginable in France where you hear the polite but firm phrase to cut off the extra serving spoonful: '*Ça suffit.*' Not only do fast food customers eat less in France, but they take longer to do so; even fast food has various gears. There is also more of a cultural norm about eating at set mealtimes. The very words used by the French for eating otherwise are American: *le snack* and *le fastfood*. And of course being overweight is *non, non, non*: not chic at all!

Wherever you do it, eating out is part of the weight problem. We eat more when there is more choice, as in a work canteen buffet or with a large menu of different courses. We eat more when food is prepared by someone else. When we eat out, the food is generally higher in calories because fat and sugar are an easy (and cheap) way to please, and we eat more when foods taste delicious as they push our evolutionary buttons. We are not the only creatures to do so. I read about one experiment in which rats, normally offered the unappealingly named 'ratchow', were then offered the more varied choice of a 'supermarket diet'. Guess which one they chose? At the talk I attended in

London, Richard Wrangham showed a sadly comic picture of an overweight hedgehog like an inflated pincushion. This happens when they favour the cooked food put out for them by humans rather than what they are meant to eat.

The reasons we cook less at home are many and varied, but there is now, said Andrew Hill, a greater 'opportunity cost' to home cooking: instead of chopping onions we could be working instead, or enjoying any number of other leisure activities. I remember talking to a French woman who had moved to England. 'The English do so many other things,' she said, delighted by our packaged-food culture. 'They have time to sing in choirs!' I'm not purist about having to cook everything all the time, but home-cooked food is still the bedrock of good eating, the peeling of carrots, the bowl of salad, and – yes – the baked potato, whatever the carb-deniers say. It gives you far more knowledge and control over what is in your food.

One of the reasons eating out so much is dangerous in terms of weight is that we consume as much food as we are given, regardless of whether we need it or not. When a Guild member asked Andrew Hill how to lose weight, one of his tips was a simple one: smaller plates. His Ph.D. was on hunger and satiety and how environmental causes override the weak internal mechanisms we have for saying 'Stop – enough!' If there is less to eat in front of you, you eat less. One classic experiment showing the opposite is the Bottomless Soup Bowl. Unwitting – or shall we say hungry – students were invited to lunch by experimental psychologists and were given bowls of soup, some with hidden tubes that replenished their bowls without them realizing. The students with these bowls kept on eating and eating, waiting to reach the bottom of the dish. The observation was, again, that we eat according to serving size, not fullness.

I went to a talk by another experimental psychologist, Martin Yeomans of the University of Sussex. He is known as the 'Meal Professor' because he lures students into his experiments by offering free pasta at lunchtime. Then he does things like pumping tomato soup with differing amounts of calories into them through a nasal tube to show how we don't know when we've had enough. 'How much we eat isn't much to do with biology,' Yeomans summarizes.

The Meal Professor, like Andrew Hill, was also interested in how a modern Western lifestyle promotes overeating. It starts in our childhood, when we are trained to leave a clean plate. Fair enough, we don't want to waste food. The key, again, is to have smaller servings so there is less waste, or even to make your own domestic 'doggy bag' and put some food back in the fridge to reheat later rather than feeling you always have to finish everything up.

Food is prone to the stresses and influences on rest of our lives, said Yeomans. 'We're being trained to go for more all the time,' he said. Advertising, economics and the hyped-up media urge us to 'max out' in every way, so why not on food? Why not have a Whopper or a Super-whopper or a Super-maxed-out-quadruple-whopper? A colleague told me about a sign in his hospital staff canteen in Oxford that used to advertise a 'Belly-busting breakfast'. Even hospitals are at the max-out game. But, hey, you bust your body and we'll try to mend it in the same place.

The clever tricks of the experimental psychologists also show why restrictive diets rarely work in the long run. The problem, of course, is that prohibition makes you want more. In one trial, more unwitting experimentees were split into two groups. One group was told it was about to go on a strict diet; the other was not. Both were given unlimited access to chocolate. The first group ate three times as much as the second. Certain kinds of restriction lead to what is called disinhibited eating, or bingeing, in other words.

Animal studies indicate another way that emotions come into play. There is a sinister breed of 'stressor rat', which are animals bred to aggravate their neighbours. The normal rats respond to being caged up with these stressor rats by eating more. It seems the higher the level of stress hormones, the less effective are the hormones that control satiety.

I wasn't so sure about this one. Stress tends to make me lose weight as I rush around doing things, or sit nervously chewing my fingernails. But there is a condition of animal stress, which I had learned about through researching factory-farmed animals, known as 'learned helplessness'. This occurs when you are stressed but know you can't do much about it. In this state – a form of depression – you do reach for the biscuit tin. It seems that hormones have a role in how we eat, and they are released, in part, according to emotional reaction; another indication that the psychological aspect of eating is an important part of being overweight and therefore of dieting successfully.

★

Andrew Hill was asked a complex question by another member of the Guild of Food Writers: what makes people change the way they eat? People are motivated in different ways, he said. Some can be scared into a lifestyle change by being shown clogged-up arteries and so on, whilst others shut off completely when they are told such stuff. I was interested that he thought the local food movement was relevant to the question, and helpful. Once you make more connections with your food and enjoy cooking and learn those skills, you are able to engage with eating in a better way, he said. It is true that when you value food more, you notice its many aspects; the very fact of awareness is helpful. No longer is it squat and gobble. Even to register you are eating at all is helpful. John Garrow used to get his students to write down everything they ate for a period, and they would all lose weight, whether they meant to or not. I was intrigued to learn that Mark Bittman, a food writer for the *New York Times*, lost 35lbs (nearly 16kg) in four months through what he calls 'aware' eating. One of his strategies was to be vegan until 6 p.m. Almost anything that makes you pause and be more aware of at least some of the 226.7 food choices that you make per day is likely to be helpful.

I began to incorporate into my life the ideas I had picked up. I now knew that my body was not going to tell me when I had had enough, or at least not straight away. Pausing before having a second helping was useful; you rarely really want one. I had some smaller plates, between a dinner plate and a side plate, and started to put my helping on one – I need to eat less than the teenage boys and adult man I am generally feeding. Slightly to my surprise, my smaller portions filled me up. I had been eating too much simply because my plate was too big.

My biggest mental shift was realizing how often I ate when I wasn't hungry. From time to time – perhaps once a fortnight – I hardly had supper, if I had eaten a big lunch and was having an early night. Again to my surprise, and this really was a significant discovery, I didn't feel hungry. However, I noticed this certainly depended on my not having a drink in the evening.

The experience of sometimes having a very light supper led me on to another aspect of eating and overeating: meal times. The rule used to be 'three square meals a day and no snacking'. But I had noticed a number of nutritionists and dieticians now advised eating a series of smaller, regular, snack-like meals throughout the day in order to keep blood-sugar levels constant rather than a roller-coaster of peaks and troughs.

It may matter when we eat, not just what. There is some evidence that eating late at night can lead to high triglyceride levels in the blood, associated with obesity and diabetes. It is also thought that a big breakfast gives you energy that you burn off rather than storing as fat, whereas going to bed on a full stomach does the opposite. There may well be wisdom in the old saying: 'Breakfast like a king; lunch like a prince; dine like a pauper.'

When I spoke to a nutritionist at the British Nutrition Foundation, she sat on the fence. The evidence on snacking and obesity, she said, is 'scarce and contradictory'. Whilst some studies show that snacking more than three times a day is associated with being overweight, eating frequently may help to control appetite and prevent overeating at meals. In the end, she emphasized the importance of having three balanced meals a day – lunch having roughly the same number of calories as dinner – and choosing healthy snacks, if needed, to keep you going in between.

It is not often easy to follow this advice. Many people work away from home during the day, snatch a quick lunch and only have time to eat at leisure at night. Alcohol stimulates the appetite and drinking and dining tend to go together.

In my own life, there was some leeway around the timing of meals. I had started to eat a bigger breakfast. Since I work from home, this can be at 9.30 a.m. or so, after I have been at my desk for a while and am properly hungry. Even if I eat breakfast earlier, it tends to be two courses, as I had learnt from my Best Breakfast research. My partner works nights and so I sometimes like to have a more leisurely lunch with him when he wakes up, when he is having a big breakfast. I found that eating more lightly at night, and earlier, felt good, so I did that when I could. Everyone else eats heartily, and I eat the same, but I am much more watchful about my portions and don't have seconds.

Because my other meals are not too big and are around about the same size, I need – and feel fine about – eating snacks in between, so long as they are reasonably healthy: an apple, some nuts, maybe some bread and cheese. The problems start when I have a glass of wine and start to feel disinhibited about the crisp packets that are hidden away in a cupboard but still present in the house.

★

Dieting is tough. You need good tactics, especially if you want to make a properly focused effort to lose weight. My first kilo came off after a few months; another one came off a month or so later. But I realized that a more concerted effort would be needed to shift a bit more.

How to do it? I came across another author who claimed to have discovered psychological tools to combat overeating. Dr David Kessler served as commissioner of the Food and Drug Administration in the US. A paediatrician by training, he has been head of the medical schools at Yale and the University of California, San Francisco. He has struggled with his weight for a long time and particularly with an addiction to fast food. His book, *The End of Overeating*, is an investigation into the source of his calories and the strategies he has developed against temptation.

Kessler is particularly good on why we fall for the mind-and-body games of the fast food industry. For a start, it is so cheap. Some American fast food deals are quite staggering. I was absorbed by a lecture on the internet, 'Sugar: The Bitter Truth', by Robert Lustig, an expert on childhood obesity at the University of California, San Francisco, that had become a surprise hit on YouTube. In it, he shows a 'meal deal' in Texas that consisted of a 60oz soda, hamburger and Snickers bar for, unbelievably, 99 cents. But it's not just about money. Kessler interviews industry insiders who tell him how sugar, fat and salt are added quite simply to make us eat more, pushing evolutionary buttons that override any other consideration, such as 'This could give me a heart attack.' Such foods signal rewards, which in turn stimulate 'feel-good' hormones, such as dopamine.

There is, to use psycho-jargon, a form of 'conditioning' to such eating. Just as Pavlov's dogs start to salivate with they get an electric shock, in anticipation of the food they are given, so we have feelings of comfort and happiness when we give in to food cravings. Kessler argues that fast food is rewiring our brains in this way, changing our neural pathways by connecting certain foods with rewards and treats, even though these could ultimately lead to our downfall – diabetes and beyond.

By far the greatest tug is sugar. People often notice that when they eat something very sweet, they immediately want more. There has been a general sweetening of our palate, not just through sugary foods but also through the addition by manufacturers of sugar to savoury foods. Even fruit breeders now aim for sweetness instead of the delicious balance of acidity and sugars that makes an apple or a strawberry so delicious. I happen to have a savoury tooth rather than a sweet one, but crisps work for me in the same addictive way. Even as I'm eating one, fingers knuckle-deep in my mouth, I'm imagining my hand rustling back into the packet.

Since we become 'addicted' to bad food habits, Kessler says we need a spell of food 'rehab'. This can break old patterns and form new ones. For example, if you always have a doughnut from a particular shop on your way to work, take another route. Some of his advice is attractively positive. He thinks we should follow our own likes rather than just deprive ourselves; and that we should focus on our food when eating, for example by sitting down to eat. As for nutrients, he advocates a diet of natural foods, with high fibre and protein and some fat.

Kessler is interesting on the issue of willpower versus rules. Willpower, in general, is very tough; a few well-chosen rules can be more straightforward to follow, so long as they are reasonable. This is perhaps one reason why ketogenic diets such as Atkins's are easier for some people to follow than simply cutting down on everything. Stick to simple rules and you won't need to exert willpower every time you sit down to a meal.

I don't have a fast food habit, but there was one particular problem that needed solving. Kessler has a problem with cakes; I have one with glasses of wine and those subsequent packets of crisps. It's not that wine is bad; drunk moderately, it is fine for your health. I also believe in moderation in all things, including moderation in moderation. The odd hoolie is all right. But the habitual glug, glug, glug of a weekday evening is not good. It slows me down and leads to eating more – far more – than I want. I wanted to crack this one; it felt like the key to the final stage of my weight loss.

I decided to adapt David Kessler's 'food rehab' tactics to my wine drinking. His steps sounded like therapy-speak, but perhaps they would be a good place to start.

Figure out what leads to overeating (or in my case, drinking).
This is Kessler's first step for rehab and immediately gets to the psychological and not just the physical.

Well, as for many people, a drink helps me relax and signals the end of the working day. It is convivial. It is delicious. It makes me feel good. The single main start to 'too much' is when

I drink without food. The glass of wine while I'm cooking is the opener. Beware – or be aware of – that one.

Limit your exposure to it.

This is difficult. A drink is a very normal part of my life. If the world is 'obesogenic', mine is also 'drinkogenic'. I don't want to stop going out for dinners and lunches where all sorts of delicious glassfuls get poured out for you. Perhaps such events could fit into my 80:20 rule.

From day to day, there are two ways I could potentially cut back. Should I stop going to the pub with my partner, or go in and not drink? I suppose I could have a tomato juice, although it's not the same at all. But we don't go very often, it's sociable and I love pubs as places, not just for the booze. The answer is probably to have a pint and then not drink any more that evening. But I wish there was more bar food other than crisps and greasy nuts, as the Spanish have tapas. Some pubs now make an effort to do interesting bar food and I try to go to them when possible.

The other frequent point of exposure is during the evening slump when I somehow drink too much as I relax in the evening at home. But it's a bad habit and one I want to stop.

First, I found a literal way to limit my exposure. Following on from Andrew Hill's plate tip, I started drinking from a smaller glass. I like to hunt around the posher end of bric-a-brac stalls, so I tried to find some old glasses that suited; then in the end I found some in the back of a cupboard at home.

There are other forms of restriction. Many people check their drinking habits by having a time of abstinence, often not drinking in January, which makes a long and miserable month even more long and miserable, but by all accounts helps, not least after Christmas excess. Others decide not to drink during the week. I thought I could manage two days off. According to doctors, these are best to do consecutively in order to give your liver a chance to recover. I wondered if I could do Monday and Tuesday. The first week I tried this out, I had to go and check out a pub that was claiming to be eco. It seemed silly not to have a half just because it was Monday. But gradually it became more normal not to drink every night as a habit.

Have an alternate plan for when such matters arise.
Just at the point when the bottle is tipping towards the third glass, my plan is that I will get up from the table, put on the kettle and make a pot of green tea. A certain amount of gobbling or drinking is what I call 'mouth hunger' – you just want to put something in there, as a child sucks a thumb or smokers have a cigarette. A cup of tea works as well as any other drink and changes your tastes: have a cuppa rather than a cool bottle.

Refuse what you can't control.
This means stopping at a big glass or two small ones, which is about what I should be drinking. It also means no spirits: too much, too quick. Well, apart from the odd late-night whisky when nothing else will do. And the odd gin cocktail.

Remember the stakes.

Martin Yeomans made the point that we are good at reading the signals of under-eating but not of over-eating: 'It doesn't kill you soon enough.' Over-drinking, however, is easier to judge, by a hangover. I'm more motivated by feeling good now. The point about alcohol that concerns me, more than my heart or cancer, is its affect on my brain. I notice that my memory is definitely damaged by even a small quantity, and that worries me. I began to see this as the high stake for me. It was almost as if I needed to work out why *not* to drink as much as why I drank in the first place. Also, drink gobbles time and there isn't enough of that.

I also dream much better without alcohol, and that's a big prize. Sober dreams can be extraordinary and revelatory short stories, and are often worth not drinking for.

Direct your attention elsewhere.

My plan was to be diverted by, paradoxically, going out. I sometimes have an evening in alone, and instead of keeping myself company with television and a drink, I resolved to get a last-minute ticket to a play or opera or go to a film. This would turn the booze-less evening into a treat.

Learn active resistance. Be conscious of your thoughts and use that to stop your urge – talk down the urge.

At this point, Kessler sounded just too much like an American football coach turned analyst. And, after all, you drink partly in order to lose control. Life is so regulated and ordered and busy; booze blurs this nicely, relaxing the synapses in a way that can be creative as well as fun, even if it is a matter of diminishing returns.

Instead of 'talking down the urge', I pondered on finding a mantra. A mantra can be surprisingly powerful. The word that came to me was 'time'. Not as in 'Time, gentlemen, please,' but the time that I crave. Time. Time and space. Time and space and zoom. When the thought of a cold glass of wine came to me, I could push it out by repeating a word a few times. 'Wine' can easily become 'time'. Then there were practical measures. I got in a stock of high-quality soft drinks, such as pressed apple juice and raspberry lemonade made by Luscombe, and started to pour a chilled one into a big Riedel glass when the urge for a drink takes hold.

This was my strategy. How would it work overall? And would it help me to shed the extra kilos I wanted to lose?

Time … change does take time. I gradually absorbed what I had learnt and found ways to incorporate the knowledge into how I ate. When I found a change hard to make – such as drinking less – I tried to find ways around that. In David Kessler's 'food rehab' he says that rules are a useful alternative to self-discipline. Of course rules are there to be broken, but they are a simple way of keeping hold of basic principles that you agree with. I found five rules to help my form of dieting.

One
Enjoy food; deprivation doesn't work for me as well as the pleasure principle. My only possible way of dieting would be the Good Food Diet.

Two

Watch portions, especially of carbohydrates in the evening. I am lucky in having a savoury tooth rather than a sweet one, so having small helpings of puddings and cakes is relatively easy. But I still enjoy them.

Three

Have two days off the booze. This proved to be a real boost to my energy levels and somehow meant I drank less in general. A measure of restraint was a good influence. My nephew Tomas, who has Asperger's Syndrome and helps me see life from a different angle, is fascinated by the concept of diminishing returns. I began to think of alcohol in this light, trying to visualize how more and more became less and less. My discovery of high-tannin, 'healthy' red wines from Roger Corder's book was also helpful, as you don't glug these as much as the modern easy-drinking wines, and you tend to have them with food.

Four

No crisps. I break this rule regularly, but I want to have it because they are my chief junk.

Five

The fifth rule is nothing to do with what I put on my plate, but I'm convinced it is the most important. When we moved house and were nearer an Underground station, my bicycle was stored in the back yard and remained there for months. Then I got back in the saddle. Walking around the park was relaxing and cleared my head. But cycling at least twice a week for half an hour dramatically and immediately changed how my body felt. Instead of slumping into supper, I ate well but not too much.

Within a month of the Good Food Diet plus exercise, I had lost two more kilogrammes and felt a great deal better. It's true what they say: once you make one change, others follow. For me, it was the exercise that made the biggest change. I had more energy, wanted to drink less, which gave me more energy, which made me exercise more, which gave me more energy and so on. Many would call this a 'virtuous circle'. I would love to know Tomas's way of conceiving this opposite of diminishing returns. It would sum up the Good Food Diet.

And then I went on one of those glorious press trips that very occasionally come my way, this time to Western Australia. Alas, it meant eating wonderful food for breakfast, lunch and dinner. A glass of champagne seemed as much a greeting as a handshake. We went to the wine region of Margaret's River and I did what I was meant to do: I drank wine.

Back home, life became stressful and for six months or so life was to be got through rather than anything more positive being achieved.

When I next stepped on the scales I weighed 65kg again.

Perhaps I am destined to find my own version of 'yo-yo' dieting, or just knuckle down like everyone else to proper deprivation rather than trying to enjoy food and lose weight. But somehow I don't think so. When I stuck to my principles, the

Good Food Diet worked, and it was a way of regulating my eating that was enjoyable and possible. I also think that, in all honesty, the good old motivators of (health) fear and vanity will help my five rules along. Change takes time, and time will tell if this approach works in the long term as well as the short. I think it will.

WHAT TO EAT?

Easy. Use a smaller plate; wait before deciding on a second helping; get more nutrition from your snacks; sit down to eat and take your time; take more notice of what you eat; be aware of sugar and other processed carbohydrates, especially at night; eat plenty of fruit and vegetables; eat yoghurt and other foods that help your healthy gut-bugs.

Worth the effort. Have a bigger breakfast and a smaller supper; don't go on a crash diet based on deprivation but work out how to tweak what you like to eat; work out the reasons why you might be overweight, thinking it through for yourself rather than following someone else's diet plan; find ways to drink well; take some exercise every day and more strenuous exercise two days a week.

Hopes and dreams. That we no longer believe in other people's diets but find our own, based on real food and sociable ways of eating; that I'll never want to eat a crisp again in my life.

8

How Can I Eat 'Five-a-Day'?

For me as for many, fruit and vegetables have become a key antidote to the problems of the modern Western diet. They contain vitamins, minerals and a great pulsing cocktail of vibrant phytochemicals; fibre to help digestion; not too many calories; a certain amount of protein to repair your cells; even some carbohydrates for energy. It is what they contain that makes them so good, and it is also what they replace on the plate. A diet high in fruit and veg is lighter than one that focuses just on meat and stodge. But that's just their underlying appeal. Most of all, I love the colours, tastes and textures of fresh produce: a scented peach, the sharp-sweet of a good tomato, a munch of peppery rocket. They bring a plate to life.

Some argue that there are healthy societies that thrive on a diet that consists almost entirely of meat, such as the Laps. I interviewed a Sami reindeer herder for a magazine article. We spoke via Skype; a slightly surreal conversation between a writer in a suburban study and a wild-meat man who herded reindeer by paraglider in the white expanses of Lapland. Olof said he could eat reindeer three times a day and also fish soups. The photographer who had met him to take some pictures described how the vegetables in the local supermarket lay wilted and unsold. But even snow-bound Arctic peoples do eat a certain amount of vegetables, not least potent greens such as sorrel. On top of this, the quality of their diet gives it a different nutritional status, with its lean wild meat, wild greens, omega-3-rich fish and a very, very large amount of exercise. Sitting in front of the television and supersizing on burgers and shakes, it ain't.

It makes sense to truly get behind the advice that we should eat five portions of fruit and veg a day. What exactly is a portion? And why five? A portion is 80g if you follow the World Health Organization's recommendation of at least 400g a day. Some of it is straightforward – a portion would be an apple; two dried apricots; two marinated artichoke hearts; a medium tomato; two handfuls of watercress. Some of it is more than you would think: half a small melon; twenty raspberries. On the whole, it is easier (and much cheaper) to get your portion from vegetables rather than fruit.

'Five-a-day' is a catchy phrase that turns out to be based on pragmatic if unscientific thinking. I read a newspaper feature that explained how the State Nutritionist for California, Susan Foerster, got together with food producers in 1998 to work out how to persuade people to eat more fresh produce. They doubled the average consumption and came up with five portions. This was adopted by the Federal Government, then the WHO, and from there went around the world. In other countries, the recommended amount is higher: seven-a-day in Australia, eight-a-day in Spain, and seventeen in Japan.

Whatever the figure, in the UK not many people want to eat up their greens (and reds, yellows, oranges and purples). In 2010 a UK government White Paper estimated that three out of ten people didn't even eat five-a-day. The questions are: why, and how can we eat more?

There are a number of reasons why people don't take to fruit and veg. There's the usual problem that we cook less at home. Vegetables in particular take more preparation than other foods. Then there's the fact that fruit and veg are relatively expensive in terms of cost per calorie. For some reason – and I wanted to know why – children often find vegetables hard work, especially if they grow up without the habit. The power of phytonutrients to build up our immune system may be most potent in kids, as I had learnt when researching the connections between food and health, so this may be an important problem.

Alongside this, I have come to suspect that there is an underlying reason for a lack of interest in vegetables – among people of all ages – that can be summed up in one word: status. People talk about 'the humble' potato, carrot or parsnip. They tend to sit at the side of the plate, not the centre. But why should they be lowly? And how can this change?

My own journey towards appreciating vegetables and fruits was fortified by three years writing on the social and natural history of plants for *Kew* magazine. Kew Gardens have one of the best botanical libraries in the world, and I would spend days clambering around its shelves and diving into obscure monographs to learn about the magic powers of cinnamon or the multiple uses of a coconut – surely the most useful plant in the world: a third of the planet's population use it, for food, drink, medicine, cooking and eating utensils and even furniture. I discovered how plants turned up in all corners of life, some of them deliciously esoteric. One of my favourite obscure plant discoveries was how an astonishing and stinky yellow paint used in Indian miniatures was made by feeding cows on mango leaves and then collecting and concentrating their urine; when you look at a picture you can see how the colour of the paint is the same as the perfectly ripe fruit.

The more I knew about food plants and where they came from, literally and historically, the less they became like fodder for the side of the plate and the more they became interesting and valuable in their own right. Then I would wander around the gardens and Victorian glasshouses and seek out the plants themselves. The banana tree in the lovely Palm House grows surprising flowers with big mouths; peppercorns are berries; and asparagus is a tender shoot that rears up suddenly (in Worcester-shire, the heartland of English production, they still call it 'grass').

Seeing food as plants made me understand how our food is part of nature. The author Barbara Kingsolver captures the way food is part of the natural world in her book on local food and self-sufficiency, *Animal, Vegetable, Miracle*. She describes her kitchen garden progressing through the year, and the way each season corresponds to different stages of growth: 'Each plant part we eat must come in its turn – leaves, buds, flowers, green fruits, ripe fruits, hard fruits – because that is the necessary order of things for an annual plant.' First come the leaves – spinach, kale, lettuce, chard; then mature heads, such as cabbage and broccoli.

May and June bring young fruits: snow peas, baby squash, cucumber, then green beans, green peppers and small tomatoes. They are followed by the mature coloured fruits – aubergines, red and yellow peppers, beefsteak tomatoes. Then come the hard-shelled fruits with seeds inside, such as melons, pumpkins and squash; and finally come the root crops that store food to take them through to the next year, such as maincrop potatoes and parsnips.

Of course it isn't just a straight line – you eat young carrots and new potatoes in early summer and so on. But Kingsolver's explanation gave me a greater sense of the natural history of food as the year runs its course. I began to see fruit and vegetables as living entities rather than objects on shop shelves, and this helped me to understand their seasons and tastes better. Once I had seen how pineapples grow up from the ground, I noticed how the base of the fruit is slightly sweeter than the top. I now slice them from top to bottom, in wedges, so everyone gets some of the sweetest part. For the same reason, when workers on the Florida orange groves take a snack from the tree, apparently they prefer the half of the fruit from closest to the stem because it is sweeter.

Since the start of my book's quest, A is for Apple, I knew that the detail of production mattered. For every plant, mass production has meant greater availability but, alas, a falling-off of quality and charm. Why were the potatoes I grew myself outstandingly delicious in comparison to the cheap ones sold in the supermarket? First of all, there has been a focus on the few varieties that suit industrial production. This is true of all produce. The popular Nairobi carrot is said to have been tested to see if it could bounce from a height into a hopper six times without being damaged. Then the cheap potatoes are grown as quickly as possible – we have fast farming as well as fast food. More water is used in commercial potato farming than you would use domestically. The potatoes are sprayed during production and again after harvest to stop spoilage by bugs and fungi. I wondered if this accounted for the slightly bitter taste I sometimes detected in shop-bought potatoes.

My hunch was that getting closer to the growing was another key to valuing and enjoying fruit and vegetables. You don't change how you eat because someone wags their finger over your plate; you do so by gradually establishing new habits and by being inspired to do so. In the case of vegetables, in particular, this is first and foremost through eating those with good flavours, bright textures and an appearance that glows with vitality. To get the very freshest, you grow your own or find a good grower. I have had allotments in the past and now grow some potatoes, lettuces and herbs in our small city garden. But I don't have a full-blown vegetable plot and am unlikely to have one in the near future. In any case, to grow produce well is a hard task and best left, in my case, to the experts. The way for me to get the best, I suspected, would be through a veg box.

Veg boxes are a vibrant offshoot of organic farming. They began in the UK in the early 1990s, when Tim and Jan Deane, farmers in south Devon, realized that to make a living they needed to sell directly to local customers rather than through wholesalers or supermarkets. This would also mean a better, fresher deal for the customer, with the vegetables no longer shuttled between farm, packhouse, distribution centre and shop shelf. The challenge for the Deanes was to produce enough variety to keep their customers interested. Tim Deane happens to be a talented and experienced grower who can coax even melons out of the Devon fields. The Deanes found 200 customers within a ten-mile radius of their home; the idea worked.

There are now around 500 veg box schemes in the UK supplying 400,000 households. Quietly, this had become a large movement. My first veg box came from Riverford Organic Farm, just down the road from the Deanes. I understood why the idea worked from my very first delivery. It was February, hardly the sexiest time of year for vegetables, but everything had more taste, more sweetness, more sappiness, more oomph that supermarket vegetables. The cabbage was greener, the carrots sweeter. There was a mineral kick in each bite that felt actively good for me as well as full of flavour. All right, you had to wash the mud off the carrots, but I discovered the soil meant such organic vegetables kept fresher for longer – the act of washing scrapes off the first 'skin' of the root that protects it. The price, as well as the quality, of veg box produce can be better than the organic vegetables that you find in supermarkets; 20 per cent cheaper in the case of Riverford.

One of the biggest hurdles to eating more vegetables is that there is more preparation – and even more when farm-fresh produce needs a good scrub. The work involved must be one reason why people don't manage five-a-day. Sure, you can cut corners and buy ready-prepared veg – peeled carrots and so on – but this sacrifices flavour and texture. The second you cut up any food it starts to lose life. Over the years, I have learnt to be a believer in what Rabbi Lionel Blue calls 'the sanity of small tasks'; those little jobs that keep you anchored in what's worth doing. I put the radio on or half-watch the Simpson re-runs on television in the kitchen as I prep. Scrubbing, peeling and chopping are certainly the longest day-to-day tasks in the kitchen. A good peeler and a sharp knife at least make the work easier, and I now don't notice the effort, just as you automatically clean your teeth.

A veg box, otherwise, turned out to be really convenient. Vegetables are heavy, especially if you shop by foot or bicycle. Now they are delivered to my door. There are nine kinds of vegetables in my box, changing with the seasons, just dug or picked and with as much variety as they can manage. You can choose to include other vegetables or make your own list. To follow the seasons, I let the farmer choose for me. So I was, like everyone else, confronted with the usual question: what do you do with the veg you don't know or like? Whatever the season, there is always a cabbage. Even though Riverford usually manage to rotate the different kinds – Savoy, red, spring and so on – my partner isn't keen on cabbage at all. I knew I'd have to find some ways through this problem.

I consulted my cookbooks and came up with some interesting flavour combinations and good techniques, the twin poles of a good recipe. The most successful dish was the most basic. Put sliced green cabbage in a pan with a little butter, just the water that the cabbage had been rinsed in, and – crucially – plenty of pepper, then fry-steam the cabbage for 3–4 minutes with the lid on the pan, giving it a couple of stirs or a few shakes. I also got into crunchy slaws, using a mixture of vegetables and a vinaigrette, perhaps with cream or yoghurt, or with Asian flavours such as soy sauce and rice vinegar. I like thin wedges of cabbage fried and then braised in cider with a base of softened onions and celery and a spice (or two, or three: it's one of the fascinations of cooking to discover how two spices together – and even more so three – completely change each other). My partner grits his teeth at red cabbage, and still refuses coleslaw, but since I tend to cook at least a couple of vegetable dishes for supper, it is optional for him and enjoyed by me. But my cabbage experiments showed me why five-a-day, variety and veg box cookery can be hard; you never want to cook unwanted food.

There is, altogether, a big difference between veg box cookery and what you might cook otherwise, and it took a while to learn how to do this. The main shift is that you have to work with what you've got. Rather to my surprise, I ultimately found this a relief. It was one route through the contemporary quandary of having too much choice. And it was true what other veg boxers had told me: I ate more vegetables simply because they were there. To use up the produce, I often steam two or three vegetables together, and slosh on a bit of olive oil and some seasoning. The question, of course, is whether this could get monotonous.

To help out, I turned to the recipes that came in the veg box.

These were well done and part of a change of emphasis by Riverford. 'I realized we were focusing too much on the growing when the cooking was much more important,' said Guy Watson, the company's founder. The company recruited a team of Riverford Cooks and trialled a series of events such as supper clubs and home classes to help people 'think inside the box' and not end up with a tatty red cabbage and mouldy swede they didn't want to eat. They also produced two good cookbooks.

The style of cooking is based on Riverford's inspirational restaurant, the Farm Kitchen. When I went to the Farm Kitchen it really did change the way I thought about vegetables. I saw how it was possible to have an '80:20' balance of plants to animal protein. To get to the restaurant, you walk along a muddy path alongside a field; it is very much on a farm. Instead of 'meat and two veg' it is more like 'nine veg and some meat' as a series of platters are passed down long, shared tables. On the day I was there, a melting duck confit was served alongside purple sprouting broccoli and grilled leeks with garlic, chilli and hazelnuts; creamed parsnips; roasted fennel with orange and ginger; sweet and sour roast beetroot and carrots; sauté potatoes and cavolo nero. It was colourful, fresh and delicious.

The Farm Kitchen is run by Jane Baxter, a cheery Midlander with a suitably mucky laugh, who is the co-author of the Riverford cookbooks alongside Guy Watson. Her style of cooking suits the home kitchen – not too many or difficult-to-get ingredients and straightforward techniques. She advised getting into cuisines that are naturally strong in vegetables, such as

Mediterranean, Moorish and Asian. Some of their techniques could be adapted to British produce. The Asian balancing of sweet and sour could be successfully applied to winter roots such as parsnip and celeriac, for example. Small details make vegetables interesting. Cook carrots with butter and honey instead of boiling them and you get a much more intense flavour, said Jane. But she didn't think such cooking had to be hard work. Her advice was not to feel you must layer up a gratin like a chef, but just throw it all in.. The Riverford cookbooks have become an ally in the kitchen. So have the quick ideas passed on in a conversation or in a leaflet in a box. Cooking is, best of all, an oral tradition, transmitted through personal recommendation. But wherever you get ideas from – recipe book, friend, television, tweet or even packet copy – all in all, to eat more vegetables it helps to start with ingredients that are at their peak.

I saw my cabbages back in their fields when I went along to an enterprise called Root Camp, held near the Riverford headquarters in Devon. This was a cooking week for teenagers. The fourteen who came were split into two groups; one group spent half the day in the kitchen whilst the other group was in the fields, and then they swapped over. They came together for the lunch and dinner they had cooked, principally using vegetables. Some of the teens had done a certain amount of cooking – a few had even thought of food as a career; others were barely past Rice Krispie cakes. I was interested to see how they would take to eating and cooking vegetables.

This was a hard-core immersion in the world of vegetables.

One morning, I accompanied a group up to what has been charmingly nicknamed Dead Sheep Field by the Riverford crew. 'There's nothing between the Moor and us,' said the farmer, and you felt the looming presence of Dartmoor and its granite-chilled winds as we stood there in November before a bobbled carpet of cabbage. The teens trailed over the field, some in shorts and mud-splattered black tights, in shearling-trimmed fashion boots or scuffed trainers, suddenly breaking out into song, like birds, or sudden bursts of laughter.

It's quite a challenge to relate food to fields – let alone dead sheep ones – but details stick. The farmer mentioned how a chemical field could be 'stale', its soil exhausted by growing, and that conjured up a sense of what the organic movement was about. But it isn't all about sweaty peasant toil. He showed off a salad-reaping machine that could harvest 200kg of leaves in an hour, whereas before they used to handpick 6kg in that time.

Back in the kitchen, a cook called Sylvain Jamois showed the teenagers how to cook, amidst their chat. One clever recipe involved mixing thick Greek yoghurt with honey and freezing it for a simple ice cream. They had to taste the mix to find out when the balance between the two was correct. It was about learning by doing with playfulness. A bowl of celeriac rémoulade, covered in clingfilm, was soon decorated in hearts and names. Leftover crumble mix was made into biscuits in the shape of letters, hearts and a giant sperm with a smiley face. There was, of course, a lesson in clearing up. 'Like anything you do, you've got to put a bit of energy into it,' the patient Sylvain told a desultory sweeper, with the extra tip that it was generally a good idea to pick the pile off the floor at the end.

Lunch was an Indian meal with coconut curry, dal, carrot salad, pilau rice, two raitas (one tomato, the other walnut and chilli) and rosebud and cardamom custard. For supper it was soda bread, carrot fritters, celeriac rémoulade, either shepherd's pie ('Yay!') or 'meadow pie' , the vegetarian equivalent. For afters, apple and cinnamon crumble was served with the Greek yoghurt ice cream.

The week had a conviviality about it that made the task of veg preparation – and there was a lot of it – both happy and companionable. The fruit of their labours was soon on the table for all to taste; a very public forum. One 14-year-old boy told me how he'd initially balked at his task, which was to make a big salad. 'I thought, why am I doing the salad that will go on the table and everyone will ignore it?' he said. 'Then it was a big hit.' The salad was composed of layers of grated carrot and beetroot on a large serving dish – it must have taken him an age to prepare. It looked and tasted great. The kids went back for more.

The playfulness had an underlying purpose. Many of the teens absorbed Sylvain's fundamental lesson that you don't have to stick rigidly to a recipe or an idea of what you want to make, but you should adapt to what you have; cooking is about creativity.

None of them seemed to mind, or even notice, that the food was predominately vegetables. Some had certain phobias – veg that 'creeped them out'. Yet in some cases these phobias were shifted by cooking and sharing the food with their peers and eating it in different ways. A few had never tried beetroot without vinegar, for example. Cassia Kidron, the creator of Root Camp, is convinced of the power of people working and playing together, as you do making music. A great deal was achieved in a day at Root Camp. 'It's made me realize how much more I can do in a day,' said one girl. 'It's made me feel I can get up and do things.'

Riverford produce is certainly of high quality because it is well grown and freshly dug or picked. But to what extent is it good because, like the contents of most veg boxes, it is organic? Organic agriculture is about a way of farming that pays more attention to nature. It means fewer chemicals on the land, such as the artificial fertilizers which pollute waterways. It should mean more wildlife and biodiversity, since animals and plants are not being poisoned by pesticides and herbicides.

Yet organic is, for some, a bogey-word, synonymous with middle-class consumers and a diet that is wholesomer-than-thou. In 2009, a report was published by the UK government's Food Standards Agency that summarized the findings of previous studies on the comparative nutritional benefits of organic and conventional produce. It concluded that organic did not deliver significant health benefits.

There was much gleeful reaction to this report, not least in the banner headlines that followed its publication. What a kick in the teeth for the smuggy-pants organic acolytes! The report also elicited an equally strong defence of the merits of organic food. I looked at the detail.

When I scanned the FSA's report, I found that, in fact, there is plenty of evidence, despite the negative headlines, that there *are* more nutrients in organic produce – more vitamins and minerals, more omega-3s. These were said to be 'not statistically relevant'. But it can't be a disadvantage, in whatever quantity. A five-year Europe-wide study by the Quality Low Input Food group based at Newcastle University, also published in 2009, showed higher levels of vitamins and antioxidants in some (though not all) organic fruit and vegetables as well as lower levels of pesticide residues and heavy metals. Organic milk was shown to have up to 70 per cent more of 'the goodies' than conventional. A French review study, looking at much the same evidence, came to markedly different conclusions to the FSA report. As well as having more nutrients, some organic vegetables have 50 per cent fewer nitrates, which have been linked to a number of health problems. They also have more natural sugars and are less pumped up with water, which means more flavour and nutrients. There is also a theory that organic production encourages more phytochemicals because the plants have had to struggle a bit more rather than being mollycoddled through a chemical world.

If you are buying organic produce just because of the phytonutrients, then the FSA's report, or at least the headlines it provoked, would have made you wonder if you were wasting your money. This is unfair, not least because the FSA report just looked at one element of organic food – and the hardest to prove in terms of benefit, namely health. What about all the other elements such as the pesticides in conventional produce? As regards pesticides, I think there are probably more significant causes of ill health as regards food – excess weight, too much alcohol and the pitfalls of a monotonous, processed food diet. But I would rather not have pesticides and herbicides added to my food, if avoidable.

Of course it's important to get a sense of perspective. The crucial front line in the way we eat is not just organic versus chemical, but more basic: fresh versus processed. The most important factor in your diet, as far as fruit and vegetables are concerned, is to eat as much and as wide a variety as possible – particularly vegetables. As far as the quantity of vitamins, minerals and other elements go, this is partly down to the soil the plants are grown in. You can get very good soil that is farmed conventionally.

On the other hand, the organic movement is based on promoting better soil, which is why its parent organization in the UK is called the Soil Association. It stands to reason that, in the long run, organic farming is better for overall soil quality, and this is the basic resource of farming, both now and for the future. Organic agriculture is designed to makes the fields more alive, whether this is about there being more insects because of fewer pesticides or the minute fungi in the ground that do not survive the chemicals put in to make crops grow faster.

I was interested to see what the American nutritionist Marion Nestle had to say on the subject of organic produce. Her view is that it is hard to quantify the phytochemicals in fruit and vegetables and their particular advantages. That is why she reckons it is good to eat a rich and wide variety of them, and to do so mainly for the best and most evident reason of all: pleasure. However, she also says that there are good studies that show how people who eat organically have fewer pesticide residues in their bodies, and this is one reason why she, personally, eats organic produce.

Does organic food taste better? To be an organic grower does not necessarily mean you are a good one, but it takes more effort, and many of those I have come across are committed to flavour as well as the environmental aspect of farming. The Riverford vegetables were certainly much fresher and tastier than those I could buy in even the poshest supermarket. They were, frankly, in a different league. The proof was in the parsnip.

I found the FSA's report to be partial in sticking a knife into the organic movement on an exposed flank. Why had the FSA not looked at pesticide residues in conventionally (or chemically) produced food, or the pollution of the water supply by nitrates, which is then cleaned up by we who pay the water company bills, or the degradation of the soil? Other European countries are much more positive about organic farming and sales have continued to grow during the economic downturn, when in the UK they fell. The Dutch government, to give just one example, in 2010 committed itself to increasing the amount of land farmed organically by 5 per cent each year. It's not about being a hippy, but about linking food production with a wider environmental agenda.

Organic is not the only way to farm in a more environmentally friendly way. There are other schemes that mean farming is 'greener'. These all owe a debt to the organic movement. Half a century after a group of farmers started to protest about the way chemicals were dosing the land and its life, the tide is moving in a greener direction. The organic movement has set the agenda and it is a good one for many reasons – environmental, taste (often), and yes, also nutrition.

'Eat more veg' is easy to say, but can be very hard to put into practice – particularly with children. I attended a Riverford Cooks' brainstorming session when the question was put: what stops people cooking, particularly vegetables – whether for themselves or family? An instant answer chimed from several voices: 'Time.' This was teased out further by a chef called Mark. 'Sometimes it's confidence, sometimes it's time,' he said. 'It's often space-in-our head time because it is something else to think about.' Sylvain, the cook I had met at Root Camp, saw taste as a motivating factor: 'I don't buy ready-made food because it tastes horrible,' he said. 'That's why it's called convenience food, not nice food.' For his own children, he thought that always putting serving plates of vegetables on the table would mean the habit would eventually seep into his veg-refusenik son. Lisa, another parent in the group, said the aversion can be to do with texture. It is true that some kids will eat crunchy raw vegetables (often the best way of all to eat them, as far as nutrition goes) when they don't like them cooked. An intriguing study showed that people will eat anything almost robotically when in front of the television. Putting a bowl of carrot and cucumber sticks and some cherry tomatoes alongside a plate of humus in front of kids watching TV certainly works.

There are a few time-honoured sneaky routes to five-a-day

for kids. One of the classics is mixing plenty of finely chopped onions, carrots, leeks, celery, peppers and tomatoes into mince, be it for bolognaise, shepherd's pie, lasagne or chilli con carne. More unusually, you can put grated beetroot into brownies, or make courgette cake, an Italian recipe along the same lines as the well-known carrot cake. Made at home, you can control the sugar level and, after all, kids are growing upwards not just outwards and need the energy. If food is well-flavoured and not overtly 'vegetarian' or burdened with the label of 'healthy eating' then it becomes much more acceptable. When I started cooking for my partner's three teenage boys, an early favourite was a tomato and bacon pasta sauce with plenty of chopped up vegetables. I guess it does have at least 'three portions', if you want to look at it that way. They just see it as 'yum'.

I started to wonder why kids found the texture of foods so difficult. After all, what could be more natural than this type of eating?

At this time, I happened to visit my cousin Honor and her one-year-old, Sophie. As we drank our tea at the kitchen table, Honor told me how she had discovered a different approach to a young child's weaning. Instead of spoonfeeding Sophie with purées, she'd gone straight to giving her what she and her husband Darren ate. So long as it was big enough for Sophie to hold, she could have it. The only rule was that you shouldn't put food into the child's mouth: they must learn how to do it. Lamb and apricot tagine, chicken curry, savoury pancakes, any kind of cooked vegetable went straight on the wipe-down table of her high chair, with a cleanable floor cover below to catch the food that fell. Patient parents (perhaps especially so), Honor and Darren coped with the mess and Sophie, over months, learnt how to eat.

I looked with delight and some awe at iPhone footage of little Sophie sucking joyously on a mango and getting down-and-dirty with a lamb stew. Darren described how his daughter looked at her first lasagne, dived down with both hands and ended up-to-her-eyebrows in the sheer delight at this new adventure in the world. All this reminded me of the joy of making mud-pies as a child and links into the sort of tactile pleasure you can get from cooking later on.

This approach is called baby-led weaning and goes against the prevailing idea that you start to give your child purées, introducing foods in mush form one type at a time (in case of allergies), then eventually moving the child – often with some difficulty – onto solid food. Honor is a person and parent confident of her own instincts and found the whole purée malarkey somewhat irksome and unnatural. The Internet led her to the baby-led weaning site. There is one book and one website because this is essentially a simple idea. The children choose what they like, develop their palate and get right into the food with all its different textures from the word go, exploring with their hands and mouth. Even at six months or so a child's gums are surprisingly hard and they can suck the goodness out of a pork chop. Within a few months they can cope with pieces of meat even without teeth.

Why did mush become the norm? The theory goes that baby

foods emerged when children were taken off the breast earlier and couldn't hold food. Even when infants are weaned later, the fear of choking and allergies puts parents off giving their child real food and there is now a big industry of kit and specialized baby foods.

Choking is your instinctive concern about baby-led weaning. But Sophie, as all the others, learnt to use her tongue and mouth to control her food. At the age of two, when I saw her next, she was remarkably dextrous and a good speaker, which may have come partly from the way she had been allowed to exercise her hands and mouth in the joyful and nourishing pursuit of food. 'They're young, they're not stupid,' says Honor. 'There's a world of difference between someone who can't do something because they are incapable and one who just hasn't learnt. It's for me to give her the opportunity to learn how to do it.'

The method also challenges the assumption that young children should be eating bland food, which sets up a situation where they eat differently from their parents and leads to two sorts of meal at the same table, which can go on for years. Pushing a spoon into a child's mouth is a slightly strange and almost invasive activity, when you think of it, and one that preoccupies the parents' time and energy in a way that splits a social and communal space.

What's more, if you've spent hours mushing up food, you want the child to eat it all, overriding their appetite, rather than trusting their instincts about what – and how much – they want to eat. 'Just as you or I might feel like carbohydrates and big stodgy food one day, so Sophie – even from six months – was the same,' says Honor. 'She'd go through a couple of days when she'd want so much protein and other days it would be all about the fruit. I wouldn't have believed that a child would have that level of preference. But she was eating properly from eight months and selecting what she wanted and in what quantities.'

Honor felt that allowing Sophie to eat autonomously meant there was no 'weird energy' put into the food and attitudes towards it. 'There are no "naughty" foods,' she said. 'So often with children it's "If you eat this broccoli you can have some ice cream." Food can become a weapon and vegetables a bit of a punishment. If you really want the ice cream then the broccoli becomes the demon.' As it happens, broccoli is the perfect food to start baby-led weaning because it has a handle and the baby can hold it and have a good suck and chew.

You would have to be quite earthy to take this approach, allowing more mess and keeping an eye on the child as you would if spoon feeding. But I could see how it would make a big difference to a child's attitude to vegetables and food as a whole and how that would be a basis for how they ate for the whole of their life.

Then there are other ways to encourage older children towards their five-a-day. I was impressed by *The Great Big Veg Challenge* by a television journalist and parent, Charlotte Hume. Charlotte took up the challenge of converting her veg-phobic son to the green stuff. The book is based on a quest to eat a vegetable alphabet, from A is for Artichoke to Z is for Zucchini. The specific challenge worked. The book is especially useful because the recipes are all simple, many with just a few ingredients. You get the sense of a busy parent feeding her kids with simple but clever combinations that wouldn't be too scary or impossible to make after work.

A certain amount of a child's eating is done at school. In the case of low-income kids, the school meal may be the most important of the day, especially if they do not have breakfast at home. Nobody remembers a golden olden past of school dinners. My own in the 1970s were full of deep-fried battered spam and sponge puddings that managed to be soggy and dry at the same time. It is hard to recall much that was green – or even a single vegetable, except for a certain smell of stale steam inside metal containers as they were opened: frozen peas, frozen sweetcorn, frozen carrots – the food was cooked elsewhere and brought to the primary school. I can recall greyish, slightly lumpy mashed potato served in hillocky ice cream scoopfuls which was only palatable once mixed with salad cream, or bled pink with vinegary beetroot.

Yet when Jamie Oliver swung into the school dinners arena in 2005, it was apparent that institutional food had got even worse. Fully processed had taken over. Kids were eating off plastic trays that dolloped gravy next to yoghurt. Even more school kitchens had gone, the budgets were pathetic and it was chips with everything. Given the choice, children have chips, making choice an illusion. They go for processed potatoes like bears to honey. Apparently the UK government doesn't allow potatoes as part of the 'five-a-day' for fear it would just mean chips and more chips (or 'Glasgow salad'), alternated with crisps.

The fight back for better school meals has begun. The Food for Life campaign, which kick-started Jamie's work and continues apace, is truly impressive. Yes, there are stories of how some kids dropped out of the healthy lunches. But there are many more examples of how, if a school really takes a lead, the staff can get most kids eating better quality school dinners. However, it takes sustained focus and effort rather than the school just offering a salad option. The most successful schools get kids tasting and voting on dishes, set up better queuing systems, do farm visits, plant school gardens and even create mini-restaurants with tablecloths and table service. In such places, food is part of a general education and a pleasure. You'd think it would be a no-brainer to feed children well, but in many cases it is seen as too difficult to do, or not a priority.

Growing is one of the key ways that schools engage children in real food. This isn't some dry leaflet about 'healthy eating'; it's the magic of putting a seed in the ground, seeing a green shoot emerge and pulling up a sweet young carrot from the ground.

In the last few years there has been a resurgence in the 'grow-your-own' movement. Even those at the very top are harnessing the metaphorical value of effort, frugality and joy that a vegetable plot entails, hence the digging up of lawns at Buckingham Palace, the White House and Downing Street in order to grow fruit and veg. Rowan Williams, the Archbishop of Canterbury, was way ahead on this. When I went around Lambeth Palace gardens to look at some bees, some nuns were cultivating vegetable plots. (The archbishop was wondering whether some goats were possible, which must have made the gardeners blanch.)

But this is truly a grass-roots movement, whether it is the Incredible Edible people of Todmorden in the north of England doing guerrilla gardening in their local graveyard, or suburbanites replacing turf with kale and tomato plants. The UK's Landshare social networking site has so far linked 60,000 people who either want to grow or have land to spare. Allotments always get longer waiting lists in times of economic downturn; this time, the demand grew before the worldwide recession, indicating that there has been a deeper tug towards the land. Perhaps as the world gets more virtual, there is a corresponding need for the immediacy of picking an apple from a tree or digging spuds from the soil.

The last time the nation got its back into growing was during a time of emergency, the 1939–45 war. In the UK, the number of allotments doubled until eventually 6 million families were being fed from 1.75 million plots by 1945. There are photographs of posh London parks turned into cabbage patches tended by ladies in hats holding watering cans like handbags. At that point, it was seen as shameful to waste food. After all, more than 30,000 merchant seamen died and 10,500 were injured bringing food to these shores. The attitudes towards food of my parents' generation were formed in these times. 'A clear plate is a clean conscience,' as one slogan went – very different from the present when a third of our food is wasted.

The reason for growing so much was necessity. Vegetables were off-ration and the most available way to feed your family. Some of the dishes that were eaten in wartime are the height of gastro-chic today: nettle soup, rabbit pie, blackberry and apple pudding. Wild food was mobilized. Some 5,800 bottling stations were staffed by 6 million members of the Women's Institute producing rosehip syrup as well as other preserves. From one of my *Kew* articles, I discovered that when the Allies arrived in Germany in 1945 they discovered the central reservations and sides of Hitler's new Autobahns were planted with roses as part of the push to get vitamin C from the rosehips.

The government's Ministry of Food paid close attention to the nutrition in vegetables, advising people that swede has the highest levels of vitamin C and recommending them to cook potatoes in their skins to preserve their vitamins, to avoid soaking vegetables in water for a long time and to serve something 'green and raw' every day. Vitamin C is largely destroyed by heat and so the swede statistic is pretty useless, but other points are worth noting, and it is as good as ever to eat something raw that's green, orange, red, yellow or purple every day.

The French do this as a matter of course, as I learnt when living in a French household for six months after leaving school. We had soup every night for supper, followed by a piece of meat or fish, followed by a vegetable or salad, followed by pudding or fruit. There's four or more of your five-a-day at one meal without further ado, simply as a cultural norm.

I have taken up the salad habit again, especially at lunchtime. It means the meal is slightly longer and you digest your food better and feel fuller by the time the temptations of pudding arrive. It is a matter of salad leaves or a grated carrot with some nice olive oil, a squeeze of lemon and some seasoning and perhaps herbs. Nothing fussy, but it makes a big difference to your overall diet.

The wartime effort gave me some clues about our attitudes towards vegetables today. There remains a sense of duty towards them – 'Eat up your greens!' – and an idea that they are a necessity rather than a pleasure, somewhat in the way the French are said to despise Jerusalem artichokes because they were part of the near-starvation diet of the war.

But were we always so miserable about veg? It's said that the Brits boil their vegetables to death and have never valued them. I asked the food historian Ivan Day whether this was true.

Ivan is one of the true food heroes of Britain. For decades, he has painstakingly researched what we really ate, not just the false historical clichés. If Ivan is researching spit roasting, he makes the spits and tries it out. If going into a historic kitchen, he takes off his shoes and walks around to feel the trackways of use. As for vegetables, Ivan says that much of the evidence wouldn't be found in cookery books because they were just too normal: you knew how to cook fruit and vegetables and so the recipes weren't written down. Where there is evidence, it can be misunderstood. For example, Mrs Beeton instructs you to cook cabbage for an hour, which certainly sounds like a massacre. But this was a whole Savoy cabbage, often a large one from your own vegetable garden, and when Ivan tried it, the timing was correct.

The historic recipes that do exist show some care and attention to detail for the likes of salad, for example in John Evelyn's *Acetaria: A Discourse of Sallets* (1699). Salad and vegetables weren't just posh food. Watercress, for example, used to be a common food amongst the Victorian working class. Some thousand sellers would gather in the market at Farringdon in London and the workmen would eat it either with bread or just from a bunch held in the hand like an ice cream. They were wise: cress has more iron than spinach, more calcium than milk and more vitamin C than oranges. For centuries, the main food of most people in Europe would have been thick soup-like dishes, or pottage, with bread. Perhaps this is another reason why vegetables and beans are looked down on as rabbit food or dull fodder.

However lowly the status of vegetables as food, the UK is a nation of gardeners, if not of cooks. I have noticed that some dedicated gardeners enjoy eating their beautiful vegetables almost as a by-product; they are eating what they grow rather than growing to eat. This part of our culture could be better harnessed in the push to encourage us to eat more fruit and veg. I came across a charity in New England that certainly used the joy of growing to great effect.

Gaining Ground is a farm just outside Concord in Massachusetts where Henry David Thoreau, the writer and proto-ecologist, was born, and a fitting place for a good and green idea to take root. The charity relies mostly on volunteers for its workforce. When I visited, this was organized by a farmer, Verena Wieloch, who at that time had two helpers, both young women in their twenties, who worked during the short growing season between April and October.

All the produce from Gaining Ground is given away to

people in need in the area. The Open Table charity in Concord uses the freshly picked organic vegetables to create a free meal. Then the produce is laid out on a table at a Food Pantry where forty local families on a tight budget take whatever they want.

The volunteers at Gaining Ground come from all walks of life. There are old people, troubled teenagers, gardeners in wheelchairs, mothers with kids who run around, singles, couples, families. By being part of the farm, they are working for what is called, starkly, 'hunger relief'. But they come, most of all, because they want to be there. I visited Gaining Ground in March, when the seventeen acres were a bleak brown. My conversations with Verena filled the scene with the life that would grow here, season by season. It was easy to see the integrity and spirit of the place and why they would want to be there.

Verena is a strong woman in her mid-thirties, her singlet showing broad shoulders. There is a steadiness to her and also a delight in her eyes as she considers a detail. After working in a high-tech industry for six years after college, she fell into farming after a life crisis when she broke up with her boyfriend, sold her flat and gave up her job. After travelling, she began to work six hours a week at a community-supported agriculture job in exchange for vegetables. She knew how to grow from her childhood – to her chagrin at that time. 'My Dad grew vegetables when I was a kid and I hated it,' she says. 'We did it because we were poor and it was weird.' Yet her childhood in the backwaters of western Pennsylvania was to stand Verena in good stead in a way that reflects the changing status of horticulture.

Verena summarized her work at Gaining Ground as twofold:

working with all sorts of volunteers and giving away all the produce. Her attitude towards volunteers is creative. 'Other places
have a more rigid classroom approach to volunteers and I really
like that here they just go out and do the work,' she says. 'They
learn so much more. You just have a conversation and see what
they are interested in.' The trick, she said, is to find what people
like to do. Everyone loves planting or digging up potatoes and
carrots. They tend to like washing vegetables, 'because they look
so pretty at the end.' Hand-weeding isn't everybody's favourite
but those of us who love it, love it, said Verena. Everyone likes
picking tomatoes and fruit in general, though they got a little
sick of the 400lb of strawberries that had to be harvested last
year. Less attractively, there was one-year-old mouldy straw that
had to be spread; but people still got stuck in.

The tasks change with the year. 'The season has this beautiful
arc,' explained Verena. 'At this time of year we're putting a few
things in the ground. Then in May you are planting a lot more
because it's warmer. By June, you are starting to harvest and the
weeds are coming in like crazy – and you're still planting. So July
you're planting as fast as you can and still weeding – and then by
August you've taken the leap off the cliff and aren't weeding any
more but you might be planting a little more stuff. Then
September it slows down, and then October it slows down
more. You come out of the gate and run as fast as you can … and
then stop.'

For all its pace, Verena's description of the acceleration of the
year, tasks shooting out their tendrils as the sun spreads light into
the longer summer days, made me understand why her very

favourite time is right at the start, the calm before the storm and
the first awakening of the year, as the maple sap rises. The farm
has a new maple syrup hut where there are jars stored from last
year, as well as popcorn from heritage seeds in many colours. On
the cusp of spring, the maple sap rises and this is tapped and then
boiled down in a vat over a wood fire to concentrate it. 'I love
maple syrup time,' said Verena. 'It's so beautiful and it's warm,
even though it's outside. You've been indoors all winter and this
is the chance to get out, and you know spring is on the way,
even though no one else knows it yet. And it's fire, it's sweet,
it's warmth and it smells good.'

The creativity of Gaining Ground is apparent in the look of
the place. 'It should just be beautiful,' says Verena. 'If it's just rows
of vegetables then it's not as magical.' She showed me a perennial
bed that was full of pieces of sculpture and objects picked up by
the roadside or from junk heaps. A large frame was ready to be
woven with vines and flowers to make a plant tapestry that
would bloom and fade each year. The main building had huge
papier-maché tomatoes on the vine, boxes of little objects and a
makeshift kitchen where they cook meals, and it felt like an
outside home. Even the huts containing the earth closets were
painted with flowers.

As we talked, two groups of volunteers arrived. One group of
lads in their early to mid-teens came regularly from a special
needs school. Their main task that day was to stack wood. When
they had finished, Verena spied a bigger job. She asked them to
move a shed from one end of the farm to be near the maple
syrup hut. There was some discussion how to do this. Eventually,

they worked together to shift one end onto the back of a truck. One of the farmwomen drove the truck slowly as the rest followed behind, carefully supporting the other end of the hut. Once the structure had been put in place, two of the lads insisted it should be moved again, just slightly, to get it exactly right.

The other volunteers that morning were what Verena called her 'pea brigade'; four little girls who had come up with their mother for an hour to farm. Buckets of peas were placed at the end of a raked and furrowed patch of earth. Verena told them to put the peas in the ground at intervals. They ran up and down between soil and bucket as if on some purposeful relay race.

The hut lads, another task finished, joined in and did their own rows, with varying degrees of competence but all with total dedication. I looked at them working and at the little green dots that now stretched out in long lines on the brown soil. Would life be much better if we simply all grew? Could the answer to some of our problems be peas on earth?

The other person whom I spoke to at Gaining Ground was Stona Fitch, an edgier character who is part of the charisma and integrity of the place and who led the organization for many years. A novelist, he grew up the son of a man who marketed Pringles. Part of Stona's childhood was bribing other kids at school to do his homework in exchange for this novel new food. A few decades on, he wants fresh organic produce to be available to everyone. 'You shouldn't have to be rich to have a nutritious diet. It should be the cheapest,' he says.

I found Stona to be a man with a delightful sense of mischief, a writer's edge of irony, and a heartfelt belief in what he was doing and what people, himself included, could get out of it. 'Writing is so solitary and boring,' he said. 'You've got to do something else. My grandfather would have loved this. He was all about people helping other people. He was part Cherokee and very supportive of people in need. He always gave things away and Gaining Ground is just my take on it.'

Other charities have been inspired by the example of Gaining Ground, now in its sixteenth year, to set up their own projects on similar lines: a couple had started up in Maine and there are some in California and elsewhere. The charity subtly influences groups to give away more produce. It is hard to put your finger on why it matters that everything is free. Yes, there is dedicated fundraising going on behind the scenes, but the farm work and food are not attached to dollars and cents. Perhaps it makes the volunteers feel as if they are in their own garden rather than engaged in a commercial enterprise. Perhaps it adds to the benevolent spirit behind the work. Perhaps it's because we're all tired of everything being reduced to just the bottom line. 'Everything's done for efficiency and if you do anything for efficiency alone you end up with something terrible,' said Stona.

Ultimately, the magic behind Gaining Ground is many-layered; but it is also down-to-earth and simple enough to be replicated. 'Even though our operation is pretty big now, you can start on a plot ten foot by ten foot, growing carrots behind your school,' said Stona. 'That's the same ethos as Gaining Ground. It doesn't have to be that complicated. We consistently push towards the real, not the abstract, and that's where you get the biggest audience, when people think: I could do that.'

To raise the status of the plants on the plate, it is important to turn, also, to the chefs. The Number One Chef In The World swung into town and I managed to get a hot ticket to see him talk. The venue was the Freemason's Hall, a stupendous Art Deco building in Holborn, London. That week it had been the venue for a Harry Potter movie party; today it was packed with a crowd composed mostly of trendy early-thirties. On arrival, we were handed whole biodynamic carrots. As we waited for the star of the show the vast hall was pocked with random crunches.

Then René Redzepi of Noma restaurant in Copenhagen appeared beside a large screen above a cooking stage and introduced his team almost as a lead singer would his band: 'On the pots and pans ...' 'On plate surveillance ...' The screen was filled with footage of flat, apparently simple Danish landscapes – a sea-marsh, woodland – and he described the richness of what he finds within them to inspire his dishes. 'Nature is the starting point,' he declared. 'It is the inspiration for how we cook.'

Specifically, the inspiration is the nature around Redzepi's kitchen. Denmark is known for design, he said; the carafe, the plate, the knives, forks and spoons in Danish restaurants are all made there. But the food and drink on the table often came from elsewhere. Why not, he thought, eat from our area? After years of working at top restaurants around the world, Redzepi decided to open his own restaurant, and went on a journey around the north to discover what was on his doorstep.

The screen on the stage showed a spruce forest. This is what the deer eat, so why not us? Redzepi mixed the spruce with some salt and discovered, as he put it, a 'northern spice'. He became interested in what people used to eat to survive: the dried fruits, seaweeds and wild greens. He discovered that reindeer moss is almost 100 per cent protein and is 'crazy delicious', and that there are numerous types of seaweeds on northern shores, all of them as different as a beet and a carrot. When one of them, dulse, is aged a year, it develops even more interesting umami (savoury) flavours. The region has fifty-nine types of edible berries, hundreds of kinds of mushrooms, and even many different varieties of horseradish. Why not use these?

What is so special about Redzepi, and why he was Number One at the San Pellegrino World's Best 50 Restaurants Awards in 2010, is the way he makes diversity-on-the-doorstep so central to his enterprise. It is a profound shift of focus. The modern shopper, with the world's larder available, knows less and less about more and more. In contrast, Noma's menus are largely based on exploring the plants, in particular, that grow nearby. He uses local oils such as pumpkin oil instead of the now ubiquitous olive oil and is proud to put a cauliflower at the centre of a dish in his high-end restaurant. 'Meat is the vinaigrette to the salad,' he says; vegetables often play lead guitar in a Noma dish.

The restrictions of the local are not always easy to deal with. Redzepi says he is a 'weather junkie', and constantly scans the Internet to see what's happening and what will or won't be available. However, this leads to many discoveries. A couple of years ago, a long cold spell meant that supplies of fresh vegetables were scarce. He phoned round the local farms begging them to consider anything at all that was edible. This was how he discovered vintage carrots. A farmer hadn't harvested his carrots but had left them in the ground, so they were two years old. By this stage they were, as Redzepi put it 'utterly, utterly shitty carrots'. He decided to cook them slowly in butter, with as much care as you would a rare and precious piece of meat, taking time and spooning over the juices with care and attention. An hour and a half later, he had a sweet, lush and luxurious dish. It was, he says, a revelation.

Redzepi's experiments with vegetables have led him towards a way of cooking that is healthier than other forms of *haute cuisine*. He worked out how to make an intense mash using a baked-potato-skin stock to enrich the purée rather than using half potato and half butter, as a number of posh chefs do. His restaurant also has a serious juice menu, alongside the wine list (the grape not being a northern fruit), and these are chosen by about a fifth of his customers.

At the end of the talk, we each opened a brown paper bag full of little packets of wild foods gathered from near London. The sprig of Douglas fir inside was deliciously citrusy. Sea buckthorn seeds were sour, then aromatic. Hogweed seeds had an aroma of Grannie's apple store. Melilot was like intense hay and sea purslane was salty and succulent. These exciting northern spices took me back to the Paleo Diet. Why do we somehow make the assumption that their food would have been basic? With their intimate knowledge of their surroundings, the caveman's food was probably more sustaining, diverse, delicious and healthy than what many eat in our modern agricultural world.

Vegetables are, increasingly, at the heart of gastronomy. I came across a huge glossy book called *Vegetables*, with photographs of the produce of celebrated French grower Joel Thiébault. It was full of the dishes his vegetables inspire, with contributions from forty top chefs. There were young carrots served in carotene butter and a carrot-cake sauce by Pascal Barbot of Astrance, a chef celebrated for his daring flavour combinations. Then a celeriac soufflé served in the scooped-out vegetable by Alain Passard, famous for his vegetable dishes at the three-star L'Arpège. The linen-covered tables at L'Arpège are decorated with vegetables from Passard's own gardens, which arrive daily, freshly picked, and they are at the centre of his cuisine. Eating here is astronomically expensive, but is an exquisite parade of tastes, techniques and textures using what grows in the ground.

Joel Thiébault is one of the few remaining 'truck farmers' who bring their produce into Paris. He grows 1,600 varieties of vegetables on his 54 acres of land beside the Seine, seven miles northwest of Paris, selling them himself with his team at markets in the smart 16th arrondissement. His family has farmed the area since the Middle Ages. Joel decided that instead of becoming super-mechanized and specializing in a few crops, he would make a virtue of variety, so he started to explore heritage vegetables, including such rarities as red and green striped tomatoes (amongst the sixty varieties he grows) and dark red carrots.

The photographs in *Vegetables* gave as much prominence to the raw materials as to the finished dishes; large type announced each vegetable was 'by Joel', just as the dishes were given the chef's name. There is a theory about how *haute couture* influences day-to-day fashion: where the high-end goes, people follow. Food is altogether a more earthy and rooted pursuit than clothes, but nonetheless this vegetable gastro-chic is a welcome celebration, a raising up from the ground of the 'humble' vegetable. Noma's celebrity will not mean we all eat reindeer moss; the food served by the Michelin Star chefs in the vegetable book are way beyond most budgets. But their attention will undoubtedly increase a background appreciation of the natural history of food and nudge vegetables towards the centre of the plate.

Chefs have a great deal to say about food, but their knowledge can seem rarefied. I was drawn, finally, to the table of a different kind of chef who combines skilful cooking and attention to ingredients with the hospitality and tastes of a great home kitchen.

Stevie Parle cuts a tall, quietly confident figure in chefs' whites, standing beside his stove. It is significant that this stove is right beside the entrance of his restaurant, the Dock Kitchen, in west London's Ladbroke Grove. This a place that challenges a few of the assumptions behind restaurants and their food.

The Dock Kitchen began as a pop-up restaurant, serving a set menu in different venues around London. Parle then moored up in a permanent home in the canalside buildings of a top designer, Tom Dixon, and continued the pop-up ethos by serving a set menu on a theme that changes according to his interest and, always, the season.

Vegetables are at least as important as – if not more important than – the meat, says Stevie. You have to give them real attention, and for him this is part of a deeply seasonal approach to food. He had cooked at the River Café for four years, the Italian restaurant set up by Rose Gray and Ruthie Rogers that takes the spirit and substance of Italian cooking seriously, not least through its focus on the best fresh produce. 'It's all about what comes in,' says Stevie. 'You look at it and say, what am I going to do with it today? How has the season moved on? How is this cavolo nero better than before we had a real frost? Being *really* reactive to what you've got in front of you.'

Parle became a chef at a very young age. As a teenager he went off travelling in southeast Asia, first with his family, then a friend, then alone, going all around Sumatra, Malaysia, Laos. His travels have continued and are the background to his cooking. The food that influences him is cooked in the home or on small roadside stoves. When he travels in India, he wants to eat at the bus stop, not the expensive restaurants. He spent three months in the kitchens of an eco-resort in Sri Lanka learning a way of cooking that used the plants that grew locally in abundance; the herbs, spices and flowers used as flavourings often came from within sight of the stove.

All this matters because Stevie Parle's travels are largely amongst cultures where meat is scarce. He echoed Redzepi's comment about meat being the vinaigrette to the vegetables. 'What I find interesting about the way other cultures eat meat is that it seems to be almost a seasoning,' he said. 'In India, it's the gravy, the sauce, that you want. The meat is a bit of boney old lamb's neck or something, but what you're really interested in is what it's cooked in. You find that in Italy as well. I've just cooked a soup today that had a hunk of salami in it that seasoned the whole dish in a really beautiful way.'

The reason for having less meat isn't just to do with availability but is also connected with a feeling that too much of it was somehow unbalanced. Stevie spoke of a festival in Chianti with T-bones and porcini, where there were huge Fiorentina steaks and fungi everywhere you looked. 'You don't eat this food every day and when you do you have a party,' he said. 'I think that's a really nice way to relate to food.' In other words, it is great to have a celebration, but nobody wants to be and to eat like this all the time. 'I think about balance in food and in a meal and how that makes you feel,' he said. 'I serve food that might be quite feast-like but the whole meal doesn't end up being incredibly rich. I don't think about health so consciously. For me it's something much more natural. If you're eating well, with variety, and if you're eating good things, that's good enough.'

A Sri Lankan meal I ate at the Dock Kitchen was, without affect, mostly vegetables simply because that is what you would eat there. A cashew nut curry; a cup of rasam, the refreshing tomato and tamarind soup that you drink or pour over rice; a carrot thoran, which Stevie explained is a quickly cooked dish that doesn't let out a lot of liquid and keeps its crispness. You start by crackling some mustard seeds in a pan, throw in some curry leaves and mix in vegetables with grated fresh coconut and onion. 'It's really simple, not difficult to make and doesn't take hours – just a different way of cooking a vegetable, like we boil a carrot,' he said. He spoke of the 'tempering' that you do to finish a dal, for example some fried onions and curry leaves and mustard seeds, perhaps some tomato, that is put on top to add a vibrant final note. This reminded me of the gremolata, a mixture of finely chopped garlic, herbs and grated citrus rind, that you use as a final bright flourish to some Italian dishes.

Cooking vegetables isn't complicated, said Stevie Parle; but the more knowledge you have, the more you get out of them. The care he took made them cherished. The Dock Kitchen isn't about show-off food, but neither is it humble. It continues, in a restaurant setting, the spirit of home, in the very richest sense of the word. Vegetables – even very good ones – are not expensive or especially hard to find. To pay attention to them is to touch base with Nature in an everyday way.

Change is often about a change of attitude. Shortly after seeing Stevie, I found myself cooking a lamb stew using four fore-shanks of lamb, the end part of the leg with nuggets of sweet, dark meat. As a child, I was always hovering around the carving board, dodging the knife to try and nick this delicious bit of meat. I'd found these at a farmers' market and they cost £1.50 each. I chopped up and softened celery, onion, garlic and carrot. I browned the meat and deglazed the pan with some vermouth that was open, and made a gravy with hot water, a spoonful of Marmite and a bit of redcurrant jelly. The veg box contained a bag of fifteen Jerusalem artichokes. I was about to chop up about a third of them and then my mind flicked over the idea. Instead, I chopped them all up. The meat became the 'seasoning': it was part of the centre of the dish; but it was no longer the only one.

WHAT TO EAT?
Easy. Find an attractive big bowl and fill it with fruit to peck at during the day; get more variety on the plate; grow some herbs in pots; eat more salads and soups; take the shopping basket off the beaten track and try something new as it comes into season; explore different varieties.

Worth the Effort. Join a veg box scheme; grow fast-cropping vegetables such as rocket; find more varied flavours and techniques when cooking vegetables; make larger quantities of vegetable dishes and keep them in the fridge so it's easy to serve several at each meal.

Hopes and Dreams. That we don't push vegetables to the side of the plate but put them more at the centre of what we eat; that the achievements of Food for Life and other school dinner campaigns become the norm; that ways are found to get kids to enjoy fruit and vegetables as a natural and unforced part of their diet; that allotments and community gardens of many kinds thrive; that the status of fruit and vegetables continues to grow.

9

What is a Green Kitchen?

A green life comes in a number of shades and some of them are dark. First and foremost is the deeply troubling state of the planet. From images of melting ice caps to the strange shifts in seasons outside the back door, climate change is there in the background all the time like a hum of disquiet with spikes of fear. There is an underlying sense that we are responsible for the world and it's going wrong.

But then there are the complicated shades of your own reaction to this slow-mo disaster. You want to do something, but what? The issues can seem both ungraspable and distant. Environmental catastrophe is one of the most important frontlines of our times, yet the approaching enemy is almost too big to see, let alone attack.

And then there's the guilt. The developed world is certainly at fault for over-consumption, and what we eat and drink is the most literal example of this. The environmental call to arms seems to demand a severe change of lifestyle: not only give up the car and the foreign holidays but alter what you eat. Does this mean we have to don a 'green hair shirt' and chew grimly on a (responsibly meagre) slice of sin-free pie?

On top of this comes a niggling thought that you cannot

heap all the problems of the world onto your own plate. The individual matters, surely, but then businesses around the world belch out pollution and carbon dioxide and the world's soaring population gobbles more and more of the planet's dwindling resources. As a mere individual, you feel hopeless before all this.

I am personally convinced by the arguments that we need to act as individuals and as a society – and soon, or else … well, that's all, folks. But I also need a better way of thinking about how to be green. I want to find a way to make the issues more concrete and manageable in the kitchen; to make changes that are possible and not sauced with guilt. To make changes that taste and feel good; changes that make a difference and will help me feel less hopeless about the situation.

To get a firmer platform, I sought a way forward that would inspire me to act in a more practical and positive way.

For me, it came in the form of a book. *Waste*, written by British environmentalist Tristram Stuart, appeared in 2009 and gave me a concrete, food-based way of looking at the issues and making changes.

Stuart delves into our bins and the way we live to discover plenty of rubbish. His starkest point is that about a third of the UK's carbon emissions come from food, yet in developed countries such as ours up to half of this food is wasted by producers, retailers and consumers. If the US, the UK and the rest of Europe didn't waste food, it is estimated that we could satisfy all world hunger between three and seven times over. It is a powerful thought, that we could feed the world and not eat less, just waste less.

Stuart discovered waste in every part of the system, be it the supermarket sandwich factory that throws out the ends of the loaves or the farmers who have their crop rejected by the retailers because it isn't cosmetically perfect. Of course I am happy to eat wonky carrots and have long discovered this is the cheap way to buy vegetables (the same quality produce is sold in 'budget' lines at a substantially lower price just because it looks a bit different). But beyond this it surprised me how much waste is down to choice per se. We are so used to super-stocked supermarkets that the shelves have to be continually loaded; some food goes past its best and is discarded. I remember going into a supermarket and being a touch huffy that they didn't have what I wanted. It suddenly dawned on me that something as ordinary as wanting everything on a shopping list could be part of the problem.

Another pitfall is that we get tempted by supermarket two-for-one offers to buy too much, and some goes to waste, particularly the likes of salad and bread. All in all, it's estimated the average household throws out a quarter of its food, at a cost of £680 a year. I thought of how I was sometimes tempted by apparent 'bargains' that were really just persuading me to buy what I didn't want or need.

There are other shopping pitfalls. Sometimes we are led to believe we should throw away food that is perfectly good, just because it is beyond its 'sell-by' or 'best-before' date. Lord Haskins, former head of Northern Foods, explained to Tristram

Stuart how these dates were originally developed to help retailers keep a track of stock. One suspects retailers are only too happy for customers to believe they need to get rid of produce that is past its package date and buy some more.

Lord Haskins was critical of how such labelling now contributes to our rubbish problem. 'If meat is five or six days out of date, I'd have a look at it and probably eat it if I had stored it in the fridge,' said Lord Haskins. 'Dairy produce, like yoghurt, if it's a month out of date and smelt and looked OK, I'd eat it.'

Best-before dates are put on produce that doesn't even legally require it, such as vegetables, encouraging us to bin them rather than making a tasty soup. You just need enough food knowledge to know what is off and to trust your instincts. The UK government is considering scrapping these labels that insidiously encourage waste. But you wonder if it will happen. There is a tendency in government to 'let Tesco decide'.

Ideally, of course, you plan your shopping to eat produce at its fresh best. This probably means going to the shops a couple of times a week rather than getting it all in one huge trolley-load. For many this would be a huge change; we are now so used to driving to a superstore for a mega-session. But wouldn't this mean more carbon emissions from more driving? And are there any local shops left as an alternative, and what are their costs and standards?

Yet avoiding waste feels like a good motivating force. Despite the profligacy of the West, on the whole we still cringe at the idea of good food being thrown out. I remember my instinctive disgust watching a woman on a television programme roast a whole bargain chicken, eat the breasts and throw away the rest. Part of avoiding waste is down to valuing food properly, and that is partly down to how much of our income it swallows. In Pakistan, for example, it can be three-quarters of the household's budget. In the UK, it is 9 per cent (in 1984 it was 16 per cent).

I wondered if my distaste for wasting food could help me to think more fruitfully about the carbon costs of my kitchen. However hard I try to think of greenhouse gases, they somehow float away from reality. But food you can hold in your hand and therefore in your head. If greenhouse gases could be translated to food and I could learn not to waste food, then that would help me to make my kitchen and my life greener.

Reduce, redistribute, recycle: this is Tristram Stuart's mantra, and in that order. It turns on its head the priorities of the person – I'll hold my hand up, in the past – who vaguely thinks that driving a car-bootful of empty wine bottles to the recycling bin is doing their bit to combat global warming.

Redistribution is largely out of the individual's hands, except as an active citizen, since it is a matter for food politics. It is more about retailers' policies and government regulations that don't allow food to be used rather than thrown away. For example, waste food is no longer allowed to be fed to pigs, which were for centuries the efficient recyclers of household scraps. Tonne upon tonne of good nutrients are being put in landfill rather than filling up animals that are fed imported grain instead.

Recycling is now familiar and tangibly closer to home. A whole section of our kitchen seems to be all about rubbish: the paper box overflowing with scribbled-over articles and chapters; the bag for plastics rather fuller than I'd expect; last week's wine bottles lying on their sides like turtled winos; a murky little box for compost that I attempt to open with one foot in the midst of the rest of the cooking whirl. All this is, of course, worth doing, whether home composting or sending peelings and bones off to the council. But best of all, says Stuart, is not to have to do it in the first place. Reduce before recycling is his message.

So, what to reduce, without it all becoming green hair shirt?

The first step was to look at my direct energy supplies. Gas has a smaller carbon footprint than electricity. I have a gas hob and an electric oven. Gas hobs are less efficient at delivering energy than electric but still better, overall. One step was to ensure that when the oven was used, it was as full as possible. This was simply down to better planning. Instead of putting only a stew in the oven, I started to put a crumble in at the same time, or roast some vegetables and bake some potatoes or make potato wedges to go with the main course instead of steaming or boiling them on the hob.

Being green is getting to grips with the small details. *The Green Kitchen*, by the food writer Richard Ehrlich, made me realize that pan lids are useful not just for bringing water up to the boil more quickly and efficiently (and cheaply), but also for keeping on the pan as the food cooks – you can then turn the heat down to a simmer, using far less energy. This is as true for sausages and chops as it is for vegetables. You can also turn the heat off earlier and let the food continue cooking this way. Richard always cooks pasta by bringing the water back up to the boil then turning it off and leaving the pan, lid-on, for the cooking time recommended on the packet. I find this works pretty well, depending on the pasta; sometimes I give it an extra minute or so of boiling at the end. As Richard points out, given how often most people cook pasta, this represents the saving of thousands of minutes of gas.

After finding use in all these tips, I reorganized my storage so the pan lids were more easily accessible rather than being piled up in obscurity. Kept to hand, I use them much more. I don't cover my food all the time, however; I like the sound and smell of food as it cooks, and sometimes you want to reduce down the juices in the pan.

Some changes in the kitchen come through good equipment and, whilst the eco-message is anti-consumption, it can help to 'tool up'. The carbon cost of production can be more than offset by a beneficial change in habits. I was interested to see that Richard Ehrlich had fallen for his microwave. I'm not sure, as yet, that I'll become a real microwave aficionado because, again, I consciously like to smell, see and even hear my food as it cooks, and the time hovering around the stove is such an ingrained part of my unconscious life in the kitchen. To change this would be like learning to walk again. But I liked the way Ehrlich approached the subject with an open mind to embrace the counterintuitive, thereby slaughtering a few green holy cows. I decided to get a cheap microwave for one main reason: leftovers. Being able to quickly and economically reheat food makes a great deal of sense. It is much more efficient (and convenient) to make more than I need of a supper dish and find corners of the week to fill with the little pots in my fridge and freezer.

Then I looked at the fresh food I threw out. Lettuce is one of the big wastes – who doesn't discover forgotten slimey leaves at the back of the fridge? Tristram Stuart's trick is to store a whole head of the long Romaine lettuce with its stem in a glass of water, like you would flowers in a vase. This really works; it keeps a lettuce fresh and crisp for a week. It helped to think of the lettuce as being 'alive', like a bunch of flowers.

Bread is another food that can get binned. I began to make eggy bread in the mornings with staleish pieces, as well as croûtons for soup – rub crusts with garlic, cut them up and toss with a bit of olive oil, then crisp in an oven that is already on for another dish. Little toasts can be made from staling bread left in a turned-off oven, and these are useful vehicles for dips and pre-supper snacks. Bread-and-butter pudding, apple charlotte, *pain perdu* (French 'eggy bread' that can be sweet or savoury) – the more down-to-earth recipe books are full of ways to use up bread. A quick whizz in a food processor produces storeable breadcrumbs. The Sicilians fry breadcrumbs and toss them into spaghetti with garlic, herbs and chilli flakes. The French put crumbs on top of gratins. I tried both ways and they have become part of my kitchen, along with a jar for the breadcrumbs. Most often they get mixed with lemon rind and Parmesan to be used to coat fish for home-made fish fingers.

I have become more canny about leftovers in general. The end-of-veg-box produce goes into soup or, chopped into small dice, thickens out a pasta sauce. The remains of a joint of meat now becomes a gratin or a stir-fry, or turns a noodle soup into a main course. The French call such an approach *bonne femme* ('good wife'), and it is satisfying to run a tight ship in your kitchen. Excess begins to feel flabby yet carefulness isn't parsimonious. Using up the end of a pot of cream bought for a weekend treat can mean a mid-week *pommes dauphinoises*. That was the key for me, I discovered: reducing waste isn't about penance but about creativity. Perhaps making a change is as much about thinking differently, with thought and action bouncing off each other, and both equally important in the end.

Household economies are useful in focusing my mind. But what would be the most effective way to make a difference to my carbon footprint? I needed a sense of perspective. I remembered how the BBC Newsnight's Ethical Man spent a year cutting his carbon footprint, then worked out that his family holiday to the Canary Islands was the same as running his estate car for a year.

My most useful guide to comparative carbon counting was *How Bad Are Bananas?* by Mike Berners-Lee, who runs an eco-consultancy out of Lancaster University. In the book he measures 'the carbon footprint of everything', from a text message (under 10g) to a war (1 million tonnes and beyond). The quantities were impossible to imagine but the comparisons were useful. Berners-Lee is not telling us what to do, but laying out some of the facts so we can pick our own battles. The carbon footprint of the average person in the UK is currently 15 tonnes. He gives advice on how to cut this down to 10 tonnes, not exactly as a target but as a way to make progress.

The most important point is that food is a big part of our carbon footprint at around a fifth of the total – and it goes up to nearly a third if you factor in an element that I'll come on to later, deforestation. All in all, how you eat is more important than leaving lights on or having central heating.

Berners-Lee lists three ways I could save 60 per cent of what I used. Cutting down waste is worth a 25 per cent saving to the average shopper, he said. I had already looked at this and found adjustments reasonably straightforward, through gradual changes in habit. Then there is the distance the food has travelled. 'Food miles' have been eco-headline news for some time. The phrase was first coined by Britain's sharpest food politics brain, Professor Tim Lang of City University London. But it was always meant to be a starting point in getting a handle on the amount of energy used by food. In some ways, food miles are less important than how those miles are travelled. Boat travel is fine – bananas and oranges – but air freight is not, for example with out-of-season vegetables like green beans. If you eat more locally and seasonably, with just some boat-freighted food from abroad, Berners-Lee thinks this is worth a 10 per cent saving. But the message isn't quite as simple as you might like. If you think that all sea freight is okay, it is important to compare like with like. Transporting lamb from New Zealand by boat may seem fine, but it's not so fine with carbon-heavy freezers on the boat. So, it depends.

The biggest challenge for me in terms of food miles was how to get enough variety in terms of fruit during the winter. Nearly all of our fruit (95 per cent) is imported. I felt good about

Fairtrade imported bananas and pineapples (both sea-freighted) and eat a certain amount of the sort of tinned fruit stored in juice, not syrup, which is convenient and is also sea-freighted. Tinned fruit is really useful for quick puddings – even if you just add it to yoghurt with some toasted nuts and a streak of honey. I have begun to find plenty of ways of using dried fruit, some of which is a value-added Fairtrade product. I soak dried mangoes in liquid – fruit juice and rum, perhaps – and purée them to make a fruit fool or soufflé. They are good in cakes, biscuits and as a snack with some nuts.

The air-freighted fruits are the light, delicate ones eaten fresh, such as blueberries. I resolved to freeze bagfuls of British-grown berries from summertime pick-your-owns, as my parents do. More than ever, I leap upon home-grown fruit in season, which is at its best in flavour as well as at its cheapest and greenest. On the whole, I had tended to be sniffy about frozen berries after buying them once or twice in supermarkets and finding them insipid. Then I realized that this was about the quality of the fruit, not the fact they were frozen. I spoke to Anthony Snell, who sells both fresh and frozen berries from his Herefordshire farm. He told me that he was able to pick berries for freezing slightly riper than those going into the fresh market. I tried some and they tasted really good. Good quality frozen fruit now has an occasional place in my freezer for smoothies and compotes. But I know that freezing has a higher carbon footprint than fresh fruit, even though this fruit is at least UK-grown and not air-freighted. You could say you should eat entirely seasonally, but that can start to get very boring. So I will eat frozen home-grown just occasionally, and tend to eat more dried and tinned to give me variety.

Interestingly, Berners-Lee says recycling your packaging is only worth a 2–3 per cent saving. Packaging is not necessarily the great no-no you might think. Packaging also keeps food fresh, and therefore not wasted. Some of the facts about recycling food packaging are also counterintuitive. Plastics can be more efficiently recycled than paper, for example, and the production of a plastic bag has a smaller carbon footprint than a paper one. Still, we should certainly avoid excess packaging. But what is this? Berners-Lee's guideline is that 'a metal dish inside a plastic tray inside a plastic bag within a cardboard box is probably excessive.' In other words, buy ingredients rather than ready-meals.

More important than any of this – accounting for another 25 per cent of possible eco-saving – is to sensibly reduce the amount of meat and dairy produce you eat. Berners-Lee is not talking about becoming vegetarian, but about avoiding the habit of having a large portion of meat at most meals. Swapping the meat for cheese is not enough; dairy cows also use resources and put methane into the atmosphere by belching and farting (as do sheep).

I scanned the chapter headings of *How Bad Are Bananas?* for references to food. By far the worst items overall in terms of carbon footprint were in the '100 tonnes to 1 million tonnes' category, which includes 'having a child', 'a swimming pool' and 'a university'. Immediately after came a food-related item: a hectare of deforestation. Cutting down rainforest largely for food production, be it cattle grazing, smallholdings or intensive agriculture such as growing crops to feed animals, is clearly an eco-no-no.

The environmental cost of meat and dairy produce was probably the most thought-provoking and challenging aspect of carbon counting I had come across. I noticed people were now talking about eating less meat, not for reasons of animal welfare but for sake of the environment. I knew this was one matter I would have to get to grips with in order to have a green kitchen.

Berners-Lee's breezy totting up appealed. Carbon counting is technical and complicated. As with nutrition label worriting and calorie counting, I would rather act on basic principles and let the numbers take care of themselves; this book gave me some useful perspective. But the sums do matter, especially as far as businesses and organizations are concerned, and I became convinced of this by a man who counts.

I first met Tom Beeston behind the counter of a deli in Ealing, Farm W5. You know that a shop is the real deal when the owner cannot stop telling you about his suppliers, whether by talking to you or writing down details on labels. Farm W5 had exceptional cheeses from small producers and shelves full of local produce, whether suburban honey or kitchen-made chutneys made by a local British Asian family. You always came out of the shop knowing more and eating well.

Tom grew up on a farm in Cheshire. His career took him from dairy farming, through sales and logistics, to becoming the head of the cheese marketing board at Dairy Crest, and from there to a job marketing, as he puts it, 'crap food to kids'. He saw the food industry from the inside and he saw its problems close-up. His career had taken him too far from his grass-roots. He thought again and Farm W5 was the outcome. Eight years later, he began to feel he was preaching to the converted. 'It's okay standing in a small pulpit but actually we need to make bigger changes,' he said. So he went to study for an M.Sc. in Food Policy at City University London on a course run by Professor Tim Lang, wrote a dissertation on corporate social responsibility in supermarkets, and then set up an eco-consultancy called Eat England. I like talking to Tom because his outlook spans every-thing from the primroses on his father's farm to the practicalities of large-scale agriculture and international food production. He puts energy into his subject, sending out a powerjet stream of thoughts, opinions and observations. If you ever felt that change wasn't urgent, Tom is one man to get you fired up.

Tom was adamant about the need for businesses to get down to the nitty-gritty of carbon counting. He decried what he called the 'ambient rhetoric' of committees and government quangos that sit about talking to each other. People need to be told ten ways to make their business greener, he said. Stories needed to be told to engage people. The time had come for ac-tion. To do that, everyone needed to get counting. 'What no-body's got about sustainability – and it's embarrassing at this stage – is that we haven't defined what it actually is,' he said. 'Every time you try to get people to put a stake in the ground and start putting some targets down, nobody wants to do it.'

Even if the calculations aren't quite right, if you have a business, you get a business plan and then adjust, he pointed out. So it should be with the business of saving the planet.

When we met up, Tom showed me some carbon counting he had just done for various food products using information on government and other websites. It was striking that dishes with beef, lamb and pork were right up at the top, along with cheese and other dairy products. A double espresso has less than half the carbon of a latte simply because of the milk. You would have thought the importing of the beans and the heating of the water would be more important. Not so – another indication that food miles are not as important as what the food is in the first place.

There were more challenges to my assumptions. Tom did what he called a 'five-minute guesstimate' of two cottage pies – one a ready-meal, the other from a posh restaurant. It showed that the raw materials were by far the biggest part of the footprint and transport was a miniscule amount – around 1 per cent. What was even more striking was that the carbon cost of processing was a much higher proportion of the restaurant meal. The economies of scale meant the ready-meal was relatively efficiently produced. I remembered being struck in Tristram Stuart's book by how acutely producers looked for ways to cut back on costs of any kind. US industry is particularly good at this, with production costs, and therefore carbon costs, cut down to the bone.

Carbon counting, Tom said, exposed inefficiencies to producers. One example of carbon and cost cutting came from Walkers potato crisps. Farmers were once paid for the gross weight of their potatoes. It was worth their while to sell the wettest potatoes they could, which the company then had to spend money (and carbon) drying before they could be made into crisps. They now pay them to produce potatoes with a high dry matter content and there is less waste all round. 'Learning to think about your own processes is good for manufacturers,' Tom commented.

Through talking to Tom, I began to reassess my assumption that 'big is bad'. Economies of scale, and therefore economies of carbon, were more likely to come from bigger producers. Tom's research had shown that Tesco's, the traditional bête noir of food lovers, with its gigantic market share and ruthless attitude towards small producers and farmers, was making great efforts to count and cut their carbon. The then chairman Terry Leahy was apparently turned on to the issues by the government report by Sir Nicholas Stern, *The Stern Review on the Economics of Climate Change*. 'It was an economist putting it in terms of economic factors and talking the same language,' said Tom. 'People like Terry Leahy and Justin King [the CEO of Sainsbury's] aren't the enemy any more. The time when the food campaigners wouldn't be in the same room as the big boys has gone.'

Perhaps small is not always beautiful, at least when it comes to carbon counting. Tom, however, was still in touch with his Farm W5 ethos. Organic livestock farming, for example, produces meat and milk less efficiently than an intensive system, if you are looking just at productivity (there are other ways that organic production saves carbon, I would discover). But when I asked

Tom the best ways to save carbon his immediate ideas were two-fold: 'Use your oven better' and 'Eat less meat.' Yet for all the talk of economies of scale, this doesn't mean just going to the most 'efficient' meat: 'What you eat is also about the ethics, the love of food and sharing the experience with family and friends – and cheap meat is crap: compound regenerated animal protein,' he said.

What happens when we eat out? Is this where all the green principles and rules get binned? Eating out used to be a treat territory and still is, even when it happens relatively often. But it increasingly feels wrong to eat completely differently from how you would at home, in terms of both health and ethics. I have often scanned a menu and realized that almost every single dish has something to worry about, particularly the meat and fish. Then there is the waste. Have you ever wondered how a restaurant can have a four- or five-page menu and produce fresh food without wastage? Can it be done? After reading Tristram Stuart's book, I began to notice the bin bags outside restaurants as I walked home late after a meal. These businesses are like great stomachs ingesting vast amounts of food and excreting endless black bags onto the street every night.

I came across a new organization that is trying to make eating out greener, the Sustainable Restaurant Association. One of the originators, Mark Sainsbury, is the owner of the Zetter Hotel in Clerkenwell, which houses Bistrot Bruno Loubert. The eponymous chef produces modern French food (in effect, lighter French food). I tried it out and found it easy to 'eat eco' from the menu, which was seasonal and unobtrusively healthy. I chose soused mackerel on a watercress salad served with buckwheat bread and a prawn butter that used up the discarded shells of prawns. Then a stuffed rabbit leg with carrot purée and seasonal summer vegetables, a dish that was very fresh and notably un-salted – so often you find yourself gulping down water after a restaurant meal not because you are dehydrated by wine but because of all the salt. It is a blessed relief to be able to go into such a restaurant and not have to worry about what you have but simply pick what you'd like to eat, as you would anywhere else. You wouldn't know from its trappings and what was writ-ten on the menu that Bistrot Bruno Loubert, for example, was an eco-restaurant; you'd just think it was a good one. This is encouraging; trend-setting food can now be good in every way.

The Sustainable Restaurant Association had already signed up 500 businesses in its first year. The bar for accreditation isn't spectacularly high, but fair enough: this is in the first place about striving to be better and not being ultra-green. The businesses are able to get advice about how to cut down on waste and car-bon and how to source food ethically. For a waste survey, the organization asked ten restaurants to put different sources of food waste into different bins to calculate where it came from. This was revealing. A huge 65 per cent came from preparation – peelings, burnt food, offcuts; 30 per cent was food left on the customer's plates; and 5 per cent was spoiled food from bad stock-keeping.

The survey showed how, on the whole, restaurateurs have to run a tight ship. If you have a great deal of spoilage or serve

outsized portions, you risk going under. The biggest waste is
that restaurant food can be inherently wasteful. I remember at
cookery school being shown how to 'turn' potatoes. There was
even a special little turning knife to get these barrel shapes that
were meant to be posh. The discards could, in theory, go into
soup for the staff lunch, but did this always happen? Turned vegetables are somewhat old-fashioned now but restaurants still
often offer a big range of food, all of which has been primped
and shaped to look special. It doesn't necessarily have the *bonne
femme* element of home food which can make use of leftovers to
good effect.

I was pondering this wastage when I noticed that I, too, put a
lot of peelings in the compost bin. This went against Tristram
Stuart's dictum that we should reduce before recycling. It seemed
especially wasteful to cut the peelings off vegetables now I knew
so many of the micronutrients are in the skin. Since the vegetables were organic, I didn't need to get rid of the pesticides, which
are also most concentrated in the skin. I began to see that in
many cases peeling was a waste of time, as well as of food, goodness and taste. Potatoes could be made into skin-on wedges.
Roasted carrots just needed a good scrub. The Jerusalem artichokes for soup or stew or for roasting were such a bore to peel
and could just be given a thorough brushing. My soup wasn't
going to be competing for Michelin stars; it was there to nourish me in the most delicious way possible. I spotted in a cookbook by food writer James Ramsden that he had never bothered
much with eating butternut squash because they were such a faff
to peel; then he discovered that the roasted skin was 'pleasingly

chewy'. It is true; you just have to get over your assumptions about what is edible and what isn't. Tom Norrington-Davies from Great Queen Street told me he now got his kitchen to use peelings to make stock. It had been quite challenging for his staff to do this, but they were coming round to the idea. Some of the SRA restaurants are now making marmalade out of the orange peel left over from squeezing breakfast juice (admittedly, not the bitter Seville orange kind, but perfectly acceptable; even the marmalade supremo at Fortnum's told me he had taken to the sweet orange type because he found it refreshing first thing in the morning).

The SRA's waste report calculated that a restaurant could save £2,000 on food bills and up to £1,700 on waste costs by being more careful. The economics concentrate the mind. In the opinion of one of the restaurateurs I spoke to, furthermore, the benefits of taking an eco-approach are clearly far greater than saving money. The effect on him has been nothing short of a revolution.

Richard Bell has been a chef for five years, and before that managed pubs for over twenty-five years. Now, finally, he has his own pub, a big Victorian boozer called The Three Stags near the Imperial War Museum in London. Such places are steeped in beery history, and as you stand at the bar you can almost hear the tales of pints past from centuries of people doing exactly as you are now. The Three Stags has a black-and-white tiled booth left as a memorial to Charlie Chaplin's dad, an alcoholic and pub owner (as well as frequenter). Young Charlie hung around pubs, doubtless observing people and getting the very best training for comedy.

Richard had been running this pub for a couple of years before joining the Sustainable Restaurant Association. He soon went on farm visits, met other chefs at sustainable food demonstrations and talks, did some 'ferocious networking', and took part in the Association's waste survey.

When we spoke, Richard was in the midst of a torrent of change brought about by his new perspective. Whilst it took a fair amount of effort to be sustainable, it was eminently worthwhile on many levels. The energy bills for his pub, with its inefficient old boilers, came to £60,000 a year. There were huge savings to be made by switching to a more efficient combi-boiler. Joining a not-for-profit business organization called the Waterloo Quarter enabled him to massively reduce his waste removal charges – £600 a month – saving around £7,000 a year. 'If I carry on like this, it's not just good to do but it'll add around 20 per cent to my profit,' he said.

The biggest breakthrough, from a food point of view, was his direct contact with farmers. Like most chefs and restaurateurs, Richard dealt with packets that arrived at his door rather than the people and places that had produced them. Crossing over to the other side had affected him profoundly. He spoke of a day-trip to Longwood, an organic farm in Suffolk where he had travelled around with a group of chefs on a trailer. They had seen the geese on the lake and gone to visit the chickens. The farmer played Radio 4 to pacify the baby chicks in their shed and when they went in, as if on cue, the day's episode of *The*

Archers started. Richard spoke with respect of how a farmer works from sun-up until sundown for hardly any profit; not unlike a chef, in fact. It was as if a dividing wall had dissolved. He was now using beautiful vegetables and meat from Chiltern Farm to make a game pudding with pink fir apples and red and white carrots alongside. There was now as much of a fuss about the side veg as the main dish. After much thought, he had decided to take fish off the menu unless he was absolutely sure that it had been caught sustainably.

Having spent much time in the Far East, Richard had a certain slant on Western consumerism. I sensed that part of the satisfaction he got from running a greener kitchen was that it would enable him to integrate some of his wider thoughts on life into his food profession. 'It's like a new world,' he said. 'We're taking staff to farms and its bloody marvellous. You go into the catering trade and you never go to a farm, you just get meat from a supplier. I'm forty-eight years old and after all these years I'm doing all these things that are how it should be. It's a great movement.'

One of the useful aspects of eco-eating is how one step leads to another. If you start to recycle, you see all the packaging in one place. You lift it up in its recycling tub and put it outside. And at a certain point you think, as you heave your box outside to be collected: did I need all this packaging? Packaging may be only a small part, comparatively, of a carbon footprint but it can start to feel unnecessary.

I went to a shop called Unpackaged in north London. The

owner, Catherine Conway, has run the business for five years, first as a market stall then as a shop. The shop has a grid of tubs full of grains, seeds, nuts, spices and dried fruits. There are barrels of oils and vinegars. On a shelf behind the counter is a super-foods section with such exotica as whole cocoa beans and pollen. You bring along your own containers – anything you like, from a tub to a small paper bag. Then you measure out your goods and pay. I first came across this idea in the 1990s in a community-run supermarket in Vermont. It seemed so logical to have little hoppers of the goods you need to restock once a month or so. This way of shopping also makes you look around for good containers – although, ironically, these often have been thrown out in the recycling bin.

Catherine described her customers as a real mix, from dark or light 'greenies' to people who use the shop daily as a local corner store. Photographs on the shop walls show the different containers people come in with. One couple who like a dram have a collection of filled-up whisky bottles; another woman brings her china rice bowl (and one customer even brings her hat for pasta). They have created solutions for impulse buys such as the sweets off the counter – pages ripped from glossy magazines make great paper cones. 'Some people are so inventive,' says Catherine. 'They'll whip out an envelope from their bag if they want to buy some nuts.'

While Catherine acknowledges there is a need for some packaging to keep some foods fresh or uncontaminated, she thinks that on the whole this sort of technology developed to support big, industrialized supply chains. If you buy a fresh, local cucumber and eat it soon because it is so delicious, then you don't need it to be shrink-wrapped so it can be flown around the world and sit on a shelf for longer.

Catherine and some of her fellow 'unpackagers' have now formed a pressure group to try to get more unpackaged bulk buying. This is a UK arm of BIG (Bulk Is Green), which started in the United States where buying commodities from hoppers is much more common. It certainly makes sense in terms of both cost and carbon. Perhaps one or two of the more enlightened big supermarket chains in the UK will take this on; it certainly seems like the future to me, as a shopper who wishes to be greener. In a way, it is retail coming round in a full circle. First you had grocers dispensing dry goods by the bagful, to order. Then supermarkets made packaging necessary because you were helping yourself from shelves. Now it looks green and modern to measure out commodities according to your needs.

Just as I was hunting around for storage jars for Unpackaged, my eye was drawn to a film by the French New Wave director Agnès Varda. *The Gleaners and I* (*Les glaneurs et la glaneuse*) came out in 2000. This documentary shows a number of people, often on the margins of society, who put to good use the thrown-away, the overlooked, the left-behind. One group of gleaners are the people who go onto the shore near oyster farms to pick up the shellfish that are scattered there after a big tide or a storm. Then there are those who gather potatoes that are missed by mechanical pickers, and the people who get the 10 tonnes of apples left unpicked in a three-hectare orchard. This being France, the right to glean is encoded in law. Varda films lawyers bearing the red volume of the Penal Code in the middle of fields, as well as on a street corner near thrown-away televisions that had been stripped of their precious copper.

Varda's film struck a chord with the new and growing eco-awareness in society and won audiences and prizes. Long before Freeganism became fashionable, Varda filmed a man who had eaten, as he put it, '100 per cent rubbish' for ten years. Educated and able to follow a profession, he had nonetheless made a conscious decision to operate on the margins of society, teaching English to immigrants and picking up the perfectly good produce left behind by market stallholders. Gleaning was part of how he wanted to live his life.

Such gleaning can be a necessity, and this was especially so in the past. One man in Varda's film describes how during the Second World War he picked up grains of wheat from the ground and pounded them to make flour. It was a twentieth-century version of Millet's famous painting 'The Gleaners', showing women in the fields, bent over and gathering the grain into the scoop of a lifted apron.

Today gleaning is not so much about necessity as about a state of mind that is in opposition to mindless consumerism. In Varda's film, even a Michelin-starred chef is at it. Edouard Loubet, then the youngest chef in France to get two Michelin stars, is filmed by Varda picking up bits and pieces from the ground for his restaurant's high-end tasting menu. He said he liked to know where his food came from. 'I don't want produce from Italy that's been in a fridge for three weeks which is sold only when someone feels like saying it is ripe,' he says.

It is not only food that you can glean. Varda's film shows artists who use rubbish, or as one of them, Louis Pons, says: 'People think it's a pile of junk; I see it as a pile of possibilties.' Varda is herself a gleaner of images for her films, catching life as it flies. This is at the heart of New Wave films with their natural light, real places and, from time to time, non-professional actors. In the documentary, she picks up heart-shaped potatoes and a clock without hands. She lets her film linger on the interesting people she encounters and plays with images captured on her new handheld digital camera. The film ends with her delight in the way the wind ruffles a canvas of a painting of gleaners, held outside by a bemused pair of staff from the museum.

Environmentalism can be portrayed as sacrifice and cutting back. Yet it can also be about really seeing what is around and using it well, rather than attempting change through guilt and fear. To get the most from what you use is a satisfying way of living, much more so than careless waste. This was the biggest shift in thinking for me. Who isn't prone to rush past, without squeezing the last bit of juice or being still enough to really look? If a green kitchen is about awareness, then this can be, like Varda, playful, creative and alive, as well as useful and thrifty.

If you want to 'eat green' and simplify matters, I kept being told, then eat less meat (or rather 'animal protein', since this includes dairy and eggs). These are easily the biggest carbon guzzlers in the kitchen, leaving aside the ethical issues in the farming of animals.

If the best way forward for me as a green eater is at least to cut down on meat and dairy, then how far should I go – cut down or cut out? Tom Beeston remarked how striking it was that many food campaigners were vegetarian. I had also noticed this to be the case amongst prominent scientists. An article profiling well-known scientists in the *Observer Food Monthly* showed many of them to be vegetarian, for a variety of reasons – health, environmental, ethical. Some 23 per cent of people in the UK are now 'meat reducers', according to a 2010 survey by market researchers Mintel. I was one of them. But how far should I go, and should I go further?

I read a closely argued book that gave me another angle on the issue. *Meat: A Benign Extravagance* is by Simon Fairlie, a former editor of the *Ecologist*. A supporter and practitioner of smallholding, he challenges the thought that meat is necessarily un-green. It depends, he says, on what kind of meat, what kind of animals and how and where they are kept and fed.

Meat, says Fairlie, has been singled out for criticism when other kinds of food – such as imported strawberries, asparagus, baby sweetcorn, tea, wine, coffee and chocolate – may be as nutritionally inefficient and also take land away from growing cereals for hungry people. He has many positive arguments for eating meat of a certain kind: from grass-fed animals such as lamb and beef, and pigs and poultry that are kept non-intensively. He argues that such animals build soil fertility by being grazed extensively on the land and that this kind of farming brings people back to the land to lead a more connected and greener life.

Fairlie's argument has as an underlying theme, the need for a retraction from the wasteful ways of 'overdeveloped' nations. Here we are, he says, despising manual labour and wanting more industrialization, and at the same time being told by the doctor to go out and take more exercise. Physical activity used to be part of daily life. It was hard to imagine that I might swap bicycling for milking a cow, but I got his general point. My version of it could be shopping more often to get fresher food, walking or cycling and carrying the food home in a backpack rather than driving to a supermarket once or twice a week.

The book is especially thought-provoking in the way it deconstructs a couple of oft-cited statistics. One is that eating meat is 'ten times less efficient than eating plants'. Some may be worse. Beef is calculated by some to have what is called a 'feed conversion' ratio of up to 20:1, that is, for every 20kg of feed you get 1kg of meat. This does seem shockingly wasteful, considering the hunger in the world. Shouldn't we just be eating the vegetable matter instead? Or, as food writer Hugh Fearnley-Whittingstall puts it, 'cut out the middle man'?

But Fairlie shows how these figures come from feed-lot beef, who are finished on a grain diet. A decent quantity of British beef is mostly grass-fed, and eating pasture that is, on the whole, grown where crops wouldn't thrive so well (or at all, in the case of sheep grazing on hillsides), so you are not taking up land that could be feeding humans directly. Grass is good, green stuff in more ways than one. It helps lock carbon back into the ground, a process known as carbon sequestration.

Beyond this, beef is less than 20 per cent of the animal protein eaten in the world. Other animals, particularly chickens, need far less vegetable matter to get the equivalent weight of meat. Non-grass-fed animals such as pigs and chickens can eat rejected food such as potato peelings and vegetable oil seed-husks that wouldn't be eaten by humans anyway, just as cows and sheep graze on grass that we wouldn't eat. When Fairlie crunched down all the statistics, and posited ways that animals could be fed most efficiently, the feed conversion rate could, potentially, be an average of 1.4:1. Neatly enough, this is the same ratio as the nutritional value of meat to vegetable food: meat – broadly speaking – is 1.4 times more nutritious than vegetables.

These figures, however, are arrived at in an ideal world, which we are far from achieving, or ever likely to. However, we could get far closer to the optimum ratio by taking various steps. For example, the amount of waste food that could be eaten by animals could be so much higher. I remember the scraps from my primary school dinner – scrapings of pink blancmange, grey mash, streaks of salad cream – being carted off in steel tubs for pigswill. But I had discovered that nowadays this form of waste feeding is banned, and is likely to continue to be. The UK government banned pigswill in 2001 because of fears of disease spreading during the foot-and-mouth outbreak. This ban was soon extended throughout the whole of the EU. Instead of going through pigs and being returned to the land to build its fertility, waste food is incinerated and sent to landfill. It doesn't have to be that way. In Cuba in the 1990s, a national effort had to go into feeding the country once Russian money disappeared. A national herd of some 500,000 pigs was fed a diet that was composed of more than one-third food waste from schools, restaurants and hospitals. Pigs evolved to eat bits and pieces. It wasn't so very long ago that urban life was full of the oinks of the backyard pig. Why do children put money in a piggy bank, Fairlie asks? It was the traditional way of saving up scraps to produce a tangible whole.

There are ways to recycle waste safely and efficiently. Tristram Stuart has great descriptions of 'waste food gastronomists' in Japan who carefully unpick the mush in bins and send it off to a new life in their gleaming high-tech factories. One commented that he is 'changing the image of food waste recycling'. But the fears about animal disease seem to make even this approach unappealing in the West. Technology could be used to make it safe, however, and the thought of food being recycled instead of thrown away is a powerful one. As so often, you yearn for much more investment in green technology for there really to be a green industrial revolution – and soon.

I came back, once more, to the statistics behind how to be green. Fairlie examines another much-quoted figure, that a single kilogramme of beef requires 100,000 litres of water. He debunks this by simply looking out of his window at the life lived by his own Angus/Jersey cross, a steer called Bramley. Bramley ate grass, which just took rain from the sky, and excreted urine as much as he took in water. He finished his days at a small abattoir that wasn't wasteful of water (as none would be, as water is a cost). How on earth could he have consumed 100,000 litres of water? It turned out that the figure came from intensively produced feedlot beef fed on irrigated crops in a dry part of California; in other words, a tiny fraction of expensive beef produced ultra-wastefully in one of the richest parts of the world. The environmentalist George Monbiot had quoted this figure in his eco-argument against meat. After reading Fairlie's book, he retracted his stance that veganism is the only green way to eat. This was a significant move for those of us watching our green waste-lines. If Monbiot thinks eating meat is, in certain cases, now all right – or, as Fairlie puts it, a 'benign extravagance' – then it is all right, so long as you eat the right kind.

So you have to be wary of statistics. Fairlie shows how oft-repeated 'facts' can originate from a hidden agenda. Another statistic came in a 2006 report by the FAO called *Livestock's Long Shadow*. Its headline 'fact' was that meat was responsible for 18 per cent of the world's greenhouse gases and was worse for the environment than driving a car. Fairlie looked harder at the 400-page report and started analysing where this figure came from. A big chunk of the figure – some 30 per cent – was due to deforestation. This was from cutting down trees in Latin America to graze cattle and to grow soya to feed factory farmed animals. Fairlie argues that the reasons for deforestation are complex, and there is less of it now than there was; the food industry turned away from feed from such sources once the scandal was exposed. In other words, it isn't right to simply point the finger at livestock. And what was behind the report's conclusion? Since meat-eating is bad news for greenhouse gases, the best conclusion is to eat meat that is produced as efficiently as possible. This means factory meat. But this doesn't take into account the carbon footprint of imported feed, the concentrated pollution from animal factory waste, the packaging of industrial food and so forth. And then, if you produce meat more cheaply, won't people simply eat more of it?

Fairlie's arguments further propelled me to get meat from a proper farmer or the farmers' market stall or butcher, when possible. If I was going to continue to eat meat, then I would have to eat less and feel that it was better on all levels – welfare, taste, overall 'green-ness'.

I found one straightforward way of doing this by simply adding on a meat order to my veg box scheme from Riverford Organics. But there was an equation to balance. I totted up the amount of money we had spent on meat in the previous week. My partner's three boys had been home for a week of the school holiday and meat, I'll admit, is the easiest way to please. We had had two packets of free-range chicken drumsticks, mince for bolognaise sauce, outdoor-reared sausages and a leg of lamb. This added up to around £30. I worked out that buying organic cooking chorizo, shin of beef and pork ribs would be around the same and, stretched out with plenty of vegetables, feed the same number of people for the same number of meals. The chorizo jazzed up a parsnip soup and added another flavour to the shin of beef stew, which was cooked with onion, garlic, carrots, leeks and celery, as well as red wine and herbs. With some roasted slices of butternut squash and a celeriac and potato mash, plus greens, the equivalent weight of meat to a couple of steaks fed seven at one meal and my partner and I at a couple of others. We had three pork ribs each, which was less than usual, but they were so delicious and chunky that it somehow felt enough, once accompanied by plenty of (skin-on) potato wedges.

The meat, I knew, came from smaller farms, though not as small as Fairlie's 'neo-peasant' model. I pondered whether to buy part of an animal directly, as part of a Community Supported Agriculture scheme. This means you are part of a group that buys a share in an animal. Such schemes enable small-scale farmers to survive and give consumers a greater sense of connection to their meat.

But I didn't have much freezer space and couldn't see myself making bacon and hams at the kitchen table. However, I like the idea of smaller-scale farming being accessible to the consumer in this way. You don't have to go 'the whole hog', however. From friends in Sussex, I now hear of ways to get hold of semi-small-holder meat and intend to make the effort to follow this up, and such meat is increasingly available in markets, farm shops and butchers. Britain tends to have larger herd sizes than other countries (and they are getting larger). In Austria and Switzerland, for example, a herd of six to eight milking cows is still normal. Even more small-scale, in Romania animals peel off into their homes as they are led back through a village from grazing in a community flock or herd. Whether the pending reform of the EU's Common Agricultural Policy will make the small-scale herd untenable is to be seen. One suspects, alas, that a way of life will be swallowed up by the likes of Smithfield's vast pig factories in the US. Instead of community grazing, and a way of life that puts humans and animals in the fields, there will be cheap meat from unhappy pigs. But if a sizeable number of people join CSA schemes, go to farmers' markets and to smaller butchers who buy from traditional farmers, and if we appreciate the restaurants that source meat from smaller producers, there will at least be an alternative.

For my home meat-eating, this swap to a meat box made sense. In terms of cost, it was about the same; in terms of taste, it was better; in terms of weight of meat, it was less; in terms of carbon, it was better than I had hoped. But, in the meantime, I also continued to buy meat elsewhere and it wasn't always organic.

The health benefits of organic food are widely held, by supporters, to be probable if partly unprovable. Its eco-credentials tend to be clearer – especially so when it comes to fruit and vegetables because the pesticides and production methods apply directly to the produce. How much greener is organic meat?

I was curious to know more and went to talk to Ben Watson, who knows most about the meat side of Riverford. Like his brother Guy, Ben is refreshingly honest about his business. This 'anti-spin' is curiously effective. You somehow believe someone more because they don't shy away from the negative.

Ben is utterly convinced, of course, that as far as standards are concerned, organic is really the only way. But he is pessimistic about its widespread future and predicted, bluntly, that organic meat may be finished as a mainstream option in five years' time.

'You could say it's served its purpose,' he said. 'Conventional agriculture is largely a lot greener and a lot of this is the effect organic farming has had over the last fifteen years.'

The question mark over organic meat's mainstream future is largely about price. Organic lamb is kept on more natural pasture and is roughly the same in price, though organic beef is a bit more expensive. But when it comes to pigs and chickens, there is a very big difference between organic and non-organic. Ben had recently bumped into a comfortably off acquaintance who had asked him if it was really worth spending £3.45 on a packet of bacon. 'Of all the things we do, this is probably the one that is *most* worth it,' Ben reflected. Good welfare makes organic pork and chicken more expensive, as well as raising the cost of the feed. It is a hard truth that the animals that are kept far better in an organic system are the ones that people shy away from buying because they cost so much more.

Ben Watson has seen the plight of the pig with his own eyes. His father was a pig farmer and over the course of fifteen years or so, the industry went from keeping pigs in the field to keeping them indoors, with the sows tethered up in stalls so they could hardly move throughout their pregnancy, and the pigs kept on slats so the slurry would just wash away. Ben's father didn't agree with this and so kept falling behind the moves needed to be profitable. 'The price of pork – until the grain shortage a couple of years ago – has been basically the same for the last forty years,' Ben explained. 'More efficiencies were forced on people because this was the only way they could stay in the business.' You could say that it is a consumer triumph that pork costs the same as it did four decades ago; but that is because the pig pays the price (and so does the consumer in terms of quality).

Riverford's meat comes from a number of smaller-scale farmers. The pigs are kept outside, then brought for the last month into big straw-filled enclosures, with no walls on the barns so there is plenty of natural light and fresh air. The animals are killed in a small local abattoir. Ben liked that fact the local abattoir killed three days a week and finished the job by 10.30 a.m., after which the workers got on with other jobs such as cutting up the meat and sausage-making; their work time wasn't all about killing.

As for the future, Ben could see organic meat working in a box scheme, but it was very hard work selling it in a shop. I had seen this myself. Why should we prefer organic when it's next door to free-range? I was about to find out.

First and foremost, it is through knowing more about our food and how it is produced. Ben says: 'The main thing is for people to be a lot more interested in what they eat. If they are, I'd like to hope that they'd make the right decisions. If eating is like going to a petrol station, it's never going to happen, is it? People treat food less well than their mobile phone. I like to think it gives a lot more pleasure.'

The reason for buying organic pork and chicken in particular is not just about the welfare; it is about the feed. That is a few steps from the plate. You are thinking not just about what you eat, but about what the animal eats. At this point you may wonder if you can stand another layer of food dilemmas on your plate. But the subject was brought home to me through one particular food in my cupboard: pots of honey.

I spent several years writing a book about bees and honey. That was seven years ago and, ever since, bees have enriched my life and helped me learn about the world. Some of their wisdom isn't sweet. The subject of bees has attracted considerable anxiety in recent years because of a mysterious bee plague. Bees all over the world have been dying in billions. In the United States, where some beekeepers lost 90 per cent of their hives, this was known as Colony Collapse Disorder. French beekeepers had, before then, complained that their bees were eating something in the fields that made them disorientated and unable to find their way back to the hive. A lost bee is a dead bee.

What is killing the bees? The story feels apocalyptic. Bees produce honey but they are much more important as pollinators. It is estimated that a third of the food we eat relies on pollination. Without the bees, we could survive on other staples but our diet would be very dull. Bees pollinate nearly all apples, and many berries and other orchard fruits. You would have meat on your plate, but with a small selection of vegetables. Carrots, broccoli and onions all need bees (I keep looking out for onion honey, but no luck so far).

But it's a far bigger story than that. Bees of all kinds – there are some 22,000 kinds – pollinate plants of all kinds. Four-fifths of the world's plants rely on pollination and bees, which co-evolved with flowering plants, are the most important pollinators. Some of the connections between particular bees and particular plants are specific, as I had discovered when looking at Brazil nuts. This interdependence can lead to a spiral of decline; fewer bees mean fewer plants; fewer plants mean fewer bees. Bees are crucial to biodiversity; if they are in trouble then so is the world.

An American radio interviewer once asked me as regards bees: 'After all this time, haven't we got anything better to pollinate plants than bugs?' It was hard to know where to start on that one. I could have turned the question round by saying everything about bees leads you into an ever greater respect for the natural world and its sophisticated interconnections. We are in their world, not the other way around, and they are far better than humans at doing an infinitely varied and complex task such as pollination.

Yet what do we do with sustaining, complex, creative, nourishing Nature, as symbolised by the bee? We poison it. Why are the bees dying? As an overall reason, I am with Willie Robson, a Northumbrian beekeeper of considerable experience, who thinks it can be summed up in one word: 'stress'. Agricultural monocultures mean the insects can be hungry; they can be handled roughly and get diseased. There's the problem of Varroa, a bloodsucking mite that invests the hives and weakens the colony. But then there are also the pesticides.

In part the problem for the bees must be because we find brutal ways to poison life. One particular kind of pesticide is now prevalent in our fields. Neonicotinoids, based on nicotine, attack the nervous system of insects such as bees. These pesticides come under various macho brand names, such as Chinook for oil seed rape and Gaucho for sugar beet. They are applied either to the soil or as a seed dressing, when they are known as systemic pesticides because they go from the seed into all parts of the plant, be it sunflowers, maize or oilseed rape. The pesticides are also used in garden products and golf courses. Look for words like imidacloprid, thiacloprid and clothianidin on the packaging.

Bees get stronger concentrations of these chemicals because they concentrate the nectar (honey is nectar that has a fifth of its original moisture). The makers of these pesticides say they have been tested on bees. But their evidence has been widely questioned, and what are known as 'sub-lethal' amounts are thought to add to the load of bees that are already under stress from pollution, disease and lack of food in the monocultures of modern farming.

When you take a bee's eye view of the typical agricultural field, it doesn't look too pretty. It doesn't look too pretty for anyone. These particular pesticides can pollute the environment, and a memo leaked in 2010 from the US Environmental Protection Agency regarding an application for one such pesticide, clothianidin, revealed that the regulatory hoops are not what you would hope. Yet such substances have become one of the most widely used types of pesticide in the world since the 1990s.

A green kitchen is certainly about avoiding such poisons, be they for yourself or for the planet. There are a number of ways to farm in a more sustainable way but organic farming takes the strongest lead. To give another example, artificial fertilizers ultimately deplete the soil and pollute water systems, and a large amount of energy is used in their production, whereas organic farmers use green manures that bring carbon and nourishment to the land. The condition of the soil is paramount to the health of the plant. If you destroy the teeming micro-life in the ground you affect the strength and nutrition of what grows there.

Then I started to look more into concerns about glyphosate, one of the most commonly used herbicides in the world. It is the main ingredient in Monsanto's Roundup product, and as it is now out of patent it is made by some five hundred companies.

Don Huber, emeritus professor of plant pathology from Purdue University in the US, gave a presentation to the UK All-Party Parliamentary Group on Agroecology in November 2011, a transcript of which I read. It made me understand more fully how serious the pollution of the soil has become. 'Over thirty years of continued glyphosate use in the USA, we find that entire groups of organisms don't exist in the soil anymore,' said Professor Huber. The knock-on effect is that plants become less resistant to disease and pick up fewer of the micronutrients that matter to their health and also, he argues, the health of the animals who eat them. His talk was illustrated by some graphic images of plants growing side by side in strips. The ones growing in soil where glyphosate had been applied were, in the words of my Scottish grandmother, 'peelie-wally', or washed out.

Of course the producers say their products are safe. But it is worth paying attention to the mainstream, if marginalized, scientists who are prepared to speak out about their concerns. In the case of glyphosate, these concerns are far-reaching.

So to return to chicken or pork, when you buy organic you are certain not to be supporting the kind of chemicals – glyphosate, neonicotinoids and others – or the artificial fertilizers that are used in order to grow crops to feed these animals. And that is a major reason why, expensive as they may be, organic meat and other animal products are a very good choice in terms of the environment.

Now, I don't always buy organic meat by any means. Partly this is down to cost and partly it is to do with having a connection to other farmers and to butchers who get meat from low-input, high-welfare farmers. The meat I buy is traditionally reared and covers many of the same bases as organic meat, particularly welfare and feed if it is grass-fed, and often when the animals are fed on cereals, too, if the crops are grown sustainably. Just because a farmer is organic doesn't mean to say he or she is the best of farmers, though you would like to think that they are people who would bother and be skilful on all fronts.

Yet there are also good non-organic farmers with a green outlook whose standards I know and respect. Tim Wilson of the Ginger Pig, for example, doesn't use insecticides or artificial fertilizers – they have enough pig muck to enrich the soil – and he feeds his animals from crops he grows on the farm. Rather than spraying all his land with weedkiller he selectively hand-sprays nettles when he's out walking his dogs. His system of farming is not one that pollutes the land or kills bees.

I do tend to eat organic vegetables, partly because they are easily available in my veg box and because they make up the largest part of my diet, at a reasonable price. Feeding four or five people on organic vegetables for a week, however, costs roughly the same as one top-quality organic chicken.

Sifting through the layers of 'what is green' has meant going into not just what I eat; not just what the animals I eat are fed on; but also what is fed into the soil that grows the crops that feed the animals that feed me. And I have come to see more clearly the concerns about the chemicals that can be used to grow animal feed cereals, be they home-grown or imported, and this has made me think much harder about organic meat.

I have long known that the standards for Soil Association organic eggs are notably higher than for free-range, and I have switched to buying them. Finding my way through this question has made me much more appreciative of organic meat, particularly chicken and pork, and animal products as well, such as milk and eggs. It has also made me want to know more about all the meat I eat, from the ground upwards.

Eating organic or high-welfare and low-input meat becomes much more possible, in terms of cost, if you eat less of it. In 2011 a useful cookbook came out that explicitly addressed the issue of eating less meat. Rachel de Thample writes recipes for another UK box scheme, Abel & Cole, and was previously a food editor on a national magazine, *Waitrose Food Illustrated*. It was from her that I had come across the useful, visual idea that you need a piece of protein just the size of the palm of your hand for lunch and supper. We eat twice the meat and half the vegetables we need: hence her idea to write *Less Meat and More Veg*.

Part of Rachel's approach is to buy a bigger piece of meat,

roast it one day and use the leftovers for perhaps as many as four subsequent meals, making use of the freezer and spreading out the meat protein with plenty of plant protein and fruit and vegetables. Roast leg of lamb might then become lamb pitas with baba ganoush, shepherd's pie, part of beetroot, pea and watercress salad and the basis of an Irish barley broth. Careful, maybe, but not parsimonious, and the book is full of flavours, good ideas and practical solutions.

Vegetables, especially roots, can take a long time to prepare and cook in comparison to meat. Rachel has risen to this challenge and has developed recipes including vegetables such as parsnips and celeriac that are cut up into smaller pieces so they are ready much more quickly, absorbing spices and flavours in the (lidded) pan along the way. The roots mouldering at the end of my veg box were sorted: they were done in ten minutes and I didn't have to turn the oven on.

Cutting down on meat does go against the grain, now we are so used to it being cheap. It came as a slight shock to see a recipe for sweet and sour chicken that serves four with just one chicken breast; this small quantity is offset by the large amount of vegetables served with fried chunks of chicken. I could imagine eating that way myself, but the rest of my home table would feel a bit short-changed. I asked Rachel how she took her way of eating into her own home with her family. 'I was the one who started with the small portions [of meat],' she said. 'I'd give them extra and then gradually less. You have to ease yourself into a routine.' Habits and tastes change, not least in terms of portion size and the proportion of meat in a dish. After a while, a huge steak seems slightly obscene and a smaller one just right.

When I bought a larger leg of lamb, I managed to control the portion size on its first outing and was planning to make some of it into a shepherd's pie and play around with some sort of root vegetable and lamb gratin for the rest of it. Then I went out one evening, saying there was *some* cold lamb and vegetables for supper, and came back to find every piece had been snaffled. Cutting down on meat certainly means portion control.

Even more challenging, it is not just meat that the book cuts back on, but also eggs and dairy produce, often the default swap for meat. Rachel had gone around a supermarket looking at prices and was struck by the relative cheapness of dairy produce. 'A pint of milk is cheaper than a packet of chewing gum, mozzarella is cheaper than chocolate fingers,' she said. 'And it's so wrong because what's gone into that milk is so much more. Dairy should be a treat.' We are in a world that is pushing towards the 'super-dairy' with its vast herds of cows kept indoors for greater productivity and lower prices. But shouldn't we reduce consumption rather than always going for more, more, more?

Western cooking is based on the products of the traditional (now factory) farm, but it doesn't have to be that way. For example, Rachel's experiments led her to use coconut milk in pancakes instead of milk and eggs, to great effect. Carrot muffins using the same approach worked out nicely. I would hesitate to call such food vegan, and it isn't that, exactly, although it comes from some of the same impulses.

★

I had come to the conclusion that a green diet is, broadly speaking, a healthy diet as well. This point was reinforced when I went to a talk by Colin Tudge given to food politics students at City University London. Tudge is an advocate of what he calls 'enlightened agriculture' and a believer that a greener way of farming can feed the world's population. He argued in his talk that we need a triple bottom line – economic, environmental and social. As a biologist, he sees that biology, or the environment, is the reality. 'That's what the world really is,' he said. Economics are flexible, in the end: an artifice that could collapse suddenly even though they are often portrayed as what is 'real', as we had seen from the Credit Crunch.

What do we need to feed the world? For the land to be very productive, in order to feed a booming population, and for that production to be sustainable in order to keep the planet going, said Tudge, who has written a book on the subject, *Feeding People is Easy*. Climate change is likely to throw us some flips and we'll need to be light on our feet and able to respond to change, he said.

And we do have a model for this sustainable, adaptable production – Nature: astonishingly diverse, extremely integrated and using minimal inputs, getting what it needs largely from what's around. Going 'back to Nature' in farming, with less intensive forms of agriculture, is not some sort of romantic joke, he said, but the way through the mess we're in. He had a pithy summary of the kind of diet this would use: 'Plenty of plants, not much meat and maximum variety.' A green kitchen means a plant-based diet and paying more attention to horticulture; this has also been the nub of nutritional theory over the last thirty-five years. Happily, it describes the basis of many of the great cuisines in the world: India, Turkey, China, southern Italy, Lebanon. 'The future belongs to the gourmet,' said Tudge; the most appealing call to arms I had heard in a long time.

I was on a personal quest to make my own diet more green. But that is, as for every individual, clearly a small part of the whole story. I kept coming back to statistics such as the fact that 50 per cent of the world's agricultural carbon emissions come from developing countries. One of the most shocking parts of Tristram Stuart's book *Waste* is the amount of waste there is in the food production of developing countries, where there is the most hunger. Often this is due to poor distribution and outdated technology that means, for example, that food can go bad through poor storage.

An article in the *New Yorker* profiled some people who were trying to invent a better kind of solid fuel stove to be used in developing countries. Half the world's cooking is done on small, inefficient stoves, powered by the likes of cow dung, and the black fumes of smoke pouring past the lentil curry somewhat negates the fact the people are eating plants, not meat, in terms of being green. These inventors were trying to find a better way. This is obviously much more important than me putting a lid on a pan.

The underlying story of green issues is a story of finite resources – water, land, oil – and the need to make the best use of them in a world with a booming population. What I do in my kitchen matters in itself, but it is just as important that it helps me to understand the bigger picture. To be really green, I should not just think about my own diet but find ways to support innovative green initiatives.

I started this chapter wanting to get a clearer perspective on my own carbon use. What you eat at home, and outside it, matters in many ways. Apart from my individual carbon use, I felt the need to personalize matters; to start with my breakfast plate rather than the melting glacier. I ended by broadening out my questions, again, by seeing food as a global issue, not just of the climate but of resources more generally.

Whilst food miles are for me no longer the be-all and end-all, I avoid food that has been air-freighted. Local food can certainly be greener. But the question still niggled me: did it necessarily make the world a better place?

WHAT TO EAT?

Easy. Cook seasonally; don't peel vegetables unless necessary; buy whole lettuces and store them in a jar of water in the fridge; put lids on pans; eat more raw and organic food; find the best dried and tinned fruits; use the oven with care and fill it up to get maximum use.

Worth the effort. Reduce before recycling; be canny with leftovers; grow some vegetables to appreciate what goes into your food; explore preserving seasonal gluts; eat less meat and fewer dairy products; know more about what the animals you eat are fed; shop more often to get fresher produce, walking to the shops rather than driving once a week; prepare food in larger quantities and reheat.

Hopes and dreams. Environmentalism will be more widely appreciated for its creativity rather than its denial; the message about pesticides, herbicides and artificial fertilizers will continue to filter down, be it to the gardener or to the shopper; organic food will stop being rubbished and will be recognized as a worthwhile cause; polluting will be fined and the true cost of cheap food will be factored in to make organic produce a more viable alternative; waste will become a taboo and everything will be put to good use.

10

Is Eating Local Parochial?

'Local food' has become a fashionable term in recent years. It also gives rise to a certain amount of harrumphing from different quarters. Some call it a meaningless term with no quality standards. Others dismiss local food as an irrelevant elitist fad since the vast majority of us shop in supermarkets with national and international supply chains.

The term 'locavore' was coined in 2005 by Jessica Prentice, a chef in California, to describe a person who bases their diet largely on what is grown locally. On very first acquaintance with this idea, it is easy to think this is impossible. If a food is produced locally, the raw ingredients may be imported. The bread at a local bakery is not local, strictly speaking, if the flour has travelled. We have been eating foods from other parts of the world for centuries, as the spice trade shows, and plenty of fresh produce in our diet is imported, especially fruit. If you want to eat what grows best locally, the joke goes that the UK could be turned into a vast cabbage patch. Not too appealing.

But a number of people have taken up the challenge of eating as much local food as possible, some exclusively so. I wanted to see how their discoveries could be relevant to my table.

There are different definitions of 'local', none of them with legal force. Certification bodies, however, set up rules, or at least guidelines. FARMA, the excellent organization which certifies some of the UK's famers' markets, says that local food ideally comes from within 30 miles, though this can stretch to perhaps 100.

Then locavores set their own rules. In 2005, two Canadians started a 100-mile diet, beginning symbolically on the first day of spring. Alisa Smith and James MacKinnon pledged to spend a year eating within this area, and wrote a series of articles to report their findings. Their adventures became a bestselling book and other people have since set up their own version of the diet.

The core of the couple's adventure was to discover what was on their doorstep and make connections with farmers. The most difficult part, initially, was to find a wheat grower within their 100-mile region. Until then, they ate an awful lot of potatoes and craved pancakes and pasta. The restrictions they set themselves may seem to stretch a point, but the diet was about 'learning by doing', and every effort that the couple had to make to stay within the rules made them understand their food better. The result was that for a year they ate the freshest of foods at their seasonal peak, and discovered not only the seasons but also the 'micro-micro seasons' as food changed throughout the year. Significantly, the shift meant they had to cook from raw ingredients, and this was part of what made the diet healthy and delicious.

The American author Barbara Kingsolver and her family also decided to eat locally for a year, and the result was her book *Animal, Vegetable, Miracle: A Year of Food Life*. This, too, was a bestseller: people clearly like to read about local food even if they don't eat that way. Kingsolver's relationship to the seasons was even closer than most because the family has a smallholding where they grow a great deal of their food. Their harvest emphasized the fact that locavores often find it crucial not just to cook but also to preserve. You can eat locally in winter, says Kingsolver, but the time to start preparing for this is in summer when you are in the midst of the glut of the land.

This leads to another reason to eat seasonally. When you source good food locally, directly from the farmer at the height of the season, it is much better value than produce flown halfway around the world. 'The main barrier standing between ourselves and a local-food culture is not price, but attitude,' Kingsolver writes. 'The most difficult requirements are patience and a pinch of restraint – virtues that are hardly the property of the wealthy.' This is true; but they are certainly qualities that go against today's food culture (and the way of the world in general).

I noticed that the 100-mile diet website has a gadget to show your own catchment area. Living in Acton, West London, my 100-mile diet would spread nearly as far as Nottingham, right to the south coast and into Somerset and Gloucestershire. It seemed like a good deal. Yet as soon as I started to think harder, I realized that it wouldn't encompass the Devon produce in my veg box, or the Fairtrade banana I had just eaten, or the organic chocolate and Fairtrade sugar in the Brownie I had for supper last night. None of these seemed bad to eat. It sounded as if the locavore diet wouldn't be at all easy to keep to, or desirable from the ethical point of view either – don't the Fairtrade farmers in developing countries need our money?

I discovered a family who had managed to make a personal leap into local food that also engaged with the wider community. Mike and Karen Small and their two young sons made the decision to eat within Fife, an agriculturally rich part of Scotland. The Fife Diet is about environmentalism, yes, but is also about culture and a sense of place. This is part of the appeal of local food for many. A 2010 survey by the Institute of Grocery Distribution showed that the number of people buying local food has doubled in the last five years to nearly a third of us. Freshness was the top reason given, but supporting local business was cited by more people (54 per cent) as a reason for going local than environmental factors (30 per cent).

The difficulties the Smalls faced were telling. Fife has a coastline with a number of attractive historic fishing villages, yet local fish was one of the hardest foods to get hold of. The nearby boats land prawns rather than white fish and most of it is exported. There are fish vans throughout the region, but their produce is landed in Peterhead, which is out of the region (albeit not very far). When Mike spoke to the fishermen's representative, he said it was easier to deal with a single exporter than a number of fishmongers, who may take a while to pay up.

At this point, you wonder whether the local food diet, though admirable, may be actually impossible. How do you turn back the clock and counter economic realities? On the other hand, the status quo doesn't entirely make sense. One of Mike's initial impulses towards creating the Fife Diet was hearing that prawns landed in Scotland could be sent to the Far East to be cleaned. It was the total disconnect between raw materials and the environmental impact that impressed him.

Perhaps it is only a matter of time before the world has to move the Smalls' way, with rising fuel prices and the growing awareness of food's carbon footprint. And if enough people want to eat locally, they can sway the economics. The number of people on the Fife Diet – now 1,000 – means they now have some collective buying power. Oats, a Scottish staple, are largely sold out of the region for cattle feed. But a farmer was persuaded to sell locally to the Fife dieters and someone has started to make oatcakes with this local product.

All in all, the Smalls found the diet was both viable and enjoyable but, again, it did mean taking the time to source ingredients and to cook from scratch. You do need to be a bit flexible on what is allowed, too. Mike and Karen started strictly, which meant buying no bananas or wine – or chocolate. Mike admitted they rather fell on guests who brought these along. But now the diet has expanded to allow the foods that can't be grown here, and a broad 80:20 guideline still means that nearly all their food is from Fife. This is not about denial, but about eating what is local when you can.

Mike Small says that the diet's followers are not especially affluent. One of the surprises for them as a family was that it had cut their own weekly shopping budget roughly in half because there are fewer chances for impulse buys in the supermarket. They spend £10–£20 a week on meat, enough for a couple of meals, plus leftovers. One of the keystones of the diet, Mike said, was to get a veg box because this enabled them to structure their meals around what was seasonal and local. Meat became a celebratory luxury, and the bedrock of their day-to-day eating was the very food that we're being told to celebrate and eat more of – vegetables. 'The biggest lesson is that you don't really need the 50,000 items on sale in the supermarket,' Mike told me. 'That concept of choice is a bit off. By limiting your choice you have a more liberating experience.'

The Fife Diet is also a sociable initiative with community meals, festival stalls and an online social network. When I was in the area, I saw the Fife Diet's quarterly seasonal cookbooks in a local café and bought one. It cost £3 and was strikingly different from the hundreds of other cookbooks on my shelf by being entirely relevant to what I could eat at that moment, right here and now. So many cookbooks take you far from your roots; this one was immediately useful.

What could I learn from this? First of all, it reaffirmed my conclusion that a veg box, far from being a middle-class status symbol, is often the foundation of a different way of eating that is desirable on several levels – health, environment, taste. Part of this is the way it can lead you into seasonal eating. Secondly, the importance of having a more local diet is a great deal to do with making connections with local producers and so making you appreciate the food more. Barbara Kingsolver writes of how local food is 'a handshake deal in a community gathering place' involving farmers with first names who 'grow trust'. She even made a craft connection with producers by making cheese, and discovered that it isn't an arcane, scientific procedure but a simple household process carried out by people all over the world. Local food led her quite naturally to learn more about a traditional food that has become 'outsourced' to the professionals but was originally much closer to home.

Of course, you can make connections with food producers wherever they are. But locavores have the added impetus of a sense of place and an ability to talk to people directly that makes the whole process of getting closer to your food much more engaging.

So the locavores are devising rules and restrictions that help them buy good, fresh food and appreciate it more. In other words, its virtues are far broader than saving food miles. But this way of eating is artificial in the sense that it takes a great deal of focus. I wanted to see a place where a local diet was more naturally part of the warp and weft of daily life.

At this point, work took me to Italy where the food culture is still greatly based on what is grown locally. Sicily is, admittedly, fortunate in its produce. Southern sun and unhurried ways tumble out the sort of vivid fruits and vegetables that a shivering northern allotment holder has to strive and pray for. In England, a tomato may or may not be good; it Italy, it just is. A fair proportion of Italy's organic supplies come from the island of Sicily, often from smallholders who have simply kept growing as they always have done, without the need for expensive chemicals. A street market in Palermo is like a river of fresh produce. When I went there in spring, bundles of fresh wild fennel sat next to spiky little artichokes and the young courgette leaves that go onto pasta. Sellers flicked water onto gleaming shoals of fish and little tender-pink prawns. The butcher had tongues and skinned goat heads, and at one of the cafés the speciality was spleen in a bun with grated hard white goat's cheese. When food supplies are kept within an area, rather than being industrialized, you eat everything.

I best understood the essence of all this local freshness from one piece of street food in particular. A big bubbling pot in front of a vegetable seller turned out to be full of potatoes cooking in highly salted water. The owner gave me a small paper coneful. That was it – no vinegar, no oil, no herbs – nothing. The flavour of these very fresh, properly grown young potatoes was quite simply enough. It was one of the most delicious things I have ever eaten.

I was visiting Scopello, a former fishing village on the north coast in the midst of the lemon growing area. My host was Gabriel David who uses the lemons to make organic lemonade for his company, Luscombe Drinks. His parents came to the village in the late 1960s from a progressive UK school to run a gap-year project that took teenagers into the working life of a Mediterranean village with one telephone and no cars or tractors, reliant only on mule power.

At that time, the stronger, younger villagers 'went north' to make a living. Scopello was slipping farther and farther behind. Gabriel's parents set up a pottery that is still going today, and helped form an agricultural co-operative. Gently and gradually, this became part of a wider change within Scopello. Returning often, Gabriel has seen the village develop a viable local economy again as people set up guest houses and bars, all independently owned.

That night, the Eve of San Giuseppe, there was a village barbecue for the saint's feast day. The vine and olive prunings from the area were piled high in the *baglio*, or village square, then set alight, and people set griddles over the raked-out embers. They cooked sausages that had been made that day by the butcher using pork belly, Pecorino and dried chilli. There were slices of wild boar shot in the hills nearby, fish landed that morning, and little artichokes, smashed so their leaves splayed open to be seasoned with salt, pepper and local olive oil, and put in the embers to roast. Everyone gathered and ate, then more cuttings were put on the fire. Traditionally, the young bucks of the village jump through the flames to impress the young women. It's spring, and this is what happens.

I sat beside the fire, watching dogs sniff urgently at the edges of the embers and children rush towards the flames to throw on more sticks. Alongside me were Katrina and Mike Power, friends of Gabriel's who had first come here as students and returned to live when their own children left home. Katrina talked of quite how local the food was. 'Each village has its own recipes that are different for the same dish,' she said. 'At first I thought it was really restrictive. But then I came to see how it's a real gift.' The way you make a dish reinforces a sense of identity, both of a place and your extended family, she said.

I noticed the way people in Scopello had a strong notion of what was good and what was bad. Sometimes, yes, it felt conservative. There was much tut-tutting in the village about how smoked fish was starting to appear everywhere in menus because tourists liked it. But they had a point. Smoked fish was imported and new-fangled. Much better was a dish that was part of the place, such as the bitter, invigorating salad of wild greens and asparagus and lemons that were all in season right now, and were put together on a plate with much success. The sense of rootedness and seasonality was a restriction, in one sense, but it made food much more of a way of life rather than a lifestyle. As with the Fife dieters, there was variety, but it came from seasonal changes rather than picking at will from a vast selection in a supermarket.

Back in London, I realized how distant I was from the source of my food. When I lived in a country town in Sussex, the connections were much more visible, be it the lamb from animals I saw on my walks or the fish landed in Newhaven. It took a bit of seeking out, but once your eye was in, such produce was clear to see. In London, it is much more difficult. I can find honey and apples, I can grow herbs in pots and some vegetables in our backyard, but it is not a meaningful supply in any sense.

London, of course, has a seemingly endless diversity of foods. Perhaps I could connect foods to a location, wherever that was, and eat 'locale food' rather than just local; and I would find these most often at independent shops, as far as possible local to where I lived. That could be my most fruitful and realizable interpretation of the term as a city-dweller.

★

At about this time, I had to write a feature about farmhouse Cheddar cheese. Looking into this subject made me realize how rich and important local traditions are – and how fragile. I came to see that respecting a food's place isn't just a marketing tool for good foods but is crucial to their survival.

Cheddar originates in the west of England, in Somerset, home of Cheddar Gorge, where the cheeses were once stored and matured in caves. The definition of a Cheddar is, broadly speaking, down to the distinctive way the curd is heated and cut, which gives it a smooth texture and particular acidity. Cheddar is now made all over the world, mostly in factories. I wondered how the original Cheddar was different and whether there was any real meaning in it coming from a particular place any more. To find out, I went to see three places still making Cheddar in its purest original form, cloth-bound and handmade using un-pasteurized milk: Montgomery's, Keen's and Westcombe, all within ten miles of each other in Somerset.

My first observation was that each of these could properly be called a 'farmhouse cheese'. Dairy, cheese-store, office: in all three cases, they were right beside the cows and off a farmyard. When I talked to Jamie Montgomery, we sat in his old-fashioned, scruffy farmhouse office in North Cadbury. A tall wall was covered by a map of parish fields, including an ancient hill fort where some their cows graze. There was mud on his boots, his hair stuck up and when he talked I could hear both the farmer and the guardian of one of the best cheeses in the world.

Nearby, George Keen is part of a family farm that is run by him, his brother and their two sons. We met outside his sixteenth-century farmhouse, which is fronted by a moss-covered wall of upright flagstones, and we talked about some new flagstones he had put up and whether they would last; his perspective was one of centuries, not decades. Farming at its best is about a rooted sense of place. The good farmers and food producers I have met know every inch of their land in a way that makes you feel they are truly its custodians.

The third cheese producer, Westcombe's, epitomized the revival of traditional kinds of Cheddar. The farmer, Richard Calver, went from making traditional cheese to a commodity product, but then returned to 'trads' in the 1990s when milk prices went up and the profits from standard cheese fell. He needed to add value to his own milk and sell it for a higher price. This meant going back to making raw milk, handmade cheese.

The three farms had recently formed a Slow Food Presidium, with a defined set of standards to keep the tradition going properly. The identity and craft of Somerset Cheddar relies on upholding quality. This means using unpasteurized milk from their own herds, wrapping the cheeses in cloth, not wax, and ageing them for a certain amount of time. 'It's given us the confidence to not change things,' said George Keen. 'What was old-fashioned and traditional is the basis of our future.'

I tasted these three different Cheddars side by side and the difference was marked. Mongomery's was sweeter – almost toffeeish, and its flavours rolled on and on in my mouth. Keen's was more assertive and had delicious grains like Parmesan. I could see why some chefs insisted on Keen's exclusively to make the best cheese soufflé as well as being delicious on a cheeseboard. Westcombe had gone for a slightly softer texture and there was a fruitiness to the best ones.

Each farmhouse made a different kind of Cheddar from the same ingredients and using the same techniques. Furthermore, raw milk cheeses are unique to the day they are made. Weather, forage and the state of the cows all make a difference to the character of the original milk. I had often heard that cheeses made from summer milk are the best because they benefit from the lovely lush grass. But Tom said that April and May cheeses were his favourite. Whilst the high summer cheeses could be delicious, they were more variable because the cows have more unstable butterfat in their milk due to a 'scratch factor' of drier forage that can irritate their stomachs. Winter cheeses could be more consistent, but fewer reached the heights than those from the milk of the first flush of spring grass.

It is not just the milk that leads to such delicious and interesting particularity. The bacteria in the cheese make a big difference to taste. Cheese-making uses a 'starter', which is a shot of bacteria. This starter used to be made by the farmer's wife (dairying was largely a female craft) who had a bowl of it in the farmhouse and kept it going.

In the 1930s and 1940s, the best starters, selected for success over centuries, were collected by a company which kept them carefully in what you might call a 'cheese bacteria' library. Then food technologists found a way to freeze-dry some of the starters so they were easier to store and use. Some starters continued to be kept in their original form, known as pint starters. The freeze-dried starters, known as direct-to-vat, don't have the complexity or the same bacteria as the pint ones. Traditional cheesemakers favour pint starters because they produce a better-tasting cheese. They feed the starters with skimmed milk powder for eighteen hours, then add them to the day's milk. 'You've got quite a lot of faff and hassle every day,' said Jamie Montgomery. 'Most of the industry hasn't got time to mess around with this crazy stuff.'

Alas, cheese starters are as prone to the same sort of homogenization as most products and processes in modern life. One particular starter, with a persistent sweetness, is used in many American Cheddars and now in British ones, too. One cheesemaker called it the 'Coca Cola of starters', and when I bit into a UK factory Cheddar it leapt out at me: the cheese was obvious, sweet and bland.

One day in the mid-1990s, the traditional cheesemakers got a letter from the owners of the cheese bacteria collection. It was too much bother to keep them going and they would stop in six months. The time-honoured genetics that underpinned traditional cheddar were under threat. Fortunately, a West Country cheesemaker called Barber's bought the pint-starter collection, and the man who was looking after them came as part of the deal. I like to think of this man shepherding his multi-billion herd of bacteria to a safe home. The traditional cheeses were saved.

But there is now another dark cloud on the horizon. Tuberculosis has been spreading through the British cattle herd in the southwest. There is a great deal of controversy about whether badgers, thought to be spreading the disease, should be culled. Bovine TB is bad in Cornwall, has spread to Devon and is now reaching the Mendips in Somerset, not far from these three cheesemakers. There have been tests showing it doesn't survive in the finished cheese, but all the same the worry was that there would be a blanket ban on unpasteurized milk. On top of this, the testing for TB is imprecise and there could be 'false positives' that would nonetheless prevent a herd from being milked. 'It's getting closer all the time because the government isn't really prepared to do something about it,' said Jamie Montgomery. 'Whether we'll be able to survive pasteurization I just don't know. I'm not sure.' It was the centenary of his family making cheese on this site, yet the future looked worryingly uncertain.

How much does this matter? Sure, nobody would starve. But one of Britain's two oldest and most established cheeses (the other being Stilton) could be annihilated in its purest form. With it, a store of tastes and traditions and stories would become part of a museum rather than continuing life. Time-honoured food has the gleam of life that inspires you and makes up the fabric of culture. The particularity of life is the basis of its richness and at the heart of the point of local food.

The longer I have looked into food, the more I have come to realize one truth: that the good stuff has certain particulars and they need to be kept going. The bad and the bland are generally the way they are because corners have been cut. Details of production are smoothed over or erased, be it in the face of overbearing regulations, time, economies of scale, fewer staff, lack of knowledge – there are hundreds of reasons why something becomes standardized and inevitably duller. You cut corners too much and you end up somewhere else. How, then, to ensure that a food does keep its identity?

One answer is to pay attention to local or 'locale' food and its technical details. One crucial person attending to these, in the area of British cheese, is the cheesemonger Randolph Hodgson. Like other cheesemongers, Randolph Hodgson saw that traditional British cheeses were in decline when he set up Neal's Yard Dairy in London in the 1980s. 'The customers in London were saying to me that the cheese didn't taste the same and so they were buying French,' he says. The first move, by Randolph and others, was to get the traditional British cheeses back on their feet and valued. A handful of these good British cheesemongers visited the farms, picked out especially good cheeses, matured and kept them well and sold them with pride and joy according to their name. They sold 'Montgomery's Cheddar', not number 447, as it used to be called by the wholesalers.

Phase two of the traditional cheese revival was to fight off health scares. Raw milk makes the most interesting cheeses. But environmental health officers with clipboards and rulebooks prefer sterile factories to mucky farmyards. The foundation of the Specialist Cheese Association helped get good cheesemakers together so they could have a collective voice and an *esprit de corps*. They fought off efforts to stop people making unpasteurized cheeses and ran shows and competitions to raise the profile of good cheeses and the standing of the cheesemakers.

Customers started to come back to buying British instead of always assuming that good cheese was French.

Phase three has now begun. Over the past couple of years, Hodgson has brought together a dozen traditional Cheddar makers and got them to talk about the details of their techniques. Hodgson had seen lots of changes even to these traditional cheeses over the years – small details that altered the cheese sometimes for the better, sometimes for the worse. He wanted to work out what the techniques were, be they what people had been taught by tradition or what they had evolved themselves over the years.

At one such Cheddary get-together in 2010, the cheesemakers looked into the particular point at which you drain away the whey from the curds. This affects the taste and acidity of the end cheese. The process is called 'pitching'. Pitching is done by feel-of-curd, sight and sometimes pH measurement. A group of Cheddar makers met at the farm that produces a new Cheddar, Hafod, in Wales. As it happened, the mechanical stirrer was broken. 'So we had to stand around and stir together by hand, like a knitting circle,' recalls Randoph. 'We were stirring and feeling the curds. Someone said, "I'd pitch now," and someone said, "Lord, no!" and someone said, "I'd have done it half and hour ago." My role was to ask: Why?'

Given that Cheddar is one of the most famous cheeses in the world, and half the cheese eaten in the UK is Cheddar, it seems amazing that this crucial point of the process can vary so much and isn't known. Yet perhaps it isn't so surprising. In France, home of 5,000 farmhouse cheeses, there are 400 technical assistants and 7 dairy schools, who are geared towards unpasteurized cheese as well as pasteurized. In the UK there are just 150 farmhouse cheeses and all the expertise is concentrated in the factory and not the farmhouse. Knowledge has become more personal and isolated than something to be discussed.

The point of these Cheddar gatherings isn't so that everyone should 'pitch' at the same time, but rather to understand a bit more about what the differences are and how different people do it. Randolph describes the process as amassing a 'seed bank' of knowledge. The discussions are immediately helpful to the cheesemakers. Whilst winemakers have the winter to reflect on what they do, cheesemakers are working day in, day out, all year. These sessions offer a chance to pool ideas and come up with some observations. 'I'm not interested in this because I think we should dress up as Victorians and make cheese as it used to be made,' said Randolph. 'We shouldn't follow traditional techniques blindly but use them as a knowledge base that is a palette of possibilities.'

Randolph wasn't at all keen on the term 'local food'. 'I've got a problem with the whole idea of local,' he said. 'I have a customer in America who visits me and the farms every year. I've got customers in Wimbledon whom I've never met. The guy in America is more "local". It's about contact. You can go to a farmers' market and be served by someone who knows nothing about what they are selling. I don't mean "telling the story" but *knowing* the food. Taste this Montgomery's and then this one made on a different day, and see they are different. The food knowledge goes up.'

It is an important point. The locavores believe in 'knowing by doing' and you can do this partly by eating and talking to the producers. I have learnt so much from talking to the people involved in food production, be it the 'boys ashore' selling fish on Hastings beach, the blessed cheesemakers or a deli owner who sources carefully. But you don't have to be local to the food to do this; you just need to hook into a network of people who care, bother and know, whether you are at home or away.

At this point in my explorations I came across a parable of localism, again relating to cheese. Lancashire is one of the most delicious traditional British cheeses and one that is still appreciated in its region. Go to a food market in Preston or Lancaster – or pretty much anywhere in Lancashire – or to one of the branches of Booth's, a northern supermarket that pays close attention to its region, and you will find several different makes. The most renowned Lancashire, championed by Randolph and Neal's Yard, is Kirkham's. It is made by Ruth Kirkham, a.k.a. 'Mrs Kirkham': she actually exists, unlike Uncle Ben, and so does her son Graham who makes the cheese with her.

Ruth Kirkham, now in her mid-sixties, can be found bending over her cheese vat, scooping the curds by hand so the whey drains well. Her face has the clean vitality of dairy folk and she speaks with modesty yet a quiet pride and determination about what they do. For decades, Ruth Kirkham helped her husband with the milking morning and night, then she made the cheese and scrubbed down the dairy to keep it spotless every day. When the cheese-grader came, she aimed and strove to get the category 'super-fine'.

Her cheese became celebrated and began to be sold under the name 'Kirkham's'. After a time, the old dairy was no longer convenient and the Kirkhams moved across the yard to a new one built for expansion. It was a disaster. In the old dairy, the cheese had 'made itself', said Mrs Kirkham. Here it was all wrong. They had expanded to cope with the cheese's popularity but in the process jeopardized what they had.

The Kirkhams tried to discover what had gone wrong. Randolph Hodgson kept visiting. Good buyers were patient but concerned. The move had meant dozens of small changes that had disrupted the cheese. One of the most crucial was the build-up of their particular bacteria in the air. Even though the dairy is spotless, these accumulate over time and help 'make' the cheese. The Kirkhams started throwing whey onto the walls, then wiping it off, again and again, to help get the bacteria to move home. Then there was 'a screwy thingy', a piece of kit that at one time was used to press down on the curds in the vat. It was no longer used because it hadn't been necessary in the old dairy. Here it was needed again. Then there was the way the milk was handled. A whizzy pump got the milk into the dairy. But Mrs Kirkham thought this was agitating the liquid too much and found a way to siphon it into the building instead. The gentle hands and ways of dairywomen throughout the centuries proved to be better than new technology.

In the end, after some tough months, Kirkham's Lancashire was back on form. The story shows how paying attention to the local, or locale, is not parochial but essential. Without attention to the details, you lose what you have. And when something is assumed, because it is what you do every day, you can also lose it when circumstances change. Randolph's project with Cheddar seems very pertinent in the light of its sister cheese in the north. The local is rich but to survive it needs to be known and nurtured.

One of the criticisms of local food is that it is too small to be relevant. I was interested to see if it could be produced on any scale.

I went to talk to Sally Scantlebury, then at an organization called Feast. A farmer's daughter, she returned to country life to work as a caterer after years as a props buyer and maker in London. At food fairs, she immediately saw that sustainable local producers were not necessarily very good at marketing what they did, and she set up an organization to help out. Sally's viewpoint was that local food wasn't necessarily small-scale. 'A lot of the messages are quite homely,' she commented. 'There's a big movement for grow-your-own and I'm all for that because it helps people understand how food is produced. But we are not going to feed people out of their window-boxes. We need commercial farming. That can be done with the highest environmental standards – there are big organic farmers.' The question is: where is the produce sold?

I was interested to learn that Sally was seeing a proper shift in thinking amongst local councils in how they wanted to buy their food. In the past, buyers could be after pencils or parsnips and it was all just numbers on a page. But once they began to understand where food came from and the values behind it, such as the environmental impact, there was a shift in culture. This was starting to happen, albeit gradually, and it was shortly to come under pressure as council budgets were slashed in the economic downturn. Almost a third of all catered meals are in the public sector and this market is worth billions of pounds every year. If local and regional food became relevant, it would mean a great deal of money going into the local economy rather than being spirited away.

Sally was adamant that local food was not necessarily more expensive and indeed could be cheaper. A fair amount of the cost of food is the profit made by the middleman. If you connect directly with local producers then you can get fresher, higher quality food for less money, she said.

Local food can be large-scale, and it can also be for the individual. Sally had helped set up two local buying groups in Nottingham, one for young mothers and toddlers and the other for widowers, to help them get local food cheaply from wholesalers. By buying collectively, they could get a big bag of fresh vegetables for £3 from local producers. It was also something of a social event, connecting communities and getting people talking, rather as used to happen on market day. She was setting up monthly stock-up cooking sessions to help make good food more cheaply. This was bringing people together, like Root Camp, to make cooking more sociable. Quite naturally, people swap ideas and share ingredients. The level of knowledge goes up and so does the sense of connection to a place and its people.

One man who has enacted this local food revolution to some considerable economic advantage is John Hughes, the catering manager at Nottingham Hospital Trust. Since he feeds 7,000 patients and visitors a day, shifting his suppliers from the globalized commodities market to the local producers of the East Midlands had the potential to make quite an impact on the local economy.

When John first addressed this issue, the hospital food was bought in from outside and the hospital also had chains on the premises that sold sandwiches and so on. He asked: Why don't we make everything ourselves, from the cup of tea to sandwiches and supper dishes, using local suppliers rather than letting corporations do it for the profit of their shareholders? Why not make the food on-site using ingredients from the East Midlands? It sounds like common sense, but it was a massive shift in thinking. John's first thought was that switching from Argentine beef to local would be too expensive. This shows what a topsy-turvy world we live in. But then he began to work out how it could be done.

The scheme was like turning a large ship round. But once the basic principle of buying local had been agreed, John painstakingly negotiated and put in place a farm-to-plate scheme that has ended up putting at least £1 million a year into the local economy. By bringing their catering back in-house, the Trust saved £2.50 per patient per day, which gave them the opportunity to use local suppliers. He estimates that if the model were adopted by other trusts, it would save up to £400 million for a cash-strapped health service. But the financial savings are minimal, he says, compared to the other benefits. 'There are huge socio-economic, sustainability and food security reasons for doing it,' he says. 'If you do not get rid of the contractors or write the use of local food into contracts you have no control over where the food comes from. If there is one thing we have learned it is that the free market drives down standards from a quality perspective.' He reckons the scheme has saved 150,000 food miles a year. The food is better, freshly made, has a local identity and pride and contributes to local businesses.

No other health trust, however, has followed the example of Nottingham. Contract catering is very big business, and turning to another more local method of feeding people is not an easy task.

Nonetheless, the buying power of government and bodies such as the NHS offers a massive opportunity for local and regional food, and nowhere is this more evident than in the case of school meals. Sally Scantlebury said when she was first looking into procurement, the food spend on school meals was as low as 32p per child per day. 'You spend more than that on dog food,' she commented. Thanks to campaigns such as Food for Life Partnership and the chef Jamie Oliver's intervention with his campaigning television show, *Jamie's School Dinners*, the budget has more or less doubled. It is still not a great deal of money but it certainly adds up if the cash is spent on better local suppliers rather than the cheapest that wholesalers can supply.

The Food for Life campaign in the UK aims to get fresh local food into schools. It has many really inspiring stories of places that have made food a central part of the day and a child's education. The notorious school dinner really can be a force for good. Currently 4,250 schools are taking part out of 22,000 primary and secondary schools in the country. There are different levels to attain – bronze, silver and gold. To achieve the gold standard, 75 per cent of the food must be freshly prepared, 50 per cent local and seasonal and 30 per cent organic. The movement has spawned farm visits, cooking clubs and playground gardens. When the school really gets behind making food special, uptake of school dinners increases radically.

The scheme can make a measurable difference to health. East Ayrshire in Scotland has been part of Food for Life since 2004, when it switched to fresh, local, home-cooked food in its primary schools. They have staff on hand to help the kids to eat fresh fruit, and dishes such as soup and have made food part of overall education, not a bought-in attachment. Over two years the number of overweight children in the region dropped by 22 per cent and the number of obese children by 30 per cent. East Ayrshire used to have the highest rate of severely obese pupils in Scotland and now it has the second lowest.

The advantages are not just for the school but also for the wider food community. For a feature, I spoke to one of the many in the Food for Life campaign, Mark Lea, a farmer in Shropshire who has increasingly become part of the local community since his farm turned organic ten years ago. Mark runs a small shop which keeps its prices low, supplies the local primary school, St Andrews, and hosts fifty to sixty schools a year for farm visits, including a course for eight-year-olds which runs for six days over the year. The benefits, he insists, are not necessarily from sales. 'We subsidize everything we do from the community angle,' he says. 'But it is without doubt the most rewarding part of our business.'

What Mark gives and what he gets are manifold. The business has grown – he now employs ten people, whereas before there had been just one. He gets a great sense of purpose from seeing the children learn about food and farming. 'My opinion is that the state of diet and public health in this country is partially caused by the breakdown of the relationship between producers and consumers,' he says. 'We have a lot of food-ignorant parents who are incapable of inspiring children in a way that would improve their diets. I hope the next generation will grow up with more connections and a greater knowledge on which to base their decisions.'

Buying local doesn't have to involve going to a farmers' market or farm shop, though on the whole this is where you'll get the freshest, best deal. Most of us are accustomed to the one-stop shop. Is it possible to marry local food with larger-scale retail? Supermarkets now say they want to cut down on food miles, and to source from the area near the store. But streamlined supply chains and regulations make this difficult to achieve effectively. One company that has managed to do this, however, is Booth's, a family-owned chain of twenty-six stores in the north of England, across Lancashire, Cheshire, Yorkshire and Cumbria.

Booth's has long set out its stall as a regional supermarket and is now looking very much ahead of the curve. It has 3,000 staff and a turnover of £240 million. At least 25 per cent of all its products at any one time are locally produced, including 85 per cent of the meat, and so its size has some significance for producers. It also makes a marked difference to the quality of the produce. What you sense in Booth's is that the people in charge really love food and know a great deal about it. When I met one of the owners, Edwin Booth, he said he was told to skip university and work in an abattoir instead. When details about meat come up, he knows the subject more thoroughly than most.

The culture of caring about food is evident in many details. Go into a store and you will see small-scale food magazines at eye-level and the television listings rags below. The store buyers tend to stay in one position for a long time, building up contacts, knowledge and relationships, and this means the smaller-scale producer really can thrive in a larger operation.

The difference in quality is easy to see. When I dropped in to look at the vegetable section in one smallish store, the potato stand alone was a joy to behold. As well as having many different kinds, loose and in bags, it displayed heritage potatoes from rare varieties. An attractive large notice explained the different types and what they were for. I had previously met Booth's kale grower, Chris Molyneux, who has supplied the company for twenty years from his farm in southwest Lancashire. He explained how most supermarkets had kale that had been chopped through the stalk. This makes it look easier to cook, with no further preparation. But his kale was kept whole, which means it stays fresh for longer; the stalk is part of the leaf and cutting it up makes a difference to the biochemistry of the leaf. The same goes for sprout stalks. Sprouts on their stalk look like some sort of medieval torture weapon, but this keeps the vegetables fresher and tastier than if they had been stored in a plastic bag. It takes a bit of food knowledge to use them, but Booth's seem to think people have that whereas other supermarkets do not.

The beer selection at Booth's was just incredible – bottles from the north in particular and also beyond as far as the eye can see. The beer buyer had just retired after decades of encouraging local micro-breweries to supply them. In the ordinary Booth's store we visited, the cheese counter had a large section just for unpasteurized cheeses. In a number of stores they have special Neal's Yard counters with the cheeses carefully matured by Randolph and his team. Booth's has trained staff to get people to taste the different kinds as much as possible. Throughout the stores there are some twenty Lancashire cheeses, including the famous Mrs Kirkham's.

On some scale, Booth's keeps a network of good, smaller food producers surviving and thriving. At a time when dairy farmers were going out of business because imported milk was cheaper, Booth's got together a co-operative of farmers who supply the supermarket at a fair price and so are kept in business. You need a genuine relationship between retailer and producer, and that comes from years of contact. It may be hard to do well, but it is possible.

The international organization Slow Food has a motto that food should be 'good, clean and fair'. In other words, it should taste good, be safe (both for you and the planet) and be fair for both producer and consumer.

The last quality, fairness, is one that is pertinent to everything you buy and yet also feels largely beyond your control. You can, of course, buy Fairtrade goods. Every time I have spoken to those involved in this movement or heard the stories of the people it benefits, I realize that buying such products is profoundly worthwhile.

I also find myself asking the question: shouldn't all food be fair? An oft-quoted figure is that for every £1 you spend in the supermarket, just 8p goes to the farmer. No wonder so many cut corners and we have not just fast food but fast farming; many feel they must do so to make a living. In contrast, when you buy local food at a farm shop or farmers' market, the producer is getting a proper deal, and often taking pride in what they do, not least because they face the people who eat the produce.

Around 85 per cent of groceries in the UK are bought in supermarkets. I am impressed by Booth's, yet there are a number of ways in which supermarket retailing, in general, has values that are miles apart from that of local food.

Most of these are unknown to the consumer. There are many shocking stories about how other retailers (posh as well as discount) treat farmers. A grower may be instructed to pay for a buy-one-get-one-free promotion, perhaps even to their loss, or they may have a crop rejected for no good reason, leaving them to plough the plants back into the ground. There's no contract and no comeback; most farmers have to take what they are given in this monopolistic world. When food is merely a commodity sold nationally or internationally, then farmers are vulnerable in a way that the so-called English sense of 'fair play' – of just common decency – should despise. In contrast, you simply cannot behave in this way to your local-food neighbour without consequences. It is hard to look at 'bogof' bargains in quite the same way once you know what can lie behind them – though of course everybody loves a bargain.

Food writer Alex Renton, in an investigation into the unfairness of supermarkets in the *Observer* newspaper, cited a farmer who got just 1p more for a litre of milk from the retailer than he did twenty years ago, despite his costs having soared. The supermarket, meanwhile, was selling the milk for nearly double the money. The National Farmers' Union has claimed that two-thirds of British farmers don't make enough money to live on. The system is wildly skewed by the power of the supermarkets to a point that threatens our national food security: if our farmers can't keep going then even more produce will be imported.

As for the shopper, food is one part of a budget that can be squeezed in tight financial times, and the supermarkets certainly look as though they offer a good deal. But they certainly make a fat profit, and you start to see that this goes to the shareholders and not to the producer – or, indeed, always to the consumer.

Supermarkets may look as though they are offering a good deal, but they are also very good at making food look better value than it is, for example by shrinking the weight of meat in a packet whilst keeping the same price. Profits are made by adding value – a pasta sauce makes more money than the ingredients for that sauce, and a ready-meal is the biggest mark-up of all. If you are a cook – and that is a big 'if' these days – then such food may be convenient, but it's a rip-off in terms of taste and price.

Whilst we are always being told that local food is expensive, it's not necessarily the case. When I did a price comparison between my local stores and a supermarket in the town where I lived, the local stores came out cheaper, somewhat to my surprise. This was, admittedly, for a wide-ranging shopping basket – fennel as well as potatoes. If you just go for bargains, supermarkets are undeniably cheap.

But what are the hidden costs of the multiples? The collective monopoly that supermarkets have on our food is a real worry, not just for producers but for local shopping as a whole. Supermarkets are moving increasingly into the territory of small, local shops by setting up convenience stores in city centres. Such places benefit from the low-cost image of the bigger shops whilst being relatively expensive. A 'local' supermarket can move into an area, drop its prices until the small local shops go out of business, and then put them up again. Such predatory pricing is illegal in the US but not in the UK. Equally, other countries are much stricter about planning regulations. In the UK, however, the government has long kow-towed to the big boys. The policy on supermarkets is often 'let the market decide', and this means the ugly fact of might is right.

Local shops are more able to tap into local food supplies. What is more, they sell plenty of food that simply isn't available in supermarkets because of the nature of their scale and supply lines. Small shops have had to raise their game to survive and you really do get better quality by shopping this way. Decent bread is best bought from a baker. The tastiest meat and the freshest fish come from specialists. It may not be easy to always shop locally but it is certainly rewarding when you do.

Increasingly it is clear that those who believe in good food must buy as much as possible from independent businesses – and do so whether the food they sell is local or not (it often isn't if you shop through the Internet). This is about more than the produce; they represent another kind of food chain that needs to be kept going as an alternative to the supermarkets.

I cannot deny that shopping like this requires effort and that most precious commodity, time. When I lived in a country market town, my local shops were a five-minute walk away; now I live in a city, it's far harder and I shop more in supermarkets. It is certainly possible to combine the two ways of shopping by doing some in supermarkets and getting weekend or weekday treats or good bread at smaller shops. It requires a bigger shift to boycott the supermarkets altogether.

Making a change to your shopping habits is down to time, priorities and knowledge, all of which feed into each other. Perhaps the decision to shop as much as possible from independents requires both the positive pull towards quality and an inner anger about what the monopoly of supermarkets is doing to our food supply. This leads me to the conclusion that local food is part of a deeper engagement with food and the part it plays in your life and the world as a whole. (The bigger point is that supermarkets should be made to behave in a better way, and that is down to government action and us lobbying them as citizen-consumers.)

Localism is an international movement. In the United States, I went to a conference about local foods in Maine. It was held in a 'Nutrition Centre' housed in a big old municipal building with a state-of-the-art teaching kitchen. Today the rooms were filled with small farmers and community activists. I got talking to Jeanne, a health educator who also grows vegetables she sells at a farmers' market. She had long grey hair and a healthy glow, what I now thought of as a 'vitamin D' tan, from being outdoors as much as possible. I got the sense she wasn't really out to make money; she kept her prices low. It was just as much a way of life and how she 'did her bit' these days. In the US, there is a term, 'social food', to describe an approach to eating that bears values other than just the economic, and Jeanne was part of that.

I listened to people going into the nitty-gritty of how to start up projects and the 'challenges and opportunities' of local food. The US seems more set up for community action than the UK, where the state, in various guises, provides more. There are highly active Land Trusts, grant-giving organizations, town meetings, volunteerism and social enterpeneurs who just take an idea and run. People were talking about a chef called Tony Geraci, often described as a Force of Nature, who was really shaking up school dinners in Baltimore, bringing in a food distributor who was buying from 200 farms in Maryland with a budget of $4 million. His good ideas included getting the kids to do meal tastings and saying what they liked. There were a number of great community and school garden projects on the go. The only problem with the latter was that the harvest was mostly in the summer when the kids were away. In time, there will doubtless be holiday cooking clubs in school to use up the produce and take the growing to its edible conclusion.

One interesting man at the event was Ken Morse, a health educator who was trying to build an effective local food network. He spoke to me of the community self-reliance of Maine, a state on the fringe of the continent that made its own way with Yankee ingenuity. In his area, there were around ten towns within a half-hour drive, with a combined population of 25,000. 'We know that we eat $75 millions' worth of food in a year,' he said. The state of Maine had adopted a food policy that it should aim to provide 80 per cent of its own calories by 2020 (at the time it grew a fifth of its food), and so they were now in the business of mapping out how that could be done. Ken fervently believed that sustainable food was the only way forward. 'Industrial food is a luxury we can't afford – the planet can't afford it anyways,' he said. 'I don't think we have any choice if we want food security.'

A contentious element has emerged in the debate on agribusiness versus local food. There are those who think the future is high-tech, or to be precise, biotech. The corporate power of genetically modified (GM) food was starting to nudge into Maine. There weren't many GM crops around, yet, but this was starting to change as biotech companies encouraged farmers to grow seed crops for oil between potato harvests. One of the organizers of the local food conference, Bob St Peter, was wearing a little kerchief around his neck, which I thought at first made him look like a young scoutmaster; he had that keen-as-mustard look on his face. But when I looked harder, it was a La Via Campesina scarf, the international peasant movement that embraces local farming. Bob said that, like his compadres in South America, he would feel like a 'landless peasant' if the corporate power of the biotech companies got a grip on Maine. I looked at his face and saw that his eyes were not just keen; they were sharpened by anger.

The GM debate is bewildering for the non-scientist. The biotech industry says it can solve the problem of world hunger and is perfectly safe. Opponents say the industry's agenda is to make money and unleash unnatural organisms into the world with unknown and possibly dangerous consequences. Who do you believe?

Sceptics of biotech say there are many ecologically sound solutions to feeding the world, and they welcomed an authoritative report that came out in 2009. *Agriculture at a Crossroads*, the UN-backed work of around 400 scientists for the International Assessment of Agricultural Knowledge, Science and Technology for Development (IAASTD), was endorsed by 58 countries, including the UK. The report, significantly, refused to back the view that big technological fixes were the answer to world hunger. This was as much down to finding ways of growing that suited the local land and local people.

I heard the IAASTD's director, Robert Watson, who is the chief scientific adviser to the UK's Department of Food, Rural Affairs and Agriculture (DEFRA), tell a Soil Association conference in 2010 that biotechnology may have a role in solving world hunger, but there were significant concerns for consumers and safety must be the top priority. There is enough food to feed the world using existing technologies, he said. The main issues are accessibility and affordability, not productivity.

Robert Watson used the measured language of science and there was a dizzy whizz of Powerpoint screens as a background to his talk. He didn't rule out GM, but he made a hugely powerful single point. The problem of world hunger is not one of productivity; it is one of fairness. There are now as many people overfed as underfed in the world, a fact that should have a logical solution. But that solution is, ultimately, about politics. The real struggle, then, is how to make the world a more equitable place.

Another day, another meeting, this one in London. An American soil scientist called Chuck Benbrook was in town. He is the chief scientific adviser to the Organic Center in Colorado and had used United States Department of Agriculture figures to show how chemical use has gone up dramatically during the time GM crops have been planted. Crops are genetically engineered so as not to be affected by particular herbicides. But the plants around them have become resistant and these 'super-weeds' need more herbicides, not fewer. Use of herbicides, and also pesticides, had increased dramatically in the past thirteen years of GM crops, with use accelerating in recent years as the problem increased. Biotechnology is often sold to the public as being environmentally sound. Yet the evidence, using the US government's own figures, was to the contrary.

On top of this, seed prices have also risen steeply as they have become increasingly high-tech. Instead of having one trait – such as resistance to a particular herbicide – they now have two or three or more and every trait has a price. Farmers are likely to pay as much as double for GM seed over conventional. Those opposed to GM say that farmers get locked into expensive, high-tech farming that can result in more chemical pollution of the soil, not less.

Present at the meeting were representatives both from the National Farmers' Union and the pesticide industry. The man from the NFU said that farmers weren't stupid and they would decide whether GM was worth backing or not – it was up to them to decide. But farmers are as liable as anyone else to get caught up in techno-escalation. Furthermore, farmers occupy land that is part of our environment, and if this leads to more pollution then it is everyone's business.

The pesticides – or 'plant protection' – representative reeled off many facts and figures as evidence that pesticide residues in water had gone down and fewer insecticides were used. The main issue, he said, was how we were going to deal with an unprecedented crisis in food as populations grew. As I left the building, he wheeled his suitcase past me at double speed on his way to Brussels and I heard him say to his companion: 'Well, we managed to move the debate on.' He was doing his job, but I wouldn't want him to cook my supper. The food crisis is being used as a pushing point by the GM crop lobbyists. But we need to be careful how we tackle the situation: that the 'solution' doesn't lead to more problems.

Whilst it is hard for a non-scientist to understand all the technical debates, it is not enough to say 'trust the experts'. The scientists concerned may decide to stand aside from the application of their work but the politics and uses of GM crops are very much the point. It is not just a question of the safety of the crops, but whether they are used for the good of the wider world or for the profit of the few.

Clearly, biotechnology is the most powerful toolbox the world has ever known. But who has their hand on the tools? The farmer-poet Wendell Berry said: 'The shift of colonial power from European monarchy to global corporation is perhaps the dominant theme of modern history.' Agricultural research used to be publicly funded but now it is carried out by multinationals who have the capital to put into it. The problem with GM can be illustrated by the fact that scientists who want to independently test its products cannot do so because commercial confidentiality means it is impossible to get hold of the seeds to do the tests. There is a great need for independent and trustworthy information and this is impossible to get. The IAASTD report certainly said that assessment lagged behind development when it came to GM.

And so, at the other end of the spectrum, we come back to

local food. Whilst large-scale technologies can play a part in solving world hunger, the local solutions that work within a community are very important. Yet of course it is more straight-forward for governments to go for the large-scale and high-tech ideas which promise to bring about single solutions. It is more complex to support a web of smaller-scale, more environmentally sound ways of farming, the sort of biological agriculture that Colin Tudge talks about. This is the essence of local food and what I, for one, want to put on my plate. Is local food parochial? In an infinite number of ways, it can feed the world – if governments and science decide to go further down this route.

The big corporations, however, argue that they can produce more food more cheaply. The argument may be won by default if they squeeze out local producers. It is clear that local food is tastier, may involve less infrastructure between field and plate, provides local employment, is less polluting and helps, often, to create communities. It may be less clear – or less simple – to work out exactly how local food can do this on a world-wide scale. One thing is certain. We should look hard at the values and opportunities of local food before it is lost altogether.

WHAT TO EAT?

Easy. Go to a farmers' market, farm shop or deli that sources local food; notice whether food comes from a specific location and producer; enjoy local and regional beers; seek out regional specialities close to home and on holiday.

Worth the Effort. Go to a local food festival and talk to producers; find a local glut and preserve it; notice how fruit and vegetables change over the course of a season; find a farmhouse cheese you like and do comparative tastings of different kinds or different ages of the same cheese; support schools that are trying to educate children about local food.

Hopes and Dreams. That schools, hospitals and local governments will get behind the local food movement; that local food systems make it possible for smaller-scale producers to thrive in a globalized economy; that more attention and research funding goes to projects that pay attention to the local circumstances and knowledge; that we feed the world rather than feeding large-scale corporations and that the GM industry will become more transparent and less aggressive.

EPILOGUE

How do you Change What you Eat?

Have I changed what I eat? The answer is yes; every chewy question has led to many juicy answers. But there is one question that underlies all the other ones: *how* do you change what you eat? Most of us already know, at the back of our minds, roughly what a good diet is supposed to be. Finding ways to make good food part of the genuine fabric of daily life is another matter.

For me, the most fundamental shift has been accepting that change is usually gradual. Like any crash diet, an abrupt alteration to the way you eat doesn't last. It is much more about small experiments, tweaks to recipes, getting into a new ingredient or making a foray down another aisle or to another shop; it is more often about absorbing a thought and adjusting a habit than a sudden, radical decision. In fact, change becomes much more possible once you accept that it takes time rather than strained effort and dramatic resolutions.

A shift in habit needs at least a few tries, over time, to see how it takes. To give just a couple of examples, once I was convinced that it was worthwhile eating fish other than salmon, cod or tuna, I needed to cook other kinds – mackerel, pollock, squid – for at least a couple of meals. When I wanted to try new grains and find ways to eat a bigger and better breakfast, I had to give each alteration a fair go, and now both are a natural part of my diet. In all honesty, it can take years rather than months or weeks to truly change how you eat.

But change does happen; and, looking back, the route to it comes through the brain as much as the mouth. For change comes, most of all, through a shift in thinking. For me, part of that has come about through being able to see what I ate more clearly. You often hear talk of a 'balanced, varied diet'. As I reassessed my food, I realized how my diet now fell short of this principle. I could gobble a hasty breakfast, grab a sandwich for lunch and drink in a pub before coming home for a thrown-together supper. I had become lazy and had fallen into food ruts – who hasn't?

My journey through each question has often been about seeing what was really on my plate and, as a result, trying to put balance and variety back onto it. Quiet and modest though these qualities sound, they are at the heart of what makes a way of eating good.

I now want more taste and more nutrition from what I eat and drink – and happily these often come together. But on the whole I now want less in terms of quantity. That helps offset the fact that better food can undoubtedly cost more, though there are canny ways around this when you cook and shop with care.

Eating less, again, has come about through a better understanding about *why* I eat what I eat. In particular, I have come to see how today's world encourages us towards too much. A food psychologist told me of how we live in a 'maxing-out' world.

We live in a consumer society and eating is the ultimate in consumption. So we have too much food, too much drink – too much dieting, for that matter. Writing this book has made me think about the unfussy and curiously unrestrictive constraints of my childhood home where we ate well, sociably and with pleasure (and certainly with pudding). But food wasn't all high days and holidays, and was all the better for it.

There is too much choice in today's food world, and the modern paradox is that despite all this we end up in ruts. Perhaps the sheer amount of choice leads us to eating the same foods over and over again – we cling to familiarity. More likely, it is partly laziness, partly lack of time and partly because modern retail, for all its apparent choice, leads us down particular paths with its economies of scale and year-round supplies. This means we end up always eating the same two or three fish (salmon, prawns, cod), or having potatoes or pasta at most meals, even if they are processed or cooked in a hundred different ways. This convenience food cul-de-sac makes me think of Andy Warhol's screen-printed soup cans: they may contain different flavours but they all look the same.

The opposite to blandification is culture. Enjoying and observing its richness and diversity is at the heart of eating well. The founder of the Slow Food movement, Carlo Petrini, says, sure, fast food is fine – but it should be different food on different streets in different places. Culture means going beyond what's pushed in front of us to see the range of what is really out there, once you focus on finding or rediscovering it.

Food culture is not something you have to pay an arm and a

leg for. It's about what is in your life, your past, your family, your country – or someone else's, if you pay attention to the grass-roots of food and not the marketeer's version.

Food undoubtedly becomes more varied once you take more interest, and variety can mean something as simple as altering a lunch or suppertime salad by adding one or two more elements – some herbs, slices of red pepper, some seeds, some fruit, even, to make the plateful more interesting and so adhere to the principle that biodiversity begins at home. My awareness that this was what I wanted to do, and of why I wanted to do it, was enough to make it happen more often.

Sometimes change is helped along by getting a bit of kit. Good-resolution shopping is suspiciously like taking out a gym membership: you feel you've done your bit without further action. But there's no doubt that good tools make short work of daily tasks. At base, all you really need are two good knives, a big one for chopping and a smaller one for fiddly bits. I have Sabatier carbon steel knives because you can get them really sharp, even though you have to wash and dry them straight away or they get rusty. Stainless steel would be easier and as good, but I now like the ritual and care that goes with the ones I've got. Without good knives, cooking would be much harder.

Beyond this, I dug out a couple of bowls from the back of a cupboard in order to make salad look attractive, and that undeniably helps me eat more vegetables. A good peeler also makes a difference and helps to ingrain the habit of prep so it is as much of an assumed part of the day as cleaning my teeth. One of the

reasons people don't eat many vegetables is that they are perceived as an 'inconvenience' food because of the preparation
involved. A good peeler and music on the radio make shorter
work of this daily task.

Two knives, a nice bowl, a handy peeler, a spacious chopping
board, a hand blender for quick soups and a couple of good pans.
That's it for kit. I should add that I am blessed with a partner who
does all the washing up (but you can't buy him at John Lewis).

Another thought I have found helpful is that change is personal
and about developing your own tastes and habits. The principles
of knowing what's good to eat can be interpreted in as many
ways as there are people – that is the joy of a varied diet and of
food itself. It's not about forcing yourself to eat something you
don't like; it is, on the other hand, about properly exploring
what is out there.

In some instances, a change hasn't taken – or not yet. I don't
find offal especially easy – kidneys were my worst 'yuk' as a
child: how could anyone eat these pissy things? But I still bother
to eat offal every so often for two reasons. First, I think that if
you eat meat, it's best to try to eat the whole animal, not pick at
what we have come to think of as the prime cuts. And then …
because it's cheap. You can feed a family on offal for the cost of
one chicken breast. I don't think I could persuade the tableful to
eat offal but I can at least serve it to adults, not least myself, and
eat ethical meat at a very good price.

And I am gradually getting more used to the interesting textures and tastes of different kinds of offal and am glad they are a

small part of what I eat, not least after learning how nutritionally rich they are. By chance I discovered that duck offal is particularly delicious, and the other day found myself ordering a duck heart risotto in a gastropub, not as some sort of good resolution but because – and this is the only reason, ever, for ordering something in a restaurant – it was what I wanted to eat.

The secret to offal is that it really should be as fresh as possible. Again, buying it at a farmers' market, or from a good butcher or farm shop, or eating it at a restaurant, pub or café that cares, makes all the different to the taste and to wanting to eat it in the first place.

In the current economic climate – and before that – it's often said that 'nothing matters but money'; that better food is a luxury most people can't afford; and, beyond that, that an interest in cooking is some sort of lifestyle choice. I don't think you'd have this argument in Italy, say, where good food is more of a given, and cheap ways to eat decent food are part of life. Yet when money is tight, food is certainly an element in the budget that can be squeezed more than an electricity bill or a mortgage payment. And as food prices rise substantially, no wonder this happens.

It is possible to budget more carefully and eat better. By eating less meat and more vegetables, it is possible to eat kinder, better quality meat and tasty, well-grown vegetables, and still pay the same amount.

The missing link in this equation, however, is cooking and an ingrained culture of eating fresh food. All my food dilemmas, and the paths through them, lead back to this one important place: fresh food. It is not a hard and fast rule for every meal and every single ingredient – passata, spice pastes and tins of cooked beans certainly have a place in my kitchen – but freshness matters as a bedrock way of eating.

Cooking is often regarded as a domestic burden. Furthermore it is one that often – though by no means entirely – falls on women, who are already hard-pressed for time and energy on the domestic front. Time, money, habit, skills, the inequalities of society and gender: all these stand in the way of us developing a better food culture.

Time and money are the big issues – and time can be about money. But both time and money can also be about priorities. This is why being interested in food in whatever way possible – but most of all through cooking, and being prepared to spend time in the kitchen – has to be part of the change towards eating well. How this shift can come about is a question that requires a great deal of chewing; it is the biggest and hardest question of all: how do you get people to cook?

For me personally, conversations have encouraged me to bother more and cook more. In a time of digital and information overload, the latest buzz in the marketing world is that people are influenced most of all through 'word of mouth'. Talk is a different sort of medium; very old technology. Somehow you take in words and they stay in your head and work their way through, eventually, to opinions and actions. Stories and conversations make the world go round, and not just money.

Stona Fitch, whom I met when looking at fruit and vegetables at Gaining Ground, made a couple of points that keep coming back to me. We were talking about how change happened. He thinks the move towards better food started as a counterculture movement that has now gone mainstream. 'We're Americans, we're shallow about looking good,' he said. 'People are driven by vanity to eat better. If you spend two hours on an exercise bike you are not going to go home and eat something terrible – it's counterintuitive.' And once an aspect of your diet has had a shift towards better quality, you don't go back.

Then Stona made another point that I found profoundly helpful. Ultimately, he said, change in food is part of human nature. 'We land on the ground anywhere in the world and generally make a go of finding something to eat,' said Stona. 'Humans are like mirrors. They reflect whatever they're eating, and if you get them to look at something new then they want more of that.' In other words, a child may not eat much veg today, perhaps, but find a way of turning that around, and that's eventually what they want. I found this a useful idea: that we are creatures of adaptation as well as creatures of habit. How you eat evolves much more than you think: compare what you ate as a child, or even five years ago, with what you eat now. The continuities of food are rich, but the changes can be, too.

I had a great number of conversations back in the UK when I attended the Oxford Food Symposium in 2010. People had come from twenty-eight countries to talk about food at this annual event, that year on the subject of fermented foods.

One headline speaker was Sidney Mintz, a renowned anthropologist who wrote a key book about our taste for sugar, *Sweetness and Power*. He spoke of how fermented foods were old, vital and complex, that this 'oldest form of biotechnology' was, for many, the taste of home.

The weekend fizzed with thoughts and tastes. When I left the conference, I happened upon Sid Mintz taking a short break, sitting down in a sunny spot with his wife. I thanked him for his talk and made to go on, not wanting to disturb their peace. But he started talking to me and I listened. Human beings, he said, have an innate taste for sweetness. After that, we start to learn. We pick up tastes and add them to what we eat. The professor, an educator even at rest, was telling me how humans are creatures of learning.

We do change what we eat, for many reasons. We learn from a parent, a friend, a television chef, a recipe or a meal. An idea appeals; a habit sticks. We are the sum of our knowledge, and our willingness to learn is part of what makes us happier, as well as human. And it is the impulse behind the many pleasurable answers to the ongoing question: what to eat?

Select Bibliography

Béliveau, Richard and Gingras, Denis. *Foods to Fight Cancer.* Dorling Kindersley 2007.

Bell, Annie. *Annie Bell's Vegetable Book.* Michael Joseph 1997.

Benjamin, Alison and McCallum, Brian. *A World without Bees.* Guardian Books 2008.

Berners-Lee, Mike. *How Bad are Bananas? The Carbon Footprint of Everything.* Profile Books 2010.

Bittman, Mark. *Food Matters: A Guide to Conscious Eating.* Simon & Schuster 2009.

Blythman, Joanna. *Shopped: The Shocking Power of the British Supermarkets.* Fourth Estate 2004.

Clifford, Sue and King, Angela. *England in Particular.* Hodder & Stoughton 2006.

Clifford, Sue and King, Angela. *The Apple Source Book: Particular Uses for Diverse Apples.* Hodder & Stoughton 2007.

Clover, Charles. *The End of the Line: How Overfishing is Changing the World and What we Eat.* Ebury Press 2004.

Cordain, Loren. *The Paleo Diet.* John Wiley 2002.

Corder, Roger. *The Wine Diet.* Sphere 2009.

Corson, Trevor. *The Story of Sushi.* Harper Perennial 2008.

Crawford, Michael and Marsh, David. *The Driving Force: Food, Evolution and the Future*. William Heinemann, 1989.

Critser, Greg. *Fat Land: How Americans Became the Fattest People in the World*. Allen Lane 2003.

Crowden, James. *Ciderland*. Birlinn 2008.

Davidson, Alan et al. *The Oxford Companion to Food*. Oxford University Press 2006.

Ehrlich, Richard. *The Green Kitchen*. Kyle Cathie 2009.

Ellis, Hattie (author and ed.). *Best of British Fish*. Mitchell Beazley 2005.

Ellis, Hattie. *Planet Chicken: The Shameful Story of the Bird on Your Plate*. Sceptre 2007.

Ellis, Hattie. *Sweetness and Light: The Mysterious History of the Honeybee*. Sceptre 2004.

Fairlie, Simon. *Meat: A Benign Extravagance*. Permanent Publications 2010.

Fallon, Sally. *Nourishing Traditions*. New Trends Publishing 2001.

Fearnley-Whittingstall, Hugh and Fisher, Nick. *The River Cottage Fish Book*. Bloomsbury 2007.

Fearnley-Whittingstall, Hugh. *A Cook on the Wild Side*. Boxtree 1997.

Fearnley-Whittingstall, Hugh. *The River Cottage Meat Book*. Hodder & Stoughton 2004.

Gratzer, Walter. *Terrors of the Table: The Curious History of Nutrition*. Oxford University Press 2006.

Greenberg, Paul. *Four Fish: A Journey from the Ocean to your Plate*. Allen Lane 2010.

Henry, Diana. *Food from Plenty*. Mitchell Beazley 2010.

Hillferty, Trish and Norrington-Davies, Tom. *Game:A Cookbook*. Absolute Press 2009.

Hume, Charlotte. *The Great Big Veg Challenge*. Vermillion 2008.

Jones, Martin. *Feast:Why Humans Share Food*. Oxford University Press 2008.

Katz, Sandor Ellix. *The Revolution Will Not be Microwaved*. Chelsea Green 2006.

Katz, Sandor Ellix. *Wild Fermentation*. Chelsea Green 2003.

Kessler, David. *The End of Overeating: Taking Control of our Insatiable Appetite*. Penguin 2009.

Kurlansky, Mark. *The Last Fish Tale: The Fate of the Atlantic and our Disappearing Fisheries*. Jonathan Cape 2008.

Lean, Michael (ed.). *Fox and Cameron's Food Science, Nutrition and Health*. Hodder Education 2006.

Litvinoff, Miles and Madeley, John. *50 Reasons to Buy Fair Trade*. Pluto Press 2007.

Mabey, Richard. *Food for Free*. Collins 1989.

McCance and Widdowson. *The Composition of Foods*. The Royal Society of Chemistry 1991.

McPhee, John. *Oranges*. Penguin 2000.

Mears, Ray and Hillman, Gordon. *Wild Food*. Hodder & Stoughton 2007.

Mennell, Stephen. *All Manners of Food: Eating and Taste in England and France from the Middle Ages to the Present*. Blackwell 1985.

Mikanowski, Lyndsay and Patrick. *Vegetables by 40 Great French Chefs*. Flammarion 2006.

Morgan, Joan and Richards, Alison. *The Book of Apples*. Ebury Press 1993.

Muir, Jenni. *A Cook's Guide to Grains*. Conran Octopus 2008.

Nestle, Marion. *Food Politics: How the Food Industry Influences Nutrition and Health*. University of California Press 2003.

Nestle, Marion. *What to Eat*. North Point Press 2007.

Ornish, Dean. *The Spectrum*. Ballantine Books 2007.

Parle, Stevie. *Real Food from Near and Far*. Quadrille 2010.

Patel, Raj. *Stuffed and Starved: Markets, Power and the Hidden Battle for the World Food System*. Portobello Books 2008.

Pollan, Michael. *Food Rules: An Eater's Manual*. Penguin 2009.

Pollan, Michael. *In Defence of Food: The Myth of Nutrition and the Pleasures of Eating*. Allen Lane 2008.

Pollan, Michael. *The Omnivore's Dilemma*. Bloomsbury 2006.

Ramsden, James. *Small Adventures in Cooking*. Quadrille 2011

Rayman, Margaret, Dilley, Kay and Gibbons, Kay. *Healthy Eating: The Prostate Care Cookbook*. Kyle Cathie 2009.

Read, Jan and Manjon, Maite. *The Great British Breakfast*. Michael Joseph 1981.

Red Herring Workers' Co-operative. *Cordon Rouge: Vegetarian and Vegan Recipes from the Red Herring*. Earthright Publications 1998.

Roberts, Callum. *The Unnatural History of the Sea*. Gaia 2007.

Saberi, Helen (ed.). *Cured, Fermented and Smoked Foods: Proceedings from the Oxford Symposium on Food and Cooking 2010*. Prospect Books 2011.

Servan-Schreiber, David. *Anticancer: A New Way of Life*. Penguin 2008.

Sinclair, Upton. *The Jungle*. Penguin 1985.

Stuart, Tristram. *Waste: Uncovering the Global Food Scandal*. Penguin 2009.

Taubes, Gary. *The Diet Delusion*. Vermillion 2009.

Thample, Rachel de. *Less Meat More Veg*. Kyle Cathie 2011.

Tudge, Colin. *So Shall we Reap*. Allen Lane 2003.

Watson, Guy and Baxter, Jane. *Everyday and Sunday Recipes from Riverford Farm*. Fourth Estate 2011.

Watson, Guy and Baxter, Jane. *Riverford Farm Cook Book*. Fourth Estate 2008.

Weber, Karl (ed.). *Food, Inc.* Participant Media 2009

Whitley, Andrew. *Bread Matters:Why and How to Make your Own*. Fourth Estate 2009.

Willett, Walter. *Eat, Drink, and be Healthy*. Free Press 2003.

Wilson, Tim and Warde, Fran. *The Ginger Pig Meat Book*. Mitchell Beazley 2011.

Wrangham, Richard. *Catching Fire: How Cooking Made us Human*. Profile Books 2009.

Acknowledgements

My journey through *What to Eat?* has had many good companions. Everyone in the book has cast light on particular issues, added thoughts and given their time, recipes and experience. To them and many others – friends, family, fellow food writers and cooks – thank you for your puzzlings, humour and insight; thank you for so generously and delightfully sharing your thoughts and tables.

The most convivial and important way to learn is through conversations, and over the past four years I have also gained much of such inspiration at events organized by the Guild of Food Writers, the Food Ethics Council, Slow Food UK and especially Slow Food Lewes, and from being part of the Oxford Symposium of Food and Cookery. Maggie's Cancer Caring Centres are about talking and listening in the best possible way and I want to thank all those I've met there, both those who come to the Centres and those who work in them and for the organization.

Thank you to the editors who commissioned articles and books that helped me on my way, in particular Richard Atkinson, Claire Bowman, Guy Dimond, Sarah Fitzpatrick, Amy

Fleming, Casilda Grigg, Carolyn Hart, Dan Jellinek, Susan Low, Jonathan Ray, Sue Seddon, Rebecca Spry and Tony Turnbull.

I was blessed with an excellent copy-editor Angela Blackburn, who picked up the pieces with much skill. Big thanks to my editor Philip Gwyn Jones and my agent Georgina Capel for all their encouragement and belief.

Once more, much appreciation and love to my father, Roger Ellis, for reading through the manuscript and making comments, and my love and heartfelt thanks to Tim Neilson for read-throughs, eat-ups, washing up and much, much more.

HE

January 2012

For more on *What to Eat?* go to www.hattieellis.com

Index